Howard Hinton

School days at Mount Pleasant

Including sketches and legends of the neutral ground

Howard Hinton

School days at Mount Pleasant
Including sketches and legends of the neutral ground

ISBN/EAN: 9783337153120

Printed in Europe, USA, Canada, Australia, Japan

Cover: Foto ©Paul-Georg Meister /pixelio.de

More available books at **www.hansebooks.com**

SCHOOL DAYS

AT

MOUNT PLEASANT,

INCLUDING

SKETCHES AND LEGENDS OF THE NEUTRAL GROUND.

BY

RALPH MORLEY.

ILLUSTRATED.

NEW YORK:
HENRY L. HINTON, PUBLISHER,
680 BROADWAY.
1871.

Entered according to Act of Congress, in the year One Thousand Eight Hundred and Seventy, by
HENRY L. HINTON,
In the Clerk's Office of the District Court of the United States, for the Southern District of New York.

DEDICATED

TO THE BATTALIONS OF CADETS, WHO HAVE, IN SUCCESSIVE YEARS, GONE FORTH FROM THE TIME-HONORED WALLS OF MOUNT PLEASANT ACADEMY, "ARMED AND EQUIPPED" FOR THE BATTLE OF LIFE.

MANY of these, alas, are now "old boys," and not a few have been placed on the retired list by that ruthless generalissimo, Death. Of those that still remain in the ranks, it is hoped that many—if the writer has succeeded in inspiring his pages with aught of the spirit of those old school-days —will take a certain quaint pleasure in living them over again. Few, it is true, of that numerous throng of old pupils will have it in their power to refer in memory to the special incidents of the single year of school-life, the record of which is here given; yet all will doubtless recognize the general truthfulness of the picture presented.

The writer trusts, moreover, that, in devoting himself to the agreeable task of narrating these reminiscences, he will at the same time have achieved a work of general usefulness to the American public, inasmuch as, heretofore, books of this class have emanated from English sources, and have reproduced the features of English schools, to which still cling many customs and peculiarities derived from feudal times. Happily freed from these, our American boarding-schools are characterized, as well in their domestic arrangements as in their methods of instruction, by features of their own, which ought to be in harmony with the wants of youth in a vigorous and expanding republic.

Is it not then time that the public, especially that more interested portion of it which includes the parents of the rising generation, should have a view of the inner workings of the schools of our own land? In this regard, the present work, whatever be its defects, may, it is trusted, be deemed a not unwelcome contribution to the fugitive literature of the day.

R. M.

New York, May, 1870.

CONTENTS.

		PAGE
I.	Reveille,	7
II.	The New Boy,	11
III.	First Approaches,	18
IV.	The Awkward Squad,	27
V.	The Feast,	33
VI.	Adventures in the Highlands,	39
VII.	The Mirage of Paradise Island,	78
VIII.	The Cloud Lowers,	86
IX.	Rain,	89
X.	Prowling,	93
XI.	Rats! Rats!	99
XII.	The Expedition,	105
XIII.	The Return,	115
XIV.	The Haunted Room,	119
XV.	The Fox Hunt,	129
XVI.	The Examination,	136
XVII.	The First Snow,	145
XVIII.	The Battle of the Snows,	150
XIX.	Remote Stars—Nebulæ,	156
XX.	The Spoiled Child,	161
XXI.	Vapors,	166
XXII.	The Vapors thicken,	172
XXIII.	Astray in the Darkness,	181
XXIV.	Derisive Echoes,	185
XXV.	Chirographic Studies.	190

CONTENTS.

	PAGE
XXVI. COASTING,	196
XXVII. PHANTOM HILLS,	202
XXVIII. THE OFFICE,	204
XXIX. THE SICK-ROOM.—MILK-SOP,	209
XXX. THE ENCOUNTER,	214
XXXI. AN OPEN SKY,	221
XXXII. TINGLING VEINS,	225
XXXIII. ON THE WING,	227
XXXIV. TRADITIONS AND LEGENDS OF THE NEUTRAL GROUND,	237
XXXV. THE SAME, CONTINUED,	273
XXXVI. TOM, NED, AND "SEVENTEEN,"	296
XXXVII. TRIUMPH AND BEWILDERMENT,	308
XXXVIII. THE FLIGHT,	312
XXXIX. STARS THAT SHOOT MADLY FROM THEIR SPHERE,	315
XL. THE ENCAMPMENT,	317
XLI. TATTOO,	324

ILLUSTRATIONS.

		PAGE
MOUNT PLEASANT,		Title.
CROTON POINT AND HIGH TORN,	Forbes,	41
THE RETURN OF THE FOX-HUNTERS,	Bonwell,	135
JOHN DEAN KEEPING THE COW-BOYS IN CHECK,	Wand,	268
THE ENCAMPMENT,	Forbes,	318

Engraved by McCRACKEN.

SCHOOL-DAYS AT MT. PLEASANT.

CHAPTER I.

RÉVEILLÉ.

With a sense of alarm I started from my sleep, awakened by the reverberating roll of the morning drum. It was the dawn of my first day at the military school. I had arrived late the preceding evening, and, tired as I was by a long day's journey, and the number and novelty of the impressions I had received on the route, I had obtained permission to go to bed at an earlier hour than was usual with the boys of the department in which I was entered. But notwithstanding my fatigue, I did not at once yield myself to sleep; I was too much excited by the change that had fallen upon the even course of my boyish life. This was to me a great event. I was enrolled as a cadet. My "uniform" had already been prepared, and on the morrow I should appear in all the brilliancy of blue and silver.

I was a boy of a rather quiet turn of mind, more fond of observing the pranks and sports of my fellows, than of entering heartily into them. I was not, however, unambitious. I withdrew somewhat, it is true, from the world of my playmates, not eagerly seeking those distinctions of the playground which they prized so highly, but with all the more ardor I nursed secret visions of future renown. These early dreams, strange as it may seem in a boy of such a turn, took a military coloring. It is the love of glory, rather than of true fame, that first captivates the heart of enthusiastic youth. The boy is enamored with the splendor that invests great actions, rather than with the great qualities, or the high and noble thoughts, from which heroic deeds originate; hence, the military career has for him the greatest attraction; the warrior is his hero.

Such, however, were not my thoughts, as I lay awake on my first night at the new school. Now that I was actually commencing a life to which I had been looking forward with so much boldness and pride, I began to feel considerable misgiving; my courage had oozed out not a little. The first introduction into a large school of boys, with whom one is compelled to associate at all hours of the day, requires no small degree of self-confidence, and is peculiarly trying to a sensitive organization. But added to my anticipation of the ordeal awaiting me, my first approach to the building which was probably to be the theater of my life for several years, having occurred after night had already set in, the great massive walls of stone, unrelieved as they were by any architectural adornment, had a very subduing, not to say, terrifying effect upon me. At the time, too, of my arrival, an oppressive silence reigned throughout the house; the boys, as I afterward learned, were at that hour collected for evening study in the main school-room, which was in a wing of the principal building.

I was ushered up the plain, well-trodden stairway to the "office," as the business room of the principal was called. I should have mentioned already that I had come alone; I had no elder brother to pull me along by his side, and my father's business did not allow him time to conduct me further than to the railway station nearest my home. I was, however, duly "ticketed" for Sing Sing, which village of the Hudson is distinguished, as my readers all know, as the site of several old military schools. Arrived here, I had but to direct the first hack-driver who thrust his eager whip into my face, to take me to the Mount Pleasant Academy, and I should be safe from all perils by the way. It was, however, with a beating heart that I, a boy of thirteen years, knocked at the door of the principal's room.

"Well, what is it?" was the answer that came from within. To this unexpected inquiry I knew not what to reply, though the voice, quick and decisive in its tones, was yet kindly. I stood doubting what to do or say, and in my trepidation would probably have awaited future developments, when the loud, cheery voice of the servant who had shown me the way up interposed with "Here's a new boy, sir."

I was bid enter, a direction which I obeyed, as you may suppose, in a very meek frame of mind; my martial enthusiasm had by this time wholly evaporated. I was reassured, however, by the gentle presence and sympathetic manner of the gentlemen into whose presence I had come; and I will here introduce them to the reader as Major Blaisdell, senior principal, and Mr. Ellery, his associate. A few simple questions were put to me concerning my family and home, more for the purpose of setting me at ease, than for the sake of information.

Such was my *entrée* into the great school, and such, as I lay restless on the bed that had been assigned me, were the new and rather dun-colored pictures which mingled in my mental vision with the warm and bright images of home which now rose up before me. At last, however, I sank into a sound, dreamless sleep, which was not disturbed even by the clattering feet and the quick voices of the more than forty boys of the department to which I was attached, who soon after were marched to bed. Nor was I molested in my sleep by those whose room I shared,—an escape from the usual trials of a first night at school, owing partly to the fact that the boys, who had enjoyed a half-holiday, were all very tired, and were glad to get abed and asleep with as little delay as possible.

CHAPTER II.

THE NEW BOY.

By way of preparation for my military career, I had read much about the Revolutionary events which had occurred on the banks of the Hudson, and during the brief interval between sleeping and waking, while the drum was yet beating, I think I must have dreamed through a whole volume of thrilling adventure.

I obtained, however, full possession of my senses in time to behold several pairs of naked legs propped up against the beds which were arranged along one side of the room, the owners of which legs were rather ruefully rubbing their eyes with their knuckles. Presently, and almost simultaneously, as with military precision, the legs were thrust into pantaloons; with a dexterous jerk, suspenders were hoisted upon the shoulders; coats and collars were caught up under the arm, and an advance was at once made upon the curtained opening, which served in place of doorway. In a moment I should have been left the sole occupant, had not a somewhat overgrown-looking fellow, happening to cast his eye upon me, cried out, "Hilloa, new boy! better get up. You'll get marked late at roll-call."

What terrible consequences would follow upon being late at roll-call, I knew not, and did not pause to consider, but jumped at once from bed and donned my clothes as fast as my limbs, unpracticed in military evolutions, could accomplish the movement. By this time the echoes of the last drum-taps had died out, and my companion, the boy who had assumed charge of me, hurriedly bidding me follow him, rushed precipitously down-stairs.

I followed my guide as rapidly as I could, and entered a large room, bare of all ornament, along the sides of which were ranged a row of wooden boxes, set upright, which, as I afterward observed, contained the toilet apparatus of the pupils. Before each of these boxes stood a boy holding in hand a wooden saucer, which contained soap, tooth-brush, etc., and having a towel slung over his arm. The teacher in charge was stationed in the center of the room, and was far advanced in the roll-call.

"Forty."

"Here!" answered the boy who had taken me, for the moment, under his guidance.

"Singular name, that!" I mentally ejaculated. But immediately numbers 41, 42, and so on, were called and responded to.

In the mean time I remained standing near the door, looking about me with a bewildered, half-scared feeling, which, however, did not prevent me from knowing that the eyes of most of the boys in the room were concentrated upon me, and that remarks of a critical character were circulating from one to another in whispers, aided by a grotesque accompaniment of nudges and winks.

Some of them, when the eyes of the teacher were not turned upon them, sought to attract my attention, and to disconcert me by grimaces, and absurd or threatening gesticulations, while others, standing near me, slyly snapped their towels at my legs. I continued to stare about me in a stupid, imperturbable way; but my heart was in my throat.

Boys are a cruel species of the animal kingdom. They will wantonly lame or destroy some unfortunate product of the lower creation,—a worm, a butterfly,—merely to watch its writhings. They will, with even greater satisfaction, work upon the tender susceptibilities of one of their own mates, and goad him without mercy. But they must not be too harshly judged; even youths of the gentler nature will sometimes indulge in this kind of sport. Who does not remember to have amused himself, in his youth, by holding a harmless fly by the legs, caught between the forefinger and the thumb, till, in its struggles to get free, one or more of these appurtenances of fly-life were detached from their sockets. The cruelty of boyhood is often a mere passing characteristic, not one ingrained in the nature; it is the exuberance of life exulting in its sense of power; this is its more satanic aspect. It is, on the other hand, the rapacity of the analytic intellect which experiments on all sides, and, in its eagerness to know, respects no form of life.

"Fall in," said the teacher in charge, a command which was almost instantaneously repeated by several voices, with the additional injunction to "close up;" and a commotion arose, out of which emerged two long lines of young heroes in martial array, prepared to make a spirited attack upon—the wash-basins. At this moment, the teacher happening to face about and observe me as I stood irresolute what to do, "Ah," he said, "you are the new pupil, whom the Major mentioned to me last night. You are to be No. 20. Here, take your place in the rear of the line."

Upon a sign from the teacher, the leading officer gave the command, repeated by subordinates, "Forward, *march*," and then in silence, unbroken save by the measured tread of the youthful warriors, the storming party advanced. The truth of history, however, compels me to state that no rugged ascent had to be climbed; on the contrary, the head of the column, leading the way through a side hall, suddenly precipitated itself down a stairway with somewhat more alacrity than had been shown hitherto. Following on, the last of the line, I found, on entering the subterranean apartment to which our march had led us, that my comrades were already deployed in open order around the room before fixed basins, into which water was flowing. The command seemed to be "Wash at will;" nevertheless, there was a considerable degree of regularity observed, for at nearly the same moment a long line of heads might be seen bobbing up and down; during a given interval of time, there was a chorus of puffings, blowings, snortings, and splashings; then soon followed, on all sides, the sharp rasping sound of the tooth-brush. I, for my part, caught the spirit of the occasion, and participated in the affair with enthusiasm. Lastly, there was a great flourishing of towels— the white flags of peace.

All now stood quietly at their places, and the commands being given to "fall in" and "close up," the line of march was directed back to the dressing-room. Here, on entering, I found my new comrades standing at their several boxes before small mirrors,—held in the hand or swung on the doors of the boxes,—in which were reflected a long row of shining morning faces, freshened by the early matutinal exercise to which they had been subjected. But I shall not dwell longer upon the minor military evolutions into which I was initiated: suffice it to say, that the several movements of combing, brushing, boot-polishing, and whisk-brooming having been performed, jackets having been donned, collars and neckties nicely adjusted, once more the order to fall in was given. At this moment began the furious ringing of a bell; this, I learned, was an announcement to the senior department of the school that the hour of morning study was about to begin. We were then marched through a passage-way leading to the main school-room.

Soon after we juniors had taken our seats on the side of the room assigned us, a heavy, measured tread was heard outside; immediately a long line of stalwart youths entered, who, compared with us, were veterans in the service. A few moments after they had taken their seats, a light, silver-sounding bell was touched, and upon the instant, the low murmured conversation ceased. The presiding teacher, having taken his place at the desk on the raised platform, proceeded to read a selection from the Bible; the reading was followed by a short prayer. This exercise ended, the bell was again touched, and immediately text-books were produced, and at once all heads were bent over the desks before them in silent study.

As I had no task assigned me, I had time to reflect upon the novel aspect of affairs. My thoughts were not the most cheerful in the world. The isolated situation in which I found myself, and the dead silence prevailing around me, were not especially conducive to a merry frame of mind. After the life of freedom which I had enjoyed, the prospect of three or four years of such marchings and counter-marchings as I had witnessed did not seem very alluring. On the other hand, fond recollections of the home I had left began to throng into my mind. I saw my brothers, and my little sister,—who was just beginning to chirrup a peculiar language of her own, half-human, half-divine,—I saw them gathering at this hour about the family breakfast-table with laughing faces and unconstrained manners; I saw the good, darling mother, restraining the excess of youthful spirits not by frowns and chilling reproof, but by the winning smile and quiet word of love; I saw the grave but genial father lifting the little prattler to a place by his side and listening with a wondering air to her divine speech; then I looked forth over the broad lawn and wide fields and down the green lanes, where I had loitered away with my playmates the dreamy days of early boyhood; I saw, too, in the distance, the school-house of modest dimensions, in and out of which we were wont to tumble without much thought of the order of our going.

All this rose before me, as I sat unoccupied at the desk allotted me, and the contrast of the absent merriment and freedom with the present silence and constraint, was not predisposing to an hilarious mood of mind. I am compelled to confess that a few stray tears stole up from the full reservoirs of youth, and dropped silently upon the desk.

The loud ringing of a distant bell, and the general stir that arose around me, startled me from my incipient homesickness, and an inward monitor advised me that this must be the announcement of breakfast.

Perhaps, I thought, that will put a different face upon the matter.

I am not going to trouble the reader to follow me in detail through the routine of the day. What he has heard will suffice to give him an idea of the kind of indoor military life to which we were subjected. He must not, however, suppose that the gloomy colors of the picture which I represented to myself during that first study hour, were true to the reality. As I afterward found, there was abundant time allowed for the free play of the exuberant spirits of boyhood. Nor, after I became habituated to it, did the precision and formality of the semi-military routine of our indoor life prove at all irksome; on the contrary, by erecting a strong and well-guarded barrier against misrule and disorder, it gave room for that internal freedom, which was more than a compensation for the external restraint. And now, as I look back from the vantage-ground of maturer years, I feel that I owe much to the habits of life to which that routine inured me.

CHAPTER III.

FIRST APPROACHES.

I SUCCEEDED in getting through the portion of the day, which was chiefly devoted to school duties, without any further symptoms of homesickness. The studies which I was to pursue had been assigned me, and my time was wholly occupied either in attending recitations in the several class-rooms, or in private study at my desk. I did not find leisure to revert to thoughts of home.

I was glad, too, of the refuge which my books afforded me. Unaccustomed to meeting new and strange faces, I found it difficult to throw off my reserve and acknowledge with freedom of manner the advances that were made to me, and as my fellow-pupils were all desirous of making the most of such intervals of recreation as occurred during the morning, I was left very much to myself. But at length the school-hours were brought to an end, the school-room was closed, and I was forced to seek a retreat elsewhere.

It was a beautiful afternoon of September, one of those delicious half-summer, half-autumn days, when living is felt as absolute luxury. A voluptuous haze of light overspread the warm earth, softening and blending all its shadows. I sat down upon a bench under one of the old apple-trees that bordered one side of the great inclosure which served at once for playground and parade. The whole space was dotted over with boys actively engaged in various sports, though ball-playing seemed to be the specialty of the season.

I sat watching them with interest, and wishing that I might somehow overcome my reserve, and enter with like ease into their free and joyous life. And yet I found a certain idle pleasure on that dreamy September day in observing the graceful spontaneous movement,—groups forming, and on the instant dissolving, others appearing, bubble-like, in some other quarter, and as rapidly vanishing, meteoric flashes of boyhood in every direction across the open spaces. As I sat watching it all, and child though I was, impressed with that vague, sad, yet pleasing sense of transitoriness to which a scene like this gives rise, my eye was arrested by the action of a boy of about my own age, perhaps a half-year older, of a generous, gallant mien, with nut-brown locks, slightly curled, and of well-knit, yet graceful form, who with an easy motion was tossing up a ball, and accompanying the action with exultant exclamations—a kind of extemporized song without words. With his head thrown back, and his eye intent upon the rising and falling ball, he kept drawing nearer to the bench upon which I was seated, when suddenly, having to make a quick spring to catch the ball, he stumbled across me, and was thrown upon the sward at my feet. Jumping up lightly, he begged my pardon and asked if he had hurt me. Upon my assuring him that he had not, before I had time to express my concern for his fall, "Why," said he, "you are the new boy. You must be lonely sitting here by yourself. Come, join me in my solitary game."

"'The Stars'—that is the club to which I belong—

do not play this afternoon," he continued, "and I am not sorry, for I like often to saunter and play at large. Here, catch the ball."

I was not loath to accept the invitation, for my seclusion was becoming tiresome enough, and I was glad of any opportunity of participation in the sports that were going on before me. I was won, too, by the easy politeness of the boy, to whom this little accident had introduced me.

"What is your number?" said he, as he tossed me the ball.

"Twenty," and I tossed the ball back. "What is yours?"

"Twenty-five."

"Why do I have so high a number when I have just come to the school?"

"Oh, that is nothing. That number happens to be vacant; so you are fitted in there. You will keep the number as long as you remain in school. The numbers have nothing to do with rank. I can not say that I congratulate you on the numeral to which you have fallen heir. Your predecessor was sent away. What a queer fellow, old '20' was! Look out for your eye, I am going to pitch straight at you. Well caught! you shall be one of our 'Stars' soon; can you swing a bat?"

I protested that I could a little, and would like to become a "Star," whereat, he tossed the ball up in the air a few times, singing the old nursery song,

"Twinkle, twinkle, little star,
How I wonder what you are," etc.

Then as he threw me the ball again, "I am not much of a Star yet, but I expect to become one of the first magnitude. Shall you?"

I thought I should.

"I say, '20,'" he exclaimed, after a little interval of silent play, "what's your name? mine's Edward Eldridge. They call me 'Ned,'—those fellows I go with. We only number each other in our public relations,— our official capacity. I'm a high private. Hurrah!" and he tossed the ball up. "Among ourselves, when off duty,—that's the military word,—then we are Tom, Dick, and Harry, or better Tom, Ned, and ——. Come now, what's your name?"

"Let Ralph complete the trio—Ralph Morley," I exclaimed, beginning to share his high spirits.

"Hurrah, then! Three times three for Ralph, Ned, and Tom, the great triumpuerate," tossing the ball high in air.

"The what?" I asked.

"The great triumpuerate. If those old ancients had a triumvirate, why can't we have a triumpuerate; it's a bigger word, and so it should be."

"Who's Tom?" I inquired.

"You shall know him in time; he's a right good, frisky fellow.

"But old '20,'" he continued, after a little interval, during which the ball was actively plied from one to the other, "that honored predecessor of yours! Poor fellow, he was not bad, but I suppose they had to send him away. Come, let us sit down, and I'll tell you all about it.

"He was older than I, and a larger boy, but he entered the school about the same time, and was in the same classes. He didn't know much; hadn't *no* book-learning, as he used to say. But take him out in the field on a fox-hunt, or upon the river, and no one could beat him. He knew all sorts of contrivances for trapping rabbits or squirrels, or catching birds, and he was great on fishing. He occupied the same dormitory I did, and what a litter we had there,—birds'-nests, cages, traps, fishing tackle and nets, besides the live victims of his wiles—birds, families of rabbits, mice, moles, and I don't know what not. Such a stench and dirt they made, you could find the room in the dark by following your nose. Finally the Major had to order a clearance of the whole collection. This almost broke Jack's heart. But he was allowed to carry them out himself, which he did very tenderly, finding hiding-places for all his traps in some of the out-houses, and transporting his numerous family to some neighboring farmer's. All this rather made him popular with the boys, and, despite his dullness in the classroom, he was liked by most of his teachers. But he would not study, and during school-hours he was often sullen and discontented. He didn't like, either, the military exercises; he couldn't seem to learn them; he was in the awkward squad almost all the time he was here, and had to take many a berating from our officers. I think his bad success at school drove him for refuge still more to his rambles over the hills and along the river. At any rate, the passion grew on him, and he at last got to playing truant and staying away over night. The first time, he claimed that, without knowing it, he got so far away—he started out on a Wednesday holiday—that he could not get back before night came on, and he had to beg a lodging in a a farm-house. We found afterward that the farm-house was an old barn. This happened a second and a third time, and his excuse was worn out. Besides, the last time he led off a couple of other boys with him; his love of a wild life was getting to be catching. I suspect, too, the farmers' roosts had to suffer on these expeditions; complaints began to come in from a distance of raids made upon the poultry-yards by boys in blue. So they had to punish him. They wrote home to his father, too, and one day I found poor Jack in tears. He had received a letter from home, scolding him pretty hard for his wild course. It was from his mother, whom he seemed to love dearly, for he often spoke of her. But he had a great dread of his father. He wished, he said, that he liked to sit still and study, as some boys do, but he didn't believe he ever could like it or get used to it. Before he came here, his father, he said, sent him to a day-school in the country, where the boys were kept in the school-room nearly all the day, and a severe teacher stood over them with a rod, and where all was gloomy and dull. He couldn't stand it, he said, and got to playing truant half the time,—he didn't care if he was whipped. And now, he said, he hated to look at a book, and knew he was a dull fellow. Here the poor fellow sobbed so fast that he could not speak, and he finally got up and went away without another word. For a while after this he tried to do better, and labored very hard over his books, and the teachers encouraged him all they could. But it didn't last long. He got to going off again on his long expeditions, and staying away nights; and other boys used often to accompany him—I don't think he asked them, for he liked going alone—but they begged to go along,—this kind of life began to have such a fascination for some of them. Finally, one holiday, a party of them got a boat, and rowed away up the river to the Highlands. They didn't come back that day, nor the next. The principals became alarmed, and sent out a scouting party of the seniors in search of them, but they did not succeed in finding them, though they heard of them here and there, and found traces of their encampments; but the birds had always flown—the nests were abandoned. Finally, the pursuing party returned, unsuccessful. The principals, as you may suppose, were now thoroughly alarmed, and feared that the boys had met with some accident in fording some stream, or in endeavoring to scale some of the precipices of the Highlands. They were preparing to send out another party in search of the fugitives, when who should appear, tramping up the road to the school, but the boys themselves; and such a ragged, jaded set you never saw,—there was scarcely a whole pair of breeches among them. Poor Jack was the last of the party, and tried, as much as possible, to keep out of sight, for he knew he would be singled out as the ringleader in the scrape. One poor fellow, younger than the rest, was so worn that he fainted as soon as he reached the school, and had to be carried at once to the sick-room. But the upshot of it all was that Jack had to leave the school. He was not exactly sent away in disgrace, for he was not really a bad fellow, but he had become such a hero among the boys that it was feared his love of a free wild life would take in the whole school,—at least all the juniors,—and there would be a general stampede for the mountains. His father was advised to send him out West, and give his passion for nature and adventure full swing, and perhaps he would come out well yet, for his heart was all right. I heard his father did so, and I shouldn't wonder if we heard more of poor Jack; he promised to write to me, but I don't believe he ever will,—he said he hadn't any fist for letter-writing. But that last expedition, wasn't it jolly! I should like to have been one of the party,—wouldn't you? Tom was, and you must hear him give an account of it, but not now, it's too late, the drum will beat for drill pretty soon. Hilloa, Tom! Do you see that fellow off there, standing on his head? That's Tom. Tom! Tom! Tom Manning! won't you come here?"

"Who calls me from above?" said the boy addressed, wheeling over upon his feet. "Are you up in the apple-trees, Ned? Prithee, speak again."

"Tom! Tom! Tom!"

"Ah me honey, is it there ye are? 'Whistle and I'll come to ye, my lad.'"

"I suppose I must whistle," said Ned. "What a fellow he is!"

"Arrah, now, sure can't ye whistle a bit?"

And whistle Ned did, bringing two fingers to his lips, whereupon Tom came bounding along. Slackening his pace, when he had advanced within a few yards, and describing a somersault over his hands, he stood before us, a good-looking, but not a handsome fellow, with a merry twinkle in his eye, yet with an evident capacity for sober sentiment reposing beneath his love of fun.

"This is my friend, Ralph Morley," said Ned.

"Then he is mine too," said Tom in his natural tone of voice.

Of course I responded to these kind advances as best I could, though I fear in a timid, constrained way. With Ned I was soon at my ease, there was something so winning and unaffected in his manner; but at first I was a little afraid of Tom, for I knew that I could not exchange brusquerie with him. He seemed, however, to feel this, and with a beautiful untaught politeness he approached me, especially during our early acquaintance, on my own more serious plane.

"I have just been giving Ralph an account of old '20,' his predecessor," said Ned. "You must tell him some time all about that expedition."

"I shall be glad to have another listener. It's fun to go over it all again. I like to spin yarns, you know, Ned," said Tom.

"There!" exclaimed Ned. "There goes the drum for drill! You're in for it now, Ralph. You'll be put in the awkward squad. Come along;" and he threw his arm over my neck in school-boy fashion, and thus led me on, while Tom ran, hopped, skipped, jumped, and proceeded, by every other known or unknown gait, in advance of us.

CHAPTER IV.

THE "AWKWARD SQUAD."

The main body of the school, which had already attained considerable proficiency in military exercises, having been marched off by companies to the parade-ground, the awkward squad, ten or fifteen in number, were left behind, in the open space back of the school-building, to be dressed into soldierly shape and instructed in the simpler movements by one of the senior officers.

"Stand erect! Incline a little forward! Eyes to the front!" were the commands of our officer, directions easy to be understood, but, nevertheless, variously executed. Fat boy on my left, the last of the line, throws his breast and belly forward with a pompous, self-approving manner, and balances himself upon his heels, describing a profile of a semicircular shape. Lean boy on my right, in his effort to incline forward, pushes his head out on a long neck, much in advance of the line, thinking that this member is competent to do service for the whole body.

Officer looks stern, stamps his foot, doesn't swear a big oath, for that is forbidden, but evidently means mischief, if this state of things isn't bettered.

"You there, '29,' draw yourself in, don't round out like a swollen porpoise."

Fat boy flattens himself in front and describes a huge semicircle behind.

"Rein your head in, '72,' don't look like a road-side goose."

Lean boy brings his head back with a jerk, which causes it to oscillate for several minutes at the end of his long neck, like an inverted pendulum; it is at last brought to a poise, and thereafter the eyes of the head are directed to the clouds.

"*Eyes*—RIGHT!"

This command had a startling effect upon the awkward squad. Fat boy, whose eyes do not move easily right or left, being firmly bedded and cushioned in their sockets, turns his whole person to the right; his shoulder and elbow, acting upon mine, force me to make a half-wheel to the left, so that I am brought face to face with my cellulose comrade. My own shoulder grating at the same time upon the lean boy causes him to half-wheel to the right, his eyes still intent upon the clouds. He, in like manner, communicates a semi-circular movement to his next neighbor. And so the right and left facings are executed along the whole line, the result of which is that we stand in couples, face to face.

Our officer, who is at an utter loss to understand how this singular arrangement, this new military movement, has been effected, pauses to take breath. Words fail him. Finally, in stentorian voice, he exclaims—

"Blockheads! As you were!—resume your former position.

"*Eyes*,—now, mind you, I say eyes, not noses.

"*Eyes*—stay there, don't move till I tell you; all I said was *Eyes*.

"Once more, *Eyes*—what are you gazing up in the clouds for, '72'? There, there, don't try to eat your own chin, keep your head straight, look in front; don't look at me. I tell you, look in front.

"*Eyes* (this time with a great increase of voice)— RIGHT!" (Voice soars upward to an eagle pitch.)

The order this time was very well executed, except that some looked to the right, others to the left, others first to the right, then to the left, while some stared with great determination straight ahead.

"FRONT."

This order was executed to perfection. The command, "*Eyes*—LEFT!" was then carried out with the same nice discrimination between the right and the left which had been already exhibited. Officer was beginning to get proud of his squad, and smoothed the hilt of his sword with martial fondness. Inclined to allow his men a little respite, he gave the order "*Rest!*" which the fat boy, nothing loath, executed with great contentment by squatting down on the ground, from which posture, much to his surprise, he was suddenly uplifted.

The officer then proceeded to describe the movement of facing to the right, and very neatly illustrated it before their eyes. Squad looked on with a mingled expression of wonder, delight, and mystification.

"*Attention—squad! Right*—FACE!"

In the sudden and energetic jerking to the right which followed the word of command, the boy on the extreme right, miscalculating his distance, brought back his right heel with great force upon the right foot of the boy behind him; the latter finding his right foot firmly fixed to the ground, sympathetically jerked his left heel back upon the left foot of the boy next in file;

the like cause produced the like effect along the whole line, and that almost instantaneously, so that the legs of the recruits exhibited, as the result of the order, a row of inverted V's united at the base.

This novel demonstration only lasted a few moments; it was quickly followed by an excited hopping about on the part of the disintegrated squad, which only ended by each boy gently caressing his wounded foot, while he skillfully balanced himself upon the sound one. The first boy of the line alone remained quiet in his place, wearing a look of innocent surprise.

That our officer was enraged, that he stormed at us with the shot and shell of explosive words, that he swaggered about fearfully and fearlessly, may naturally be expected and needs not my relating. His anger having at last somewhat expended itself, leaving only the smoldering flame, and quiet being restored, he once more throws out from his manly chest—

"*Attention*—SQUAD!"

Each young recruit braces himself in a soldier-like attitude with evident intention to do or die.

"*Right*—FACE!"

Not to mention a few blemishes, such as that some in the enthusiasm of the action, wheeled clean about; while others, having in sad remembrance the result of the last trial, instinctively turned to the left—barring such little blemishes as these, the movement was well executed. Our officer's stern features began to relax, a smile of satisfaction seemed to lurk about the corners of his mouth. However, he caused the movement to be repeated several times, and was evidently pleased with the proficiency attained.

"Now, my lads," said he, "let us have this movement executed once more, and then we'll try you on facing to the left.

"*Attention—squad! Right*—FACE."

On this occasion the movement would have been carried out to perfection, had it not been for a little incident or accident which marred the effect of the whole. The fat boy on my left, being in danger, in consequence of the unwonted energy of his action, of losing his balance and falling backward, made such a vigorous effort to regain his equilibrium, that he projected himself with great weight against my back; I, in my turn, was thus thrown upon the lean boy in front of me; lean boy, in like manner, communicated the impetus to the boy before him; and the motion thus originated proceeded without any noticeable lapse of time along the whole line, so that all fell, as one man, face downward, one overlapping another. Fat boy was slow to move, and being the last of the line, kept us locked fast in our humiliating position. Meantime, our officer, having had time to recover his first surprise, in the anger of the moment, could not restrain himself from taking advantage of the fine opportunity, and, placing his foot upon the neck of the prostrate fat boy, with the flat of his sword, severely castigated that portion of his body which, as he wore no coat-tails, was especially exposed. Sir Officer, having then rolled off the fat boy, proceeded to administer similar military discipline to the next incumbent, and thus continued along the whole line.

We rose smarting with pain and chagrin. Our officer, folding his arms across his heaving breast, and assuming an attitude *à la* Napoleon, with right foot thrown out and chin well-reined in, looked at us as who should say, "There, my fine fellows, how like you that? Is it fitting?" Fortunately, at this moment the signal was given for the close of the drill.

Casting a glance toward the parade-ground, I saw that the whole school was drawn up for military review. And a gallant sight they presented. Our officer dismissed us in time to run forward and see the Major receive the military salutes of the Captains. The several companies were then bid to " break ranks ;" and at once, amid the merry beating of the drum and whistling of the fife, there was a general dissolution of the bright array, and soon the whole green was sprinkled with gay, careering youth. The soldier was thrown off, and the boy was once more in the ascendant.

CHAPTER V.

THE FEAST.

"Hurrah, Ralph," exclaimed Ned, meeting me on the parade-ground one Wednesday afternoon, soon after our return from a long ramble,—Wednesday was the regular weekly holiday,—"Hurrah! I have just learned that a box of good things has arrived for me from home, and I have obtained permission for you and me and Tom to spend the evening together in our room. We'll open the box and try the dainties, and then Tom shall tell us the story of that last expedition of poor old '20',—you know I promised he should the other day."

This proposition—as well the dainties as the story of adventure—appealed strongly to my fresh boyish appetite. We waited impatiently for the bells which should call us successively to evening prayers and to supper.

This was only my second week at school, yet, owing to the pleasant attentions of Ned and Tom, I already felt at home. Under other circumstances it would have been many weeks before my naturally shy and reserved nature would have adapted itself to the new mode of life. We had spent the holiday in rambling about the neighborhood, mutually confiding to each other the brief experiences of our lives,—where we had lived, what kind of schools we had attended, what were the eccentricities of the teachers we had been under, what scrapes we had been engaged in. My two friends took pride, too, in taking me to those places where the surrounding country could be seen to the best advantage. We were all just of that age when to youth of a generous turn, nature begins to speak a spiritual language, whose meaning is felt, if it is not understood. Nature, however, was not so much a spectacle to be enjoyed, as a kind of food to be appropriated to our sustenance; we did not hold up our hands before it, and express ourselves in animated phrases; we tasted it, drank it in, as something that should make a part of ourselves.

The brief remainder of daylight that was left us after supper, we spent in the open air upon the playground, for we were avaricious of all the day we could get. But when the first stars began to come forth, while the orange hues were still warm in the west, the school was called in for the night. My friend Ned hastened with me to the appointed place of meeting,—the room occupied by himself and Tom. Two other boys were also invited to the entertainment. We had been there but a few minutes, when we heard Tom bounding up, two stairs at a time, followed by the two other guests whom he had remained to seek, and who proved to be the fat and the lean boys of the awkward squad.

No words were lost in idle ceremony, for we were boys. We gathered around the box with eagerness, as Ned lifted the cover, which had been already loosened. Ned had spread a clean white sheet of paper, of ample size, upon one of the beds; he now proceeded to pull forth a frosted pound-cake, a jar of preserved fruit, a jelly-cake, a second jar of preserves, a box of almonds and other nuts, oranges, bananas, half a dozen bottles of sarsaparilla, finally a silver fruit-knife, with his name chased on it. All these things Ned set forth on the bed in such a manner as best to please the eye and excite the palate.

The ceremony had proceeded without words, occasional suppressed exclamations alone giving vent to our agitated hearts. When Ned had finished his arrangements, he stepped back behind the rest of us to contemplate the display at a little distance. We, meantime, set up a noisy expression of our admiration and delight. Looking back to Ned, I saw that his eyes were filled with tears; he was thinking of the dear ones at home,—the darling mother, the sweet sister,—whose hands had devised and prepared for him this pleasure. These delicacies appealed in him to a finer sense than that of taste, and made his eyes water, as they made our mouths.

But remembering at once his duty as host, Ned bade us "fall to," and seeing us wait for a leader, "Come, Tom," he added "do you cut the cake." Tom obeyed with alacrity, and soon a more contented set of boys you never saw, two of us seated on the beds swinging our legs backward and forward, two others straddling chairs, another perched on a trunk placed on end, each having in hand a formidable piece of cake.

"Why," said Tom, "are we like that poor family down the street opposite the grocery store?"

"Because," he added, finding us all too seriously employed to pay much heed to his conundrum, or else too well satisfied with our condition to perceive any points of resemblance between it and that of the poor family mentioned, "because ours is a very hand-to-mouth life," saying which he stored away a huge mouthful of cake.

After the cake came a course of preserves,—we liked one thing at a time in those days, we believed in a concentration of gustatory enjoyment, not in a dainty dissipation of it. To serve these, Ned had obtained a sufficient number of saucers from the housekeeper, whose good graces he knew how to propitiate.

"Look-a-here, Sambo," said Tom to the fat boy, whose name by abbreviation was Sam, "I want to propound a conundrum to yer. Now you jist scratch yer wool over dis—Why are we fellows like the boys in the 'jug' this morning?"

The "jug" was the purgatory of the school; it was the name given by the boys to a small room, of a peculiar shape, in which delinquents were confined.

"Yer can't scratch that out, Sambo, no use tryin', it's too deep, ha! ha!—'Cause we're well preserved."

"That's an ill-preserved joke," said Ned, "'t wont keep."

Fat boy and lean boy occupied themselves seriously with the work in hand.

Joke-cracking was interrupted by a very lively cracking of nuts, moistened by an occasional sucking of oranges.

"Why," said Ned, "are we like those biscuit we had for supper this evening? There, Tom, you joke-cracker, crack me that."

"I'm cracking a nut just now," said Tom.

"Because we are nut crackers, and neither were they," explained Ned.

"By cracky! that joke came out between your teeth, and was cracked in coming. Feel his head, Ralph."

The nuts, fruit, and bon-bons having been liberally dealt with, while more such boyish wit was tossed about among us, Ned, perceiving that the gustatory energies of his guests were beginning to flag, produced glasses, and said we must now test the virtues of the sarsaparilla.

Each boy armed himself with a bottle, and it was agreed that we should all draw the corks at the same moment, and see how loud a report could be made.

"But before you draw," said Tom, "I propose that this combined report shall be considered as a salute to our entertainer, and that we drink the foaming glass in his honor. May the report of his virtues go over the earth! Now then, ready! one—two—*three!*"

Pop-p-p-p-p!

Such a concussion was made that Mammy Hunter,—the matron,—who was then sorting out clothes for the wash, in the room beneath us, lost her breath for several minutes; recovering it again just in time to prevent a collapse of her mortal frame, she started to go up-stairs, to learn the cause of the alarm, taking, however, the precaution to furnish herself with her medicine-box, and some linen bandages and lint, a store of which she always kept on hand.

Meanwhile, as Mrs. Hunter was a large, fat woman, and didn't find getting up-stairs a very easy task, Ned had time to express his thanks for the honor paid him.

"And now, my comrades," he added, with a slight tremor in his voice, "let us drink to the loved ones at home."

"We will, we will," said all, "and hope they may send each of us, soon, such a box as this."

"Well, my fine fellows, what's all this. You've nearly taken the life of me. Is any one hurt?"

"Yes, yes, Mammy. Terrible calamity!" said Tom. "Do you see those fellows on the bed?" pointing to the bottles; "their heads suddenly flew off, and there's no longer any life in them. Alas! alas!" and he wrung his hands.

"And look here, Mammy," said Ned, "here's the way it happened," saying which, he drew the cork of the remaining bottle, and held a foaming goblet to her lips. Mrs. Hunter appreciated the joke, and smacked her lips upon it; then, helping herself to the fat piece of cake which was tendered her, the good soul retreated from the room amid the applause of the company.

A lull then occurring, I ventured to propose that now was the time for the story.

"Yes, yes, the story!" said all.

"Clear your pipe, Tom."

CHAPTER VI.

ADVENTURES IN THE HIGHLANDS.

Tom cleared his throat, and began in epic style.

Sing, O muse! sing the wrath of offended Minerva, goddess of schools, and the direful ire of her high-priest in this temple of learning, who inflicted stinging blows upon the truant subjects of the goddess, and long time confined them in the cruel jug, and one he drove forth an exile; this one, impelled by fate, wanders perchance over interminable western wilds, a prey to biting remorse and the snaky furies.

"Hold, hold!" cried Ned, "I pray you descend; you have left us all a-gape here on the ground."

You groveling souls, must I then limp along in modern prose? Then be it known to you, that on a certain Wednesday morning in the month of June last, when nature was looking very fine, a party of young scamps, the present narrator one of them, met at a place agreed upon, beyond the limits of the village. They were all evidently bent on a distant expedition, for their knapsacks bulged out with supplies,—bread and cheese, doubtless,—and blankets were strapped to their shoulders. Their meeting in an out-of-the-way place, with no one of the teachers among them, as well as a certain uneasy expression of face, indicated that they were about to undertake something forbidden.

We—for I find I can not ride the dignified gait of

the third person much longer, and would better at once take up with the less ponderous trot of the "first"—*we* stole our way to the river by a circuitous route, fearful lest we should meet some one of the teachers, who might question us unpleasantly about our intentions.

One of our party—it was old "20," or Jack, as he was called familiarly—had gone in advance, and had obtained a boat, which he had rowed about a mile above the wharfs to a secluded cove, shut out from sight by overhanging rocks, and only reached from the land side by a winding and rugged path leading through a dense wood. It was Jack, who, thoroughly acquainted with the whole shore, had selected this spot as the most favorable for our escape. Here we all embarked, and immediately pulled with all our vigor into the open water. We were not a great way from the mouth of the Croton river, and on our right, Croton Point extended far out into the Hudson. Along this long neck of land we coasted, keeping thus as far from the village wharfs as possible, nor did we look back, until we had got some distance out. Then Jack took from his pocket a spy-glass, which he always carried with him in his expeditions, and directed it toward a group upon the shore, a little distance above the wharfs. He distinguished, he said, one of the teachers,—Mr. Homans, he thought,—who seemed to be holding a pebble in his hand, and to be reading sermons from it to the group of boys that surrounded him. But what we cared most to learn was, whether we were observed, and, satisfied on this point, we took to our oars again, and pulled vigorously without rest, until we had reached the end of Croton Point. Our original intention was, to row di-

rectly across the river to High Torn, and climb to its highest crag; but we had no sooner passed the Point, than we were caught in the current of a flood-tide, and borne rapidly up the river. A strong breeze too, was blowing from the southwest, which, with the tide, set the waves quite high, and frequently dashed us with spray. We were not daunted, however, and headed the boat as much as we dared, toward the opposite shore. We had made but little progress across the stream, when looking up from our rowing to take our bearings, we found that we had already been carried far above Croton Point, up Haverstraw bay; the wind and the tide were set against our reaching High Torn.

Jack, who was at the helm, surveyed our situation with a great deal of composure; Will Cutting, Joe Hallam, Ben Wolff, and myself tugged at the oars, while little Walden, who begged so hard to go along, sat at the prow.

"Boys," said Jack, "what's the use wasting your strength trying to get to High Torn? We shall have to land away above it, or turn the boat's head down the river, and row against the tide which is setting in so strongly. I don't believe you fellows can do it—you haven't the muscle. And what's the use? Why not ride on these waves to the Dunderberg yonder? we can reach it in an hour, and then this afternoon the ebb-tide will bring us back again as quickly. What do you say, fellows?"

"Just the plan!" "That's it!" "I'm for that," exclaimed several of us at once. " Hurrah for the Dunderberg!"

Yet, seen from the bosom of Haverstraw bay, those great, silent Highlands, in whose hollows great, dark shadows couched, seemed to have a threatening aspect, that filled us secretly with fear, while at the same time they seemed partly to allure us on, partly to draw us to themselves by a power which we could not resist, just as they seemed to draw the river into their fastnesses and hide it mysteriously from our sight.

Jack now insisted upon taking an oar, and Joe Hallam, who was considerably blown, was glad to yield his place. Jack was a skillful oarsman, and his well-directed stroke soon made itself felt; with the waves setting their shoulders to our boat, like so many Tritons—those puffy fellows we read of in Virgil—we were borne rapidly up Haverstraw bay. As we neared Stony Point, Jack pointed out to us the low ground, over which "Mad Anthony" led his few brave followers to the midnight assault of the fortress that once crowned this bold headland. Shooting swiftly by the Point, through the channel that separates it from Verplanck's Point, Jack bade the steersman incline the boat's head toward the left. A few strokes of the oar brought us into the smooth water, which was sheltered from the tide by the projecting bluff which we had just passed. The mountain towered up before us; looked at from the level of the river, it seemed almost to have a life of its own and to be rising up with a sensible motion from the breast of the waters. We rowed gently along, seeking a suitable place in which to moor the boat. At last Jack's experienced eye discovered the spot wanted. It was a recess in the shore, inclosed by great fragments of rock, which had been evidently detached from the sides of the mountain and had rolled to the water's edge; they were thickly covered with moss and lichens, and between them trees had taken root and grown to a considerable size, and now with their branches overhung the water. Great bowlders of rock, too, had rolled out into the river bed and shut in this little retreat almost completely from the waves; we were barely able to get the boat through one of the wider channels. The waters there were so still and quiet that you could look down in them and see another world set up against the world above and around us, and seeming almost as clear and as real. Little Walden in particular was delighted, and was sure some water-nymph inhabited this retreat, and he looked around somewhat fearfully as if she might be peeping upon the intruders from behind some jutting rock, or might be hidden somewhere in the watery realm of shadows below. You know, Ned, what a poet the little fellow is.

But Jack, who was, of course, our leader, proceeded at once to business, and with a stroke of his oar bringing the boat alongside a low shelving rock, bade us jump out; then pushing the boat back till it lay midway between one of the outlying bowlders and a point of rock that jutted out from one side of the cove, he threw out a line from the bow of the boat and bade us make it fast to the trunk of the tree that grew in a cleft, then telling Will Cutting to leap out and climb over to the bowlder, he threw out another line from the stern and showed Will how, by running the rope through a split in the rock and then tying a knot at the end, the line would be securely fastened. Jack permitted the ropes to slack a little, so as to allow for the fall in the tide. It was a question now how Jack was to reach the land without getting wet, and we began to raise a laugh at his expense. But Jack had already thought of this; taking hold, as far out as he could, of the line which was attached to the outlying rock, he swung himself clear of the boat, and went hand over hand, with his feet dangling in the air, till he reached the rock, upon which, by availing himself of jutting foot-holds, he easily clambered.

We all now started at once to push our way amid the broken rocks and through the bushes to the steeper rise of the mountain; but Jack, who was not to be hurried, and was always calm and steady, checked us. We must not, he said, rush wildly up the mountain, like maddened boars, or we might not reach the top after all, and only dash our heads against insurmountable precipices. Mountains were to be approached circumspectly and respectfully; they had a quiet, dignified way of resenting all hasty and inconsiderate advances.

This was a large speech for Jack to make, and the boys regarded him with open eyes, and seemed about to break into a laugh, but instead of that they began to look sheepish and foolish at the thought of their boyishness. In fact, Jack appeared like an altogether different fellow out in the open country, engaged in the present undertaking, from what we had been accustomed to considering him in the school-room, and he easily took his place as our captain.

Jack pointed out that it would be almost impossible to scale the mountain by direct ascent, that though we could proceed successfully for the greater part of the distance, we would eventually be brought to a stand before an impregnable wall of rock, which, on examination through the glass, presented very few foot-holds to the climber, and was altogether too dangerous of ascent for inexperienced mountaineers; if he was alone he might undertake it, but it would not do for us to attempt it. He went on to show us that, by aiming a little to the left, we would find a weak spot in the defenses of the citadel, whence doubtless we could easily make our way to the highest battlements; and as this more accessible point, which was easily seen from where we were standing, would be lost to sight as soon as we penetrated the woods, it would be necessary to determine its direction by the compass. Saying which, Jack pulled out his pocket-instrument, and showed us that we should have to take a course west by north.

Jack's words left nothing more to be said, and he led off at once along and up the mountain side in the direction indicated.

Looking back as we climbed, we could see the river lying apparently almost within a stone's-throw, though it was now nearly a mile out from us, for you must know, of course, that we were not climbing that part of the Dunderberg which slopes on its eastern side down to the water's edge: our outlook was to the southeast, in the direction of Stony Point and Haverstraw bay. It was pleasant thus to catch through the trees a glimmering view of the waters as they sparkled in the sun, and of the white sails of schooners wafted by, and of the broken and receding line of hills upon the opposite shore; yet this incomplete view, these peepings here and there, were tantalizing and made us the more eager to get to the top of the mountain, whence we could take in all with one sweep of the eye.

We had just succeeded with much toil in climbing a formidable ridge of rocks and had attained, all panting and athirst, the open space at the top, when Jack, who was as usual in advance, cried out, "Hark, fellows! I hear bubbling water; there is a spring somewhere near by; scatter about and search the ground." Soon a shout from one of the boys brought us all together around the object of our hunt. In a moment we were all down on our hands and knees with our faces dipped down to the cooling waters, and such delicious draughts, I think, I never drank before. For some moments not a head was raised; at last, first one, then another was lifted up, while watery globules of light dripped from our faces into the transparent pool, from which, in turn, distorted fragments of faces looked up in grinning mockery, and through the pebbly basin you could see the blue heavens and wavering clouds, and the green shimmer of leaves. When we had at last slaked our thirst, and had thrown ourselves back upon the herbage, or variously disposed ourselves in cozy and comfortable nooks in the bed of rock, we permitted ourselves to take in lazily the beauty of the place. We were shaded by a group of trees, through which the sunbeams slanted down, flinging gules of light around us and on us, which, as the tree-tops swayed to and fro in the breeze, danced merrily over the mosses and lichens on the rocks, over the quiet pool that looked up from the world beneath, over the forked and knotty roots of the trees that seemed to gripe hold of the rocks with a savage force, over the moist, green herbage that filled all the more open spaces, and, finally, over the winking eyes and the noses of us truant boys, who were strewed about in attitudes almost as twisted as the roots of the trees. Walden, our young poet, lay on his back, looking up through the trees to the snatches of sky and floating cloud, while a stray sunbeam was playing with the tip of his boot; he was, I suppose, conning fancies in his brain which unconsciously took their rhythm from the ripple of the waters that, after stealing silently out of the pool, danced merrily over the fragments of rock that interrupted their course. Of a sudden a great shadow fell over us all; the play of sunlight had ceased. We were startled from our attitudes of rest, and looked up to see if a thunder-storm were not gathering over us; but the sky was clear. It was the shadow of the mountain that had imperceptibly stolen upon us: the sun, though still high in the heavens, had fallen over it.

Jack jumped to his feet and said, we must move on, it was getting late; we had engaged not to open our knapsacks till we had reached the top, and he, for one, was getting hungry. We stretched ourselves and rose, Walden last of all, loath, I suppose, to leave his reveries.

We were now about to set off afresh, when our attention was arrested by the singular manner of Jack, who kept walking about this way and that, peering through the trees, and scanning the mountain side and the ground about him with one eye and the other, like a thoughtful chicken. Finally, "Boys," said he, "look-a-here! this little ripple of water joins a larger stream a little to our left, which runs down from the point toward which we are aiming; by striking this large water-course we shall have an easier and quicker ascent the rest of the way, for water always chooses the easiest paths." There was so much decision in Jack's words that we did not think of objecting. Jack led off at once, and we trudged rapidly after him, keeping upon the same terrace of the mountain side, though it seemed to be leading us down rather than upward.

We had not gone very far before we heard the sound of running water, and presently we found ourselves standing on the edge of a stream which was precipitating itself with great spirit over the ledge of rocks upon which we stood. The fall was not very great, but the water was caught and broken up so much by projecting rocks that when it reached the bottom it was enveloped in a cloud of spray, which the currents of wind that played about the cascade blew back into our faces. It was a lively scene, but we did not stay long; we turned up the stream and dashed on with an animation which we seemed to catch from its waters. Sometimes we followed the banks, where they were sufficiently clear of brush to allow an easy passage, but generally we had to leap from rock to rock along the bed of the stream, while the brook kept up its constant chatter under our feet, sometimes dashing up at us from beneath some rock with a kind of "ha-ha" in its voice, as if it sought to mock and affright us. We leaped forward and upward, as if some goblin of the stream or wood were pursuing us; and, indeed, what with the gloom that overcast the mountain side, and the jagged and dark rocks, often grotesquely shaped that bordered the brook, and the incessant clamor of the brook itself, which, as it coursed under and among the rocks, filled the air sometimes with hollow sepulchral voices, sometimes with sharp contending ones, added to a lingering sense of guilt which the pleasures of the day had not wholly driven from us—what with all this, it was not wonderful if a feeling of fear pervaded our little band. Every now and then some one of us would look back over his shoulder, as if he heard other steps than those of his companions. We held our way with few words, each one sought by his silence to conceal his fears. At length, looking a little a-head, we saw before us a mass of rocks which seemed to cut off our further progress, unless we essayed to climb them; nor did we, as we expected, hear the sound of falling water. What trick was the brook now about to play us?

As we approached, we found our mysterious companion flowing seemingly right out from the rocks at a spot where there was a little thicket of low bushes. Was this the cradle of its merry life? Jack, stepping forward to explore the mystery, broke away some of the brush, and revealed a cave-like opening in the rock, large enough to admit a fellow of my size by stooping; from this the brook was flowing in a leisurely, self-contained manner, which seemed to say, "I know what I know, and keep my own secret"—for so the poet Walden interpreted its voice; as for me, I don't pretend to understand the lingo of the brooks. But one thing is certain, we all felt a great desire to penetrate this subterranean passage and learn what this provoking little stream was babbling about, all to itself.

Jack was the first to propose this, and though most of us, I dare say, notwithstanding our curiosity, felt much secret trepidation, and would gladly have left our curiosity unsatisfied, we loudly asserted our readiness to follow. Jack stooped and entered, and was almost immediately swallowed up in the greedy shadows that crouched a little way back from the opening of the cave; we stole cautiously after him like a gang of thieves. After our eyes had become accustomed to the light, we picked our way over the stones among which the brook was rumbling, without much difficulty. We had not gone far, when we heard, though faintly at first, a peculiar roaring noise, unlike any thing we had ever listened to. The further we went, the louder became the noise, while the light kept diminishing in intensity. Pretty soon we were wrapped in almost impenetrable gloom, and what with the darkness and the hollow resounding din that filled the cave and swept by us, our hearts began to quail.

At this moment Jack cried out, "Light ahead! let us on!" The word was passed from one to another,—for it was impossible for all to hear him amid the din; our courage revived, and we proceeded with less timid steps. In a few minutes, there was a sensible lifting of the darkness, and, advancing now at a quicker pace, we presently entered a spacious, dim-lit chamber, at the remoter part of which, where the light got admission, we could discern, though but faintly at first, a gleaming and a flashing as of falling water. The whole air was filled with spray, which we could feel upon our cheeks, though we could not see it. The floor of the cave was nearly covered with a pool of water,—how deep we could not tell;—its surface was only slightly disturbed by the falling stream, and as we strained our eyes gazing upon it, it seemed to glisten with a deep black look of treacherous malignity. Through all the din that filled the cave, we could hear the slow waves of this pool, as they wound round and lapped the stones at our feet, break up with a cold, dripping sound. A shudder seemed to affect us all at the same moment, as we stood there grasping each other by the hand, wrist, or shoulder, as happened. There seemed to be a power of fascination in this dark, glistening pool, drawing you toward it, and I could feel the impressible Walden, as I held him firmly by the wrist, lean forward as if about to yield himself to its cold embraces.

Jack, who was more master of himself than we, broke the spell by bidding us to feel our way along the wall of the cavern, by the narrow space between it and the edge of the pool, to the opposite side, where he thought we could climb the rocks over which the stream was tumbling. He could scarcely make himself heard, and it was more by gesture than by speech that he made himself understood. On our reaching the farther part of the rocky chamber, we climbed without much difficulty up the rocks, beside the waterfall, though there were points at which a misstep might have precipitated the adventurer into the dark pool beneath. Creeping through the low arched opening at the top, we found ourselves in still another rock-walled apartment, which was even larger than the one from which we had just emerged; and through an opening nearly opposite the place of our entrance, could be seen the open sky. As you may suppose, after mole-ing our way for such a distance in subterranean darkness, we all rushed eagerly forward to greet the light, and breathe the pure air. My companions uttered a shout of exultation when they discovered that they could look off upon mountain heights beyond that which we had been climbing, and that, therefore, they had at last gained the crest, if not the highest point.

Some of the boys were about to scramble out at once, when our attention was drawn by Walden, who had lagged behind, to some singular phenomena which the cave presented. The floor of the cave was comparatively smooth, as if it had been in some earlier time washed and worn by water: on this surface we could trace out, graven in the rock, what seemed to be the foot-prints of some wild animal ; so real-looking were they, that we could hardly trust our own senses and believe that we were walking over solid rock ; and they could be easily tracked from one part of the cave to another. Mr. Ellery afterward told me that we were probably right in conjecturing these marks to be the foot-prints of some wild animal. He said that in some early age this cave was probably flooded with a mud of clay and sand, and that while the mud was yet soft, some wild beast had entered and left the prints of his claws in it; that afterward the mud had hardened into solid rock, for almost all rock, he says, is only hardened mud.

The brook, now a very diminutive stream indeed, had worn a channel through the middle of the cavern floor ; it issued out of a recess of the cave, on the right, across which a deep shadow fell ; examining the recess more closely, we found the water gushing out from the wall of the rock through a narrow crevice, and what a pleasant, yet plaintive lullaby it made, as it bubbled over upon the rocky floor. But what was our surprise to find that it was caught in a basin formed in the rock apparently by artificial means, for the stone was not simply worn away, as by the waters themselves, but was chipped off in places, as if some intelligent being had sought to aid nature in her slow work. But our astonishment was greatly increased, when one of the boys, as we were kneeling about the basin in the dark, placed his hand upon a piece of stone, which had been evidently hewn by human skill into the form of a rude bowl. This was not the work of a white man, we all said; the cave had been inhabited in early days by some Indian hunter, and this was the bowl he drank from.

After our first surprise had subsided, we dipped the bowl in the water and drank all around in turn. Peace to the shade of the old warrior and happy hunting-grounds be his!—such was our sentiment.

Our curiosity being now greatly aroused, we began to search for other memorials of our Indian chief. Soon one of us discovered upon a little natural shelf in the wall a number of arrow-heads, very symmetrically shaped. But we had hardly had time to examine these ancient weapons and pass them about from one to another, when a sudden cry of alarm, almost of horror, from one of the boys, brought us all around him in a moment, begging to know what was the matter.

"There! there!" said he, pointing with his finger, while he averted his head. We peered into a dark recess, which had not been observed before. At first there was nothing but darkness visible, but as we gazed steadily in the direction our terrified comrade was pointing with head averted, there seemed to come forth, as it were from the night, a—human skeleton. We were held immovable in the peering attitudes in which we had placed ourselves, but instinctively clutched each other by the hand or arm, as happened. It sat bolt upright against the rock, and its frame-work of bones now shone upon our excited vision with a kind of sepulchral light. The skull which surmounted it seemed to us in our excitement to be inhabited by some demoniac spirit, which gleamed out from the cavities of the eyes and breathed through the sunken nostrils. As we gazed fixedly, rooted to the spot by terror, the grinning jaws seemed to chatter with a vain effort at speech. We started convulsively, almost as if we heard its empty gabble, and on the instant broke loose from each other with wild shouts, that were repeated in unearthly echoes, as it seemed, from numerous subterranean channels. We rushed pell-mell to the mouth of the cave, and out. Having reached the light of day, we sped away in a body, without thought as to our course, nor did we regain our courage, till we were some distance from the spot; neither did we care to return, though bowl and arrow-heads, which we meant to show with so much triumph to our school-fellows, had been forgotten in the flight.

But lest some of you be tempted to go off secretly in search of this wonderful cave, I must tell you that a party of us, some time after this truant expedition, set out from the school in company with Mr. Ellery, prepared to make a thorough exploration of it. We followed the brook to the ridge of rocks, whence it issued, but much to our disappointment we found that great masses of rock and earth had slid down and blocked up the opening. The stream, however, had worked its way through, and seemed, as it leaped over the outmost obstacle, to shake its crested neck for a mad chase down the hill-side, but entrance for human being there was none. We climbed up the mountain and looked for the opposite opening of the cave, but our search was vain. I, who acted as guide to the party, had been too greatly scared to take note of the spot.

To return to the story of our adventures, though the sun now dipped well to the west and the fresh air of the mountain awakened a sense of hunger which the excitement of our journey had thus far overpowered, we determined to keep good our word and reach the highest point of the mountain before we unbuckled our knapsacks and relieved them of their contents. We were no long, however, in accomplishing this, for the going along the mountain-crest was unimpeded by broken rock or rank, entangling vegetation, and hunger was a spur in our sides.

On reaching the point aimed at, we did not wait to look about us, but each boy, unstrapping his knapsack and disposing himself as best he could on the rock, fell upon the contents with vigor. When I had satisfied the first cravings of appetite, I looked up and saw—bread and cheese disappearing with remarkable rapidity. There was no room for words. Then each fellow, as he finished his repast, laid himself back on the rock, and with his hat drawn over his eyes to shield them from the sun, gave himself up to the luxury of rest.

How long we lay thus I do not know; to us, fatigued as we were, the time seemed short enough, but when at last we rose, and, with long yawns, stretched our legs, to our surprise we discovered the sun low down in the sky; in an hour, perhaps, it would set. What was to be done?

You must know that when we set out on our escapade, no one of us acknowledged an intention to be gone longer than till evening roll-call, though it is possible that most of us secretly thought how grand it would be to pass a night under the open sky. At any rate, it was evident that so far from getting back to roll-call, it would take us till late in the night to reach the school. The gloom of twilight would be upon us before we could get down the mountain-side, and with the weird recollections of the brook and the fearful memory of the cave haunting us, the thought of retracing our steps affected us with the horrors. We were all agreed that it was necessary to spend the night upon the mountain, and accordingly we began to look about us to see what we should do to make ourselves comfortable.

Our first demand was for water; we had had but a dry dinner; bread and cheese require a little moistening. We dispersed ourselves like a band of skirmishers at a distance of thirty or forty yards from each other, and moved cautiously along the northern slope of the mountain, examining the ground about us. It was not long before a shout from Jack, who was always the luckiest, brought us all together, and we were soon slaking our thirst in a spring of delicious, ice-cold water.

Our next care was to prepare our couch for the night. For this purpose, following Jack's directions, we stripped off the lower branches of a group of hemlocks which grew a little way down the mountain, and spread them on the hard rock of the mountain-top, laying down, first, a layer of the larger branches, and upon these the light and feathery twigs in such a manner that a smooth, evenly arranged, and springy surface was formed; upon this we spread our blankets, ready for use. And not until all our preparations were completed, did we pause to look around on the splendid scene which our elevated position commanded.

The sun was just setting. His last lingering rays shot aslant through the passes of the hills, and deep shadows crouched in their hollows as if preparing to spring upon the heights, their prey. Suddenly the sun was gone, and at once the whole heavens flamed up with an orange light, and the hills were crowned with a purple splendor; the shadows crouched lower. Then, as if by magic, islands and reefs of islands, floated out in the west, catching up and dividing the light and flinging it from one to another, and heavens deepened beyond heavens, each with its peculiar glory. We looked northward, and saw the noble Highland brotherhood, their heads encircled with a halo of light; we looked southward, and saw the long billow of the High Torn range with its broken crest; and beheld the broad expanse of Haverstraw bay, its waves leaping up everywhere, like frothy tongues, to lap to themselves so much of the fleeting glory as they might; and beheld Croton Point reaching out into the waters and seeming to pulse in the wavering light, and beyond it the gentle swell of Mount Pleasant with its company of hills, all sparkling in reflected light, as if the hour was a festive one.

We gazed about us in silence. It seemed, at that moment, as if our own souls were expanded like the heavens above and around us, and were filled with a like splendor, and as if a word, a whisper, a breath might break the divine illusion.

Presently, one by one, the stars came out in the deepening blue, while the earth faded away in the gloom below us. "Are not these," at last said Walden, in a low voice, pointing solemnly to the sky, "are not these the eyes of the Universe, looking down upon us?"

Then we lay down upon our bed of hemlock, and drawing our blankets over us, with the light of the sun still lingering softly in the west, and the stars gathering in bright companies above, and the darkening mountains stationed like hooded sentinels about us, slept.

The next morning we rose with the sun, and I am sorry to say, that, notwithstanding we were naughty runaways, we felt as gay as young larks; indeed, standing on our mountain-top with the world still in shadow below us, we fancied that we, like Shakespeare's lark, were "at heaven's gate," but as our American lark does not sing, we also refrained from that amiable kind of exercise, contenting ourselves with our naturally wild, discordant shouts.

We kept our place for a little while, watching the sunlight steal down the hills north and west of us, and then, at a suggestion from Jack, proceeded to the spring which we had discovered on the preceding evening, and following the stream that issued from it, a little way in its course, till we reached a favorable spot, we freely dashed the water over our faces and necks, and shook or rubbed them dry. Returning to the fountain-head, we seated ourselves about it on the rocks and moss, and produced from our knapsacks the remnants of our bread and cheese. The supply was hardly adequate to our appetites, but we drank of the water of the spring, and each one professed himself satisfied.

Thus far there had been no word spoken concerning our course for the day; we all wanted at heart to continue our explorations, at least during the morning, not returning to the school till the afternoon. But no one summoned up the courage to make the proposition; each of us waited for another to speak. The result was, that when we were done eating, we wandered along in a random way without any plan, but strangely enough, at the end of fifteen or twenty minutes, we all found ourselves some distance down the mountain-side, a fact which did not look like returning at once to the school. We had followed pretty closely the course of the stream which had led us in a north-easterly direction, and had not as yet made a very rapid descent; now, however, it quickened its pace, and the little mad-cap precipitated itself down the mountain-side in the most reckless way, now butting with much froth and foam against the impediments in its bed, now leaping wildly over a ledge of rocks, now ducking out of sight beneath the mold and dead leaves or rocks, and reappearing at a distance, all the while filling the woods with its many-throated clamor, which was at one moment loud and defiant, then half-suppressed. When we had followed the brook to where it began its more rapid career, we seemed to be simultaneously seized with the same passion, and, as it were, gave chase to the fleeing stream. With a mad vehemence almost equal to its own, we swung or tumbled from one tree to another along the borders of the brook, or, like it, slid or leaped over the rocks, rolled over the great worm-eaten logs, dived under the thick underbrush, clumps of which sometimes lay in our course, and so continued till the brook, having almost reached the base of the mountain, flowed with a more gentle current.

We now paused to take breath in an opening in the woods, a spot where the brook circling round formed a quiet little pool. We could not help laughing in each other's faces at our mad descent of the mountain, as well as at the tacit manner in which we had come to an understanding with respect to our course for the day.

"Well," said Will Cutting, "we are not going back to school this morning, that's plain."

"I agree to it." "And I!" "And I!" exclaimed the others, in quick succession.

"At any rate," said Jack, "we must go on till we get into the valley. There we shall find some farm-houses, and something to eat. We can take an early dinner, and then turn our faces homeward." This counsel had a pleasant savor, for one can not chase a brook down a mountain-side on a light breakfast, without incurring a premature hankering for dinner.

We continued our descent through open glades in the wood, following the course of the stream, which now purred to itself in a quiet way. The sun, by this time, stood well up in the heaven, and poured rich floods of light, here and there, through the leaves. The mold, however, where it was exposed to the sky, was still wet with the dew of the morning; and the trees, which now grew more luxuriantly, harbored innumerable birds, that filled every leafy recess with their jubilant songs. We had not gone far, before a noise like that of tumbling waters was heard, in a new direction. Our ears did not deceive us; the little brook we were following emptied into a larger stream, which flowed from the west around the base of the Dunderberg. Keeping, now, along the course of the larger stream, we soon emerged into the open valley land, not far from where a solitary farm-house was standing.

It was a delightful spot before which we thus suddenly found ourselves,—a gently undulating plain, divided by straggling fences into green meadows, in some of which cattle were almost knee-deep in grass. The house was surrounded on two sides by an orchard of apple-trees, which grew in that rambling way common in all old-fashioned orchards, where each tree has an inclination, or quaint twist, of its own; they gave to the place an air of kindly, if somewhat rude and knotty, freedom. The mountains which rose on every side, seemed, from our point of view, to shut in completely this little scene of quaint, quiet domesticity; and the transition from the rugged wildness of the former, to the comparative gentleness and repose of the latter, was as startling as it was agreeable.

We gazed for a little while in silence on this island of humanity in the midst of untamed nature, then pursued our course some distance down the stream which bordered it. At last our leader sagely said:—

"There must be a road over there, leading past the house. I have always noticed that roads have a certain affection for your old Dutch houses like that one, and sidle up as closely as possible under their eaves. Let us go over and see. A trodden way would be a pleasant change. Besides we must get our supplies here, for we may not find another larder just when we want one."

We accordingly crossed two or three fields, and, as Jack anticipated, struck a road. It was evidently not a great thoroughfare, for it was overgrown with grass, through which you could hardly trace the ruts; but after having traversed mountains, we found the going now very easy. We presently approached the house, which was one of those queer Dutch structures, having a broad front, with at least three front doors of equal size and pretension, and with a few diminutive, sleepy-looking windows. Seen from the road, the house had two stories, but in the rear, the roof ran away off and down, till it almost reached the ground. It was originally painted red, but time and rain had worn off the edge of this color, and numerous weather stains had mottled it with brown. A few cherry-trees constituted the only shade, and some lilac and snow-drop bushes, the only shrubbery. There was no fence before the house, and the road ran quite close to it. We were greeted by a great cackling of hens, and scared up a sow with her litter of pigs, that turned to look at us for a moment, with that thoughtful air so becoming to youthful swine, and then, with a simultaneous grunting, scampered down the road. The shutters were drawn over the windows like half-closed eyelids, if you can imagine eyes whose lids run up and down. No sign of human animation was apparent; but an array of brightly scoured milk-pans, spread out to air upon the inclined doors, covering the stairs to the cellar, and a board spread with sliced apples, secured between the window-sash, and the sill of a window on the sunny side, gave evidence that behind this quiescent front there was an abundance of Dutch cheer.

Before making application for a share in this abundance, we determined to go on a little further and see in what direction our road went; perhaps it would take a turn which would lead to another opening in the valley with a farm-house of its own as the central object. We had not gone far beyond the house, before the road crossed a stream, which evidently united with the one we had lately abandoned. Passing the bridge that spanned this stream, the road turned northward, obliquely climbing the mountain that confronted it, along the side of which we could trace it to some distance, now lost amid trees or behind jutting rocks, now reappearing; for, as we stood on the bridge, we looked up a deep ravine between two parallel mountains, through which the stream came brawling. Glancing down into the water, Jack's keen eye discerned a speckled trout glide under the shadow of a large stone. Jack was at once all a-flame; he always carried his fishing tackle with him on his expeditions, and now having dug it up from his ample pocket, in his excitement he began dropping his hook into the water without thinking of bait, and was only made aware of his absurdity by the loud laugh we simultaneously raised. However, Jack was not going to be disconcerted, and instantly set about finding bait, a task in which, after having our laugh out, we eagerly participated; and soon, by turning over stones by the way-side, and rooting up the soft, rich mold with sticks, we obtained a fine supply of good fat worms, all life and motion. Two others of us, at Jack's suggestion, had included fish-lines in our kit, and by cutting one of them which was longer than necessary into two parts, and bringing into use the fish-hooks of which Jack, of course, had an extra supply, all but two of us were prepared to drop our speckled friends a gentle line, the worm being a "Yours respectfully."

It was arranged that the two of us who were unemployed—myself and Walden—should return to the farm-house and obtain some bread-stuffs. Walden and I, having retraced our steps, knocked long at first one and then another of the numerous front doors of the old farm-house, and listened in vain for approaching footsteps; at last we ventured to peep around the corner of the house; finding all silent, no enemy in sight, we advanced cautiously till we had turned the further angle of the building, and now, putting on a bolder front, we presented ourselves at a low, opened door, which looked into a shiny, well-scrubbed kitchen; the glitter of pots and kettles and tin pans in orderly array, was something to see, and seeing, to remember. But we had little time to delight our eyes with these things, for the good dame, dressed in a blue calico diversified with white spots, with her hands firmly resting on her ample hips, drew herself up before us. We took off our hats and made her a low bow, and I, who was to be the spokesman, apologized with my politest phrases for intruding so unceremoniously by the back door. Perhaps she didn't understand me, for her reply was not much to the point.

"Vol, you be's fine buben. Vo be yous come from? Ach, been't yous dwo little sojers from dat vone great school over der hill, an der rivfer?"

She meant West Point; and we didn't correct her mistake, for we felt in haste to get back to our companions. We proceeded to explain what we wanted, but her attention was so distracted by our bright military buttons, that we had to repeat our story a second time. At last, after telling us that her man had yoked up the oxen, and gone to the mill with his grist, and that her son, Hans, was one gross bube, and was out planting der corn, with many other particulars, she ended, almost out of breath :—

"And you be fine buben too, put not so gross as mine sohn Hans. You's soll have mine brot. How much you want? Two loafen? See here!" She opened her oven door, and pulling out a huge loaf, held it a moment against her nose—

"Goot! ist baked genough;" saying which, she pulled out with a hoe five other such loafen, subjected them to the same test, and arrayed them with great satisfaction on the table.

"Dere, dat ist fine! Now you can take von-two of dese. Shtop, you must have butter."

She lifted a trap-door and disappeared quickly

below the floor. In a few minutes she reappeared, bearing in one hand a roll of butter and in the other a Dutch cheese. She placed the butter in a broken saucer. Having then paid the good dame her price, Walden shouldered one loaf, and I another, one grasped the butter, the other possessed himself of the cheese, and thus loaded, we had got as far as the door, when our generous hostess called out:—

"Shtop! you soll hab some sauer-krout."

And when we politely declined and advanced a few steps from the door, she exclaimed, hastily—

"You soll not pay any ting vor it; you soll not pay any ting!"

We persisted, however, in our refusal, and left the good woman standing in the door-way utterly confounded at our ability to resist the fascinations of sauer-krout.

Walden and I had a staggering time of it under those two great loaves of bread. When we reached the bridge, our companions were no longer there, and we had great difficulty in picking our way, with the load we carried, among the rocks that encumbered the course of the brook, and we, as well as our loaves, ran great danger of getting water-soaked. At last we came upon a waterfall, and there, above, seated upon the rock, were our comrades. They uttered shouts of welcome, which, I think, were excited by the sight rather of the loaves than of the carriers. We reached up the former, also the butter and cheese, and then, nimbly climbing the rocks, placed ourselves beside our companions.

We found some of them busily employed cleaning the fishes, of which they had caught a large mess;

others were collecting sticks for a fire; but Jack still continued fishing, for he thought it prudent to lay in a supply for future use. I don't think he had much expectation of getting back to school that day. In about half an hour we had our fish broiled, and our table, which was a great flat rock, having been duly spread, around it we placed ourselves in Chinese fashion, having armed ourselves, in lieu of forks, with chop-sticks. The dinner was a jolly one, I tell you. The bread and butter were delicious, and the trout needed no seasoning, for our keen appetites were both salt and pepper to them. It was, I should think, about half-past eleven when we had finished our meal.

The understanding had been, you remember, that, as soon as we had obtained a dinner, we should turn our steps homeward, and it was now the general wish that this plan should be put into execution without delay, for much as we enjoyed this wild kind of life, there was a secret voice, whose reproaches gave us a great deal of uneasiness. Jack interposed no objection, but suggested that it would be a dull proceeding to go over our old tracks again, when we could just as quickly get back to our boat by crossing the mountain on the right, and so gaining the good road which, he knew, ran parallel with the river, and along which we could travel with great expedition to the base of the Dunderberg. There was a spice of novelty and fresh adventure in this counsel which pleased our fancy, and though some of us secretly feared that scaling a mountain was not going to be so brisk an affair, none liked to show the white feather. Certainly the proper course would have been to follow the stream, which would have brought us to the river, not far from the base of the Dunderberg, around which we could pick our way to the boat; but this looked like sneaking off, whipped back by the mountains. No, that big hill on our right was a standing challenge to a wrestle, and we were bound to get it under. So at it we went, first having divided up what remained of the loaves and fishes.

After some pretty hard wrestling, we gained the road, which, you remember, we saw from the bridge running along the side of the mountain, and we paused to rest a little and congratulate ourselves on what we had thus far accomplished; but looking up from the cleared space in which we found ourselves, we could see that by much the greater part of the height remained to ascend, and the sun, now verging westward, admonished us that there was but little time for delay, so we plunged again into the thickets.

Climbing the side of a mountain without a guide is not such plain work as the novice imagines, and as we found to our cost. The course, you think, is a direct one,—you have simply to keep going up; but consider that in your prescribed path lie huge ledges of rock which you can not scale and must find a way around; you are thus diverted to the right or left. Then the mountains have a trick of throwing out spurs on their flanks, which, so to speak, trip up the wrestler; when he imagines himself to be climbing directly up the mountain, he is facing in a different direction and simply ascends some such side spur. I tell you, there is a great deal of craft in those old mountains, and they are not going to let you plant your feet on their tops without a hard struggle. So we found it, for after having climbed and climbed, enough, we thought, to have gone thrice the distance which we had measured with the eye from the base,—and having, at last, all panting and torn, gained, as we thought, the crest, we looked in vain for the river; we saw nothing but mountains on all sides of us, so interlapped and spliced, that it was long before we could get any clew to our stand-point. We felt as if either we or the mountains were bewitched, most probably the mountains, for they had evidently turned themselves about in strange wise and got the sun on the wrong side of the heavens. We looked at each other, and looked at the mountains, and looked at the sun, and looked at each other again, and laughed, and then looked blue.

At last, Jack's more cultivated instinct divined the lay of the land, though I incline to think that he knew what he was doing all along; he didn't use his compass and we forgot all about it. Submitting to his guidance, we threaded our way through the thick underbrush, along the highest line of this mountain-spur, in the direction of what seemed a distinct mountain, but which finally proved the real mountain—our own mountain; our course was again upward. Unluckily, the heavens were now becoming overcast, great masses of cloud were rolling up, and deep shadows lowered on the mountain-sides, and the rumbling of distant thunder, momentarily bursting nearer and nearer, announced the quick advances of the storm. We had barely time to find shelter under an overhanging rock, when a bolt of thunder seemed to explode right over our heads, letting loose at once the whole wrath of the tempest. We huddled together as closely as we could under our rock, and succeeded in keeping pretty dry, but the atmosphere was so filled with the driving rain, that the mountain-forms, which were before visible to us, became dim and unreal, and the trees, tossing their branches in the wind, had a weird, spectral look. Meantime the lightnings crashed in quick succession all around us.

The first fury of the storm was soon past, but the rain continued to pour down for some time in such abundance that we did not care to expose ourselves to it. At last, however, the clouds broke, a flood of moist sunshine shot through the trees in front of us, making the rain-drops that hung upon their leaves resplendent as diamonds. We crept forth from the shadow of our sheltering rock, and gaining an open place, where we could view more of the sky, we saw that the storm was rapidly gathering up the skirts of his great robe and fleeing southward. After this enforced rest, we pushed on with redoubled vigor, yet our headway was not very great. The spiteful old mountain seemed to fling, on purpose, great ledges of rock right in our path, and when, with much difficulty, by grappling the trees that grew in their clefts, we succeeded in climbing them, we would perhaps find ourselves confronted by dense masses of shrub-oak, through which, or rather over which, our going was at a snail's pace.

At last, however, we gained the top of our mountain, and found a clear space and rocky floor upon which we could move about with ease and recover our breath. We were the victors; we had the mountain under; but a sad-looking company of victors we seemed, foot-sore and sorely scratched, our jackets half torn from our backs, our trousers ignominiously rent, our boots gaping at the toes and bursting at the sides, and our entire garments sodden from top to toe with the moisture they had brushed from the leaves. And now, to crown our discomfiture, the sun was already low in the heavens; to get back to the school that day was out of the question. The affair was taking a serious turn. A second night from school! What would be the consequences of all this? We began to feel, as we said, "a little skeery."

Under the circumstances, we were not in a favorable mood for enjoying the grand lookout in all directions which our position gave us, unless Walden be excepted, whose enthusiasm no personal considerations could repress. On all sides the hills swelled up, and interlapped or broke in confusion, like great waves. There, on the south, were the Dunderberg and Anthony's Nose, and toward the north the Boterberg and Crow-nest and Breakneck, and in front and back of us many another mountain, which we could not name, across which, and through the ravines of which the sunlight broke in long, slanting shafts, illuminating the vapors that curled up here and there on their sides—the wraiths of recent storm-clouds. In the midst of all wound the river, gleaming in scaly armor like a thing of life; it could be seen only in snatches through the breaks in the hills, and its flashing, yet silent and remote course, affected you with a kind of sadness,—so Walden said.

At last Jack aroused the boys from their sulks, by reminding them that they had trout in their knapsacks which needed to be eaten, and he proposed that we should build a rousing fire, which would serve not only to broil our fish, but to dry our clothes and warm our limbs, that now began to be chilled by their wet envelopments. We set about the task very briskly—made our fire, cooked our fish, dried our clothes, and warmed our limbs. When we had done eating, not a morsel of the bread we had brought with us remained, and only a few fish-bones were left as memorials of the ravages we had made.

By this time the sun had set, and the heavens were all aglow, and the hills purple in the distance. But wearied with our day's tramp and arduous climbing, we set at once about making up a bed on the rocks in the same manner as on the previous night. The fires in the west gradually paled, and again, one by one, the great host of stars came forth to renew their watch. My companions dropped to sleep like lead. For myself, a little restless,—uneasy, I confess, in conscience,—filled with unpleasant thoughts at the possible issue of our truancy, I lay awake till the thronging shadows had widened and merged into the great night. Our fire was still burning. I rose and added some of the fuel which was lying near. Presently the flame shot up with renewed life, and the blue smoke, rolling up in clouds, floated off into the night. The light of the fire strangely illuminated the tree-trunks and undermost leaves, and the grim lichen-stained faces of rock, and the bodies of my sleeping comrades; it even shot unsteady rays to great distances, and brought out here and there from the surrounding gloom some point of rock into startling boldness. It was something to make one shudder, the glamour of our lonely fire upon the mountain-top, in the midst of a dim shadowy mountain world under the silent stars. I hastened to my place on the leafy couch, and closing my eyes upon the terrors which my imagination called up, was presently overcome with sleep.

We rose in the morning somewhat stiff in limb from the unwonted exertions of the two preceding days, but determined to take the shortest possible route back to school, and to listen to no suggestions from Jack, or any one else, which might divert us from our prescribed route. We were obliged to set off on empty stomachs, but we purposed to remedy the deficiency at the first opportunity; and we plunged down the mountain-side with not the less vigor that we had our breakfast yet to win. It is astonishing how rapidly one can descend a mountain which it takes hours to climb up; nature favors a descent, but you must overcome nature when you climb.

When we had gone half way down, and the slope had now become more gradual, we suddenly came upon a road leading along the mountain-side. We hailed this with joy, for a road suggested the abode of man, and this suggested breakfast. Following the road for a little distance southward, we emerged from the woods, into cleared and fenced ground, and, soon after, we came to a small house, which, evidently, had had a hard time of it up on the mountain, and looked about as scraggy as its surroundings,—doorsteps slouched on one side, window-panes smashed in, clapboards loose, chimney half in ruins.

We succeeded, however, in getting a couple of loaves, and some butter, and were hastening on to find a comfortable spot to break our morning fast, when we observed a small boy following us at a respectful distance, and eyeing us very curiously. The boy's costume was very simple, consisting of a shirt,—which, flying open at the neck, displayed his sunburned breast,—a pair of cotton pantaloons of faded blue, hanging upon one suspender, and ragged up to the knees, and an old straw hat, which had evidently protected the paternal head from many a summer's sun, and was now very much shorn of rim. After having inspected us pretty thoroughly, we, meanwhile, proceeding on our way in haste for breakfast, he at last cried out:—

"Hello! Be you the fellows wot's run away from that big school down the river?

"Cuz, if you be," he added, not getting an immediate reply,—"cuz, if you be, they'm after you."

We stopped short. What did the vagabond mean? We advanced toward him, but he seemed to be suspicious of us, and backed up the road. "Wait," said Will Cutting; "I'll fetch him." He pulled a couple of bright pennies from his pocket, and began tossing them up in the air.

"Golly! where did yous'en get them aire," said the boy, and his eyes twinkled.

"Lots more, where those came from," said Will Cutting. "Would you like one?"

"Like as not I would," said the boy, with a chuckle.

"Come, then, tell us all about those boys who have run away from school, and who they are that are, as you say, *after* them."

"By darn, I was just goin' to tell yer, if yer hadn't chased me up the road. A gang of fellows in blue coats, jest like yourn, only brighter, came up here about sundown, asking if anybody had seen a parcel of fellows like yous'en. I reckon you'm the boys. Wasn't it you's wot kindled the bonfire up yonder? Wall, I tell you wot, those big fellows reckoned how it wor you, and they'll be down on yer, if yer don't tek keer; they camped out only a little way up the road, and dad's went up that way, since you's fellows come along."

4

We looked scared, and the little boy grinned.

"Throw him the pennies, Will! Throw him the pennies, and let's off."

The boy picked up the pennies with remarkable rapidity and eyes full of wonder, while we scampered down the road in great precipitation; nor did we cease running till we had turned a corner of the road which concealed us from view. Here, following Jack's lead, we hastily climbed a great rock around the base of which the road wound, and paused at last to take breath and consider the situation. Jack, however, to whom we looked for guidance, was quite stolid about it, and insisted that we should eat our breakfast first of all; from our rock, we commanded a view of the road above and below, while we ourselves were concealed from view by the trees and brush that grew in the clefts of the rock, and were, therefore, said Jack, safe enough.

We ate our bread and butter in no very comfortable frame of mind; we thought over the penalties that were inflicted upon deserters, for such we would seem to be, and, while we congratulated ourselves that the military government of the school was not so complete that we could be taken out and shot, yet we recalled to mind that corporal punishment was a part of the discipline, and we already felt uncomfortable sensations, in anticipation of the uncertain number of lashes that might be administered; and perhaps, we thought, our commanding officer was with the pursuing party, and might then and there attend to the business. Any way, said we, it would be pleasanter to put off the day of retribution, if we could; besides, to be ignominiously dragged back to school was not agreeable to our pride: so we determined not to be caught.

We had scarcely, however, finished our meal and our deliberations, when one of our boys, who had been stationed at a projecting point, to keep a lookout, cried in a whisper: "Hist! Hist! Lie low!" and he himself plunged hastily into the thicket behind him.

We lay still as death, and a moment after heard the tramp of our pursuers on the double-quick. Peering through the leaves, we recognized the adjutant of our school as the leader of the band, which included five of the largest and strongest of the seniors.

"Hark! what is that?" said one of them, as they passed under our rock. One of our boys had stirred loose a fragment of rock, which had rolled off among dead leaves, making a confounded deal of noise.

"It is only some squirrel up there on the rock. Steady! double-quick! pass that bend of the road, and we'll be on them," said the adjutant.

We held our breath in suspense till we saw them vanish around the next turn in the road. At that moment, however, their regular tramp ceased. They were surprised, perhaps, at not seeing their prey in sight, and had missed our foot-marks on the road. A moment after, and we saw them again appearing, with their faces turned toward us. There was at once great consternation in our ranks, and without stopping to deliberate, we plunged into the woods back of us, and climbed some distance up the mountain-side. A shout from our pursuers brought us to a stand; they had reached the rock which we had just abandoned; and now, for the first time, we remembered that we had left there the remains of our breakfast, among them an entire loaf; it was these tale-tellers which had excited that cry of triumph.

After a few moments of silence, we heard them again in pursuit; they had discerned our trail through the forest, and had perhaps heard the crackling of branches and dry leaves, which we could not avoid making. Jack, who alone remained cool, now led us in a new direction; he coasted along the side of the mountain southward; happily, we came upon a small water-course, which ran down the mountain in an oblique direction, following the peculiar lay of the rock. Jack at once took to the bed of the stream, and in a short time we were again in the road, while our pursuers were beating about in the woods above us, evidently at a loss. Having now a clear road before us, we ran down it with great rapidity, taking care, however, to keep in the grass by its sides, so as not to leave any tracks.

When we had gone a considerable distance, and were sure we had gained much on our pursuers and were out of their hearing, we once more abandoned the road, and burying ourselves in the woods, hastened down what remained of the mountain slope. In about half an hour we found ourselves on the border of the wood, with tilled land before us; crossing two or three fields, we came to a road which evidently was a considerable thoroughfare. We felt that we were beyond danger of pursuit, and that our course was now a plain one; we had but to follow the road till we reached the base of the Dunderberg, that swelled up right before us.

But I shall not dwell upon the subsequent incidents of our journey; we had turned the bright side of our enterprise, and the remainder of the way was darkened by gloomy forebodings of the consequences. As we approached the base of the Dunderberg, we passed some old revolutionary redoubts, which we supposed were the remains of Fort Montgomery. Here we had to swim an arm of the Hudson of considerable breadth, and beyond which we came upon the remains of Fort Clinton. We did not climb the Dunderberg, but made our way around its base. We found our boat as we had left it, and after a row of two hours or less, with the tide in our favor, we reached the Sing Sing wharf, and wearily trudged our way to the school, with, I should think, half the idle fellows of the village following us, laughing and hooting at our singularly rough and ragged look.

We had not eaten since our breakfast on the rock, and were completely exhausted; indeed, one fellow— it was Walden—fainted away just as we reached the door of the school, and he did not recover his strength for two or three days. I shall not linger on the punishment we received. Jack, you know, was withdrawn, and as to the rest—I don't like to think of it, it isn't a pleasant recollection.

Tom concluded his story in good time, for a few moments after, the drum beat the tattoo, and we hastened to gather up the fragments of our repast and join the ranks of our schoolmates in the old school-room.

CHAPTER VII.

THE MIRAGE OF PARADISE ISLAND.

I must now return to the story of my own school-life. Though not rich in striking characteristics or events, it is yet the chain to which the experiences and observations are linked which I have undertaken to relate. Who, if it were in his power, would not wish to recall, in all their vividness, the inner life of his early youth— his emotions, his thoughts, his aspirations, the impressions that men and things first made upon him, the wonder which the grand ebb and tide of nature wrought in him?

On the morning after my friend Tom had narrated the adventures given in the preceding chapter, I awoke with confused recollections of a dream made up of tottering mountains, maniacal waterfalls, huge rocks grinning with demoniac faces, knotted roots of trees, suddenly animated with motion and writhing like serpents, water nymphs issuing from fountains and vanishing behind the rocks, a company of goblins leaping up the brook, thunder, lightning, and rain, a human skeleton springing forth from a cave and stalking along the crest of Dunderberg. But not to make further mention of the dream, I woke.

We had passed through the terrors of inspection, a ceremony for which we were drawn up in line immediately before school was called in; the drill-master, who had won his shoulder-straps as a volunteer in the Mexican war, had paced up and down our lines and examined us severally from top to toe with a critical eye; every thing had met his approval,—our faces, buttons, and boots all shone resplendent in the morning sun.

It was, as I commenced to say, just after this inspection, when the ranks were breaking up, that Ned came running to me all agog with the announcement that all the juniors who received no marks either for bad conduct or deficient recitations during the ensuing school-week, were to be allowed to go on an excursion to Paradise Island; he had just heard it from the lips of Mr. Ellery. The announcement, Ned thought, would be publicly made, as soon as school was called in. He, for one, didn't mean to get marked, and he hoped that Tom and I would try not to, so that we might all enjoy the expedition together. Tom coming up at that moment, we all agreed to do our best, and in a few moments the bell rang summoning us to the school-room—the battle-field upon which our resolution and self-control were to be put to the proof.

Ned showed by his manner that he felt perfect confidence in his success. Accustomed to having his wishes gratified, participation in the excursion seemed to him an enjoyment already assured. Generally successful in his undertakings, and that, too, without much effort on his part, but rather by reason of a happy constitution of his nature, he rarely contemplated failure as possible. Life was to him a sunny day.

Tom, though merry and jocose as usual, was more self-contained in his manner; he did not seem to feel so sure of success in his own case, nor did he act as if failure would greatly afflict him; there were other days in the round year besides next Wednesday, and other excursions to be made besides that to Paradise Island; and there was a roguish twinkle in his eyes which seemed to insinuate that even Ned might slip up in his expectations. As for myself, the trial was a new one; but it did not strike me as a very hard undertaking to get through a single week without a bad mark.

During school-hours, with the exception of those specially devoted to study, there were but few of the pupils in the general school-room at one time; the greater part were engaged either in one or another of the surrounding recitation-rooms, or in the music-room, or in the library, where one of the principals presided. Those, however, whose duty did not call them at certain hours to any recitation, were, of course, obliged to remain at their desks and give their whole attention to the work of preparation, and it was the business of the drill-master, who, it may be here mentioned, was known and addressed as "Captain," to be present and keep order.

Among my school-mates was one, whom I remember as "69;" his name, if I ever knew it, has escaped me. He was a round-faced, chubby fellow, overflowing with animal spirits, such a boy as you will meet in every school, good-natured, though ready for a quarrel, good-hearted, mischievous, always in trouble himself and getting others in trouble.

At the desk in front of him sat one of those wiry, alert, fidgety fellows, not mischievously inclined, but always prompt to share in whatever was going on, whatever its nature, prepared to take his own part and resent offenses, no matter what the consequences—a boy whom it was necessary to keep constantly employed, or he would be in trouble. I remember him as "6."

Now the first of these boys, "69," had begun the week, as he usually did, with a firm resolve to go through it without getting marked, not that his conscience moved him to it, but because the prospect of an unbroken holiday was very captivating; if an opportunity occurred of perpetrating a piece of mischief without being perceived, he was apt to avail himself of it, but as his cunning was not equal to his love of fun, he was very frequently discovered, and by the end of the school week, he had generally accumulated marks enough to keep him in the "jug" several hours of the day. On this occasion "69" had set his teeth to it that he would be one of the party on the excursion to Paradise Island.

The greater part of the morning passed with him very quietly and successfully. Finally, however, he began to grow restless: if he could have one little piece of fun, he would settle down quietly to his work again. He was not long in finding an opportunity. "6" had half risen from his seat to pick up his pen which had fallen on the floor; the temptation was irresistible: "69" glanced hastily over his shoulder to see if he were observed, and perceiving that the Captain's attention was engaged elsewhere, quickly took from his desk a pin so bent that the point would set up, and placed it on the chair from which "6" had risen. "6," on resuming his seat, was not long in comprehending the cause of the sudden and sharp irritation that affected him in the rear. His first care was to remove the instrument of his torture; he was too much master of himself to utter a cry. His second care was, quick as a flash, to administer a vigorous cuff to the cheek of "69," who was

4*

quietly studying his book. "69," seeing from the corner of his eye what was coming, partly in his effort to avoid the blow, partly in consequence of it, rolled off from his seat with a loud thump upon the floor. The attention of the whole school was at once called to him, with the exception of "6" himself, who was too busy with his "French" to notice the catastrophe. It was in vain that "69" looked up very innocently from his seat on the floor, and protested that it was a mere slip; he was booked for an hour on Wednesday. Thus were all his anticipations of Paradise Island cruelly nipped. This little incident was not one of much importance in itself, but it had consequences which affected others besides the offender. "69," losing all hope of Paradise Island, lost all his good resolutions, and though the prospect of still other hours in the "jug" on Wednesday was disagreeable, the courage was all taken out of him; Wednesday was a great way off, life was uncertain, and it was better to enjoy it as it goes.

But now the scene shifts. The bell sounding a change of classes, I caught up my Latin exercise and my grammar, and hastened into the appropriate recitation-room. The class to which I belonged consisted of nine or ten boys, among whom was included my friend Ned. Tom belonged to a higher form. Though fond of study, Latin and Greek were branches which I had not yet learned to like. The method of these languages is so wholly different from that of the English, that as they are, or were, commonly taught, the learner for a long time is utterly bewildered. He finds himself groping, or rather led, blindfold through a seemingly interminable labyrinth of forms, to which no guiding principle affords him the clew; and when at last a little light breaks in, he is often too thoroughly disgusted with the spiritless task to which he has been subjected, to pursue it with animation any farther than he is compelled to do so. He has been dosed with "words, words, words," till a surfeit has been induced. A surfeit is stupefying. How often has a fine brain been retarded in its growth, if not seriously impaired by the dull, soulless methods of instruction which have been entailed upon us as the fruit of the matured wisdom of our ancestors! Light, free and abundant light, is essential to the healthy growth of the animal organism. In like manner is that mental light which is radiated by a perception of rational order, of active organizing principles, necessary to healthy, mental growth. The attempt, by addressing the memory alone, to build up in the mind of the boy a complicated structure of, to him, meaningless forms, while it checks the growth of the reason, blunts the edge of memory itself, and deadens the mind's general vitality. The spring and elasticity of the youthful mind is something which should be carefully preserved; and to this end dry food is not conducive.

Our teacher of Latin and Greek, Mr. Weston, was not a mere pedant; in his presence there was something of the inspiration of nature. With him the grammar of the languages he taught was subordinated to the languages themselves. He sought in the outset to inform the mind with the spirit and method of classic speech, so that our knowledge might have an element of growth in it, instead of being a mere accumulation of the memory. Under his guidance I soon found the study of Latin and Greek quite a different thing from what I had been accustomed to consider it; and the dry bones of what little grammatical knowledge I had been able to acquire, began to take life. Of course there were boys in the class, who still found the pursuit distasteful, but that was not the fault of the teacher, nor of the school, but of unwise parents, who sought to adapt their sons to occupations for which they were not naturally designed.

But to return to my intention, which was to show what ill-luck poor Ned had in the Latin class that day. Ned was well prepared in his lesson. Ambitious and quick as he was industrious, he generally took the lead, and had become the favorite pupil of his teacher. But on that morning Ned felt such confidence in his knowledge that he yielded to the temptation of permitting himself to think about Paradise Island. The name took his fancy. He pictured to himself a spot of earth swimming in beauty, one in which nature had striven to hide all her choicest sweets. The waters rippled upon the green shore; the gentlest breezes fanned the leaves; the air was filled with the songs of birds, and quickened with the scents of flowers; golden fruit hung from the boughs ready for the plucking; and airy clouds hovered over it, in a sky always serene, and filled with a delicious languor. In a word, the island seemed to float before him in an atmosphere of unalloyed delight.

He was suddenly awakened from his reverie by receiving a nudge in the side from his neighbor, and hearing at the same time a question put to him. In the confusion of mind that ensued, he was unable to collect his thoughts in time to give the correct answer, and the question was passed on. Ned's chagrin at his apparent want of preparation was so great, that when a second question was immediately addressed to him, with the kind purpose of giving him an opportunity to redeem himself, he was too much disconcerted to reply with his usual alacrity; he hesitated, blushed up to his ears, and finally stumbled upon an answer which it was not in his mind to make. With surprise and evident regret, Mr. Weston was compelled to mark him for imperfect recitation. Ned might, perhaps, have got clear of the mark after all, if he had chosen to represent to Mr. Weston that he had become confused, and had answered he knew not what, and by offering to present himself for private examination, but he had too much honorable pride and self-respect to seek to avoid the consequences of his thoughtlessness and inattention. He despised too much the habit which many of his fellows had of begging off from marks, to be now willing to show the same pusillanimity. Nevertheless, he left the recitation-room in a very dejected frame of mind. A heavy leaden cloud had settled down on Paradise Island.

CHAPTER VIII.

THE CLOUD LOWERS.

But Ned's misfortunes were not yet at an end. Cast down from his light-hearted self-confidence to a very doleful mood, he became a little peevish and fretful, and was just in a condition to fall a prey to the mischievous propensities of his school-fellows.

The morning hours were brought to a close, and the bell had sounded for "the wash," preparatory to dinner. Ned was proceeding in the performance of his duties in a mechanical, abstracted manner; he had marched in the line to the foot of the stairs leading to the wash-room. This spot was a favorable one for the perpetration of mischief. In consequence of a turn in the stairs, it was shut out from view; accordingly it was frequently the scene of lively by-play. On this occasion our friend "69," who, since his accident in the school-room, had fully recovered from its disheartening consequences, and had now determined to have his fun out, on reaching this favored spot, unobserved by the officer in command, quietly stepped out from the line, to watch his opportunity for mischief. Presently, perceiving Ned coming down the stairs, and, in his downheartedness, taking note of nobody, "69" pitched upon him as an appropriate subject, more especially as Ned was his inferior in strength; for, though not of the brutal, bullying type of boys, still "69" always had an eye to the preservation of a whole skin.

As Ned was about to take the last step, "69," watching his chance, quickly bent low down in his way, and Ned suddenly found himself sprawling over "69's" back. Ned saved himself, however, from being thrown upon the floor, by grasping "69" about the neck and pulling him down beneath him. All this happened so suddenly, that the boys following in the line either had not time to check themselves, or, prompted by the innate aptitude of boys to seize hold of any favorable occasion for sport, tumbled or were pushed upon their prostrate comrades, until there were heaped up several layers of boyhood. The approach of the teacher in charge to the head of the stairs, being telegraphed rapidly along the line, no further additions to the sprawling mass at the foot were made, and its elements quickly disengaged themselves from their chaotic entanglement.

Ned, however, was in no mood to relish the sport, and, on rising to his feet, grappled at once with "69" who, having had to sustain the entire weight of the mass, was quite out of breath, and in a state of great mental confusion from the unlooked-for denouement of his experiment, and could therefore offer very ineffectual resistance. Ned pushed him violently to the wall. Here, however, his excitement beginning to subside, and, the helpless condition of his adversary being apparent, he was relaxing his hold; it was too late: at this moment the strong hands of the teacher nabbed them both. They were very summarily helped into the wash-room, and there placed face to face in the middle of the room for inspection.

As neither of them had suffered any material harm, and as the affair was apparently one of those unpremeditated ebullitions of temper which the best boys are liable to, the teacher contented himself with setting marks to their names in his note-book. "69" explained it very simply and innocently; it seems, he had unfortunately slipped and fallen as he reached the bottom of the stairs, and "25," that is, Ned, had fallen over him, "25" thought he had done it on purpose, and got mad.

Ned, though he could not help showing by his manner his contempt of the cunning subterfuges of his opponent, scorned to save himself at his expense. Besides, he felt ashamed of his exhibition of temper; he had been long enough at school to learn that it was always the better policy to take practical jokes in good part; to this also his own good-nature generally inclined him; his present loss of temper was an evident surprise to his fellow-students. Ned, therefore, submitted quietly to the marks, and taking the place left vacant for him, he concealed the tears, which he could no longer restrain, by bending low over the wash-bowl and quickly dashing his face with its contents.

CHAPTER IX.

RAIN.

I LOOKED around in vain for Ned that afternoon on the play-ground. He had been, it is true, detained half-an-hour on account of the marks he had received, but that time had long since elapsed, and I had as yet seen nothing of him. At last, I determined to go in search of him, for Ned, though a faithful student, was not fond of moping in the house all day; there must, then, be some serious cause for his absence; he was probably taking his discomfitures too much to heart.

I looked for him in the dressing-room, or, as it was called, the "old school-room," from its having been used as the general school-room in earlier days, before the buildings were enlarged; but no Ned did I find there. Getting permission, then, to go up-stairs, I went to the room Ned shared in, and, as I expected, found him. He was sitting there alone by the window, with his elbow on the sill, and his chin resting in the hollow of his hand, gazing abstractedly over the play-ground, where, through the intervening apple-trees, the boys could be seen here and there intermingling in earnest sport; their outcries seemed to shoot up like balls in the air from all parts of the field, while at times, as if by preconcerted arrangement, their voices rose in a united uproar, like that of a great wave crashing against the cliffs.

Either because of the noise, or because he was deeply absorbed in his own contemplations, Ned did not become aware of my presence till I touched him on the shoulder. He turned and greeted me with a pleasant, though not very merry smile; he had evidently been brooding over his ill-luck.

"Come," I said, "let us go out; they are having a gay time down there."

"No, no, not yet, I have been thinking about home, and don't feel like playing. I am a little homesick this afternoon."

"Oh, that's because you have been so unfortunate to-day. Don't mind it, Ned."

"Well, I suppose that is the reason, but I can't help my thoughts. It is so different at home. If any thing happened wrong with me there, and I got a little out of sorts, I was not afraid to go to my mother, or my father either, and explain how it all came about, and they would always set me right with myself again, and get my ill-feelings all soothed down. But I have no one to go to here. I knew my Latin this morning, and yet I failed and got marked. I didn't cause that mischief in the hall, and yet I have been placed on the same footing with '69.' I know I lost my temper, and that it all grew out of my thinking too much in the class-room about Paradise Island; but how can I explain all this, and what difference would it make, if I did? The boys would say I was favored, if I should be excused. Besides, I don't want to be excused,—that wouldn't take away the disgrace. I wish I was home." And Ned's eyes filled with tears.

I knew not what to reply to my friend—therefore I sat still by his side as he gazed wistfully out of the window, and waited for a favorable turn. But, in the mean while, I remember representing to myself, not indeed in so many words, but in a dreamy, boyish way, that this, after all, was one of the great lessons of life, to learn to endure calmly those mishaps that flow partly from untoward fortune, partly from our own wayward moods, not seeking nor expecting sympathy, but remaining patient, self-reliant, steadfast. I recalled my father's saying to me, that a school can not be a home and ought not to be. "You will come back," he said, "with a thicker skin; but see to it," he added, warningly, "that the heart beneath remains warm and tender." Ned was receiving his lesson in life to-day, mine, perhaps will follow soon. But happily I was so constituted as to learn by the experience of others.

Ned having silently indulged his grief for a little while, suddenly rose and said he was a great fool to be troubled so about the matter, and offered to go out with me. As we were passing through the doorway of the lower hall into the open air, we met Tom, all aglow with the excitement of a game of ball in which he had been engaged. He had come, he said, to find Ned and pull him outdoors.

"Poh! poh! Ned, don't look so glum. What if you have had a fall, you are on your feet again. Come, try a little ground and lofty tumbling. Let's to the gymnasium. I tell you, it's a great art to have the knack of coming right side up, on your feet again, in the twinkling of an eye. You're proof against fortune then. Away to the gymnasium!"

Ned couldn't resist the good-humor of his friend.

Tom fairly crackled with electric sparks, and it was impossible to come near him without experiencing the titillation of minute shocks.

As we were hastening to the building which was specially fitted up as a gymnasium, it happened that "69" met us; "69" always had the faculty of happening up in the wrong place and at inopportune times. Of course, too, he must speak to Ned, who was passing along without appearing to notice him.

"Hilloa '25,' what's your hurry? Such a coming down-stairs I never did see. But that wasn't fair, to tackle me so before I got my breath. You wouldn't like to try it again, I guess."

Ned's face flushed, and he seemed about returning an angry reply; he, however, passed on, merely directing a single, somewhat scornful glance upon his interlocutor; he was in no mood to bandy words with him on his own level.

"You are a mighty proud fellow, you are!" said "69," half to himself. "Can't take a joke from a fellow! Guess I'm as good as you are, if I don't hic-hæc-hoc like you. Its all the same out here. Well, I'll be even with you yet." And he looked at Ned, who was now out of hearing, with an expression in which there was an equal mixture of injured self-love and simple love of mischief.

CHAPTER X.

PROWLING.

The bedrooms which the juniors occupied, were ranged on each side of a wide hall running through the upper floor of the main building. They were shut off from the hall, not by doors, but by curtains drawn upon iron rods placed across the top of each entrance. They received their light at night from the gas-lights in the hall. At one end of the hall, two or three of the teachers had apartments, and upon these, in succession, devolved the superintendence of the pupils while undressing for bed, and whatever other after-care was necessary for the preservation of order.

On the night of the day the events of which have just been narrated, the tattoo was beaten, as usual, at a quarter before nine, and we were marched up in line to our quarters. About ten minutes were regularly allowed for undressing and private devotions, when the command was given by the teacher in charge of the hall, " Draw the curtains," a command which was executed by the " monitors" of the several rooms. The only other duty which distinguished these monitors from their room-mates was that of giving every morning to the officer of the day a report of the conduct of themselves and their room-mates; they were not, however, expected to report disorder, unless the teacher " in charge" authorized them to do so. If a disturbance occurred in any quarter, the teacher merely designated the room, and it was then the monitor's duty to report the guilty ones; if he failed to do this, then all the occupants of the apartment were considered as implicated, and received equal punishment.

Immediately after the order to draw the curtain was pronounced, the lights were put out, and all conversation at once ceased; not a whisper was allowed. Generally, the teacher in charge remained ten or fifteen minutes in the hall, during which time, the boys, tired out by the work and play of the day, willingly dropped to sleep. Not always, however; it often happened that some effervescent spirits were not yet resigned to being bottled up in sleep. The silence, disturbed only by occasional snores of doubtful sincerity, which reigned over the community of sleepers, was often illusive; it was the silence of the forest, in which wild Indians lurk, watching their chance.

When the teacher in charge had retired to his own room, the door of which he left ajar, then, perhaps, if sleep had not by this time gained complete mastery, daring deeds would be committed under the cover of darkness; stealthy expeditions would be undertaken across the hall; secret conferences held in remote apartments; conspiracies hatched; plans laid for pleasure on the morrow; plots contrived for new and startling mischief. Or perhaps the stillness of the night would be interrupted by the rolling of a marble across or down the hall, or by the jingling of a bell. The hazard which attended these adventures, gave to them a spice of romance which sometimes sharpened the appetite for them even among boys whose conduct was generally good. The punishment inflicted sometimes followed close on the deed; thus, if a boy was caught out of his room, he was ordered to report at once at the "Office" on the floor below, and then sometimes, though rarely, the echoes of the great halls would be awakened by a succession of sharp, elastic sounds, which made the boys cuddle snugly within the bed-clothes in the enjoyment of a delightful sense of security. The silence that followed was made all the more intense, by the low sounds which interrupted it, like that of the bursting of bubbles on the surface of boiling water; then sad footsteps would be heard on the stairs.

But to come to the events of the evening. "69" was not yet satisfied with the sports of the day; the amusements in which he had been engaged, with the exception of the accidents in the school-room, and at the foot of the stairs on the way to the wash-room, were all permitted ones; his happiness would not be complete till he participated in some that were forbidden, and, besides, "69" had a fondness for prowling. Man is naturally a beast of prey, and in the boy the instinct to prowl sometimes crops out like the original rock which the disguising hand of nature has not crumbled into the tilled land of civilization. "69" lay restless and uneasy on his bed, waiting for the time when the teacher should leave the hall, in the mean while turning over in his mind what he should do to satisfy his craving for fun, taking counsel, too, with his fear of possible consequences. In the midst of his deliberations, it occurred to him that he had promised himself to be even with "25," who had treated him with such scorn.

That should decide the matter. Now for some sport! At length the teacher "in charge" was heard to with draw to his own room. "69" breathed more freely. He rose quietly from his bed, and peeped out aside of the curtain, to see if all was clear. No enemy could be discovered through the darkness. Only the heavy breathing of sleepers, heard here and there, broke the silence, or rather seemed to make silence itself audible. Having waited and listened a few minutes till he felt perfectly sure, "69" stole forth in his stocking feet, and with such scanty covering as his night-shirt afforded. As the boards of the hall-floor were given sometimes to creaking in a very treacherous way, our prowler got down on all fours, so as to divide his weight as much as possible. Proceeding in this manner, he reached Ned's room in safety, gently pushed aside the curtain, and crept under Ned's bed, which was the one nearest the entrance. All was quiet, the occupants of the room seemed to be asleep. After having waited long enough to satisfy himself of this, "69" softly stole his hand under the bed-clothes at the foot of the bed, and pinched Ned's toe.

Ned started, awoke, and peering through the darkness, to the bed next below his, he cried out in a whisper,—"Tom, Tom, was that you? Are you playing tricks?"

Receiving no answer from Tom, he settled down again, and, persuading himself that he had been dreaming, was soon once more asleep. "69" having patiently bided his time, for he had no lack of patience in affairs of mischief, repeated his experiment, adding, however, a little more pungency to the pinch.

Ned awoke with an involuntary cry. "Tom, did you do that?"

"What?" said Tom, now also awakened. But the

approach of Mr. Weston, who was in charge of the hall that night, cut off further colloquy.

"Report this room!" was the order, and then the footsteps of the teacher were heard receding toward his own apartment.

Our prowler lay perfectly still, while Ned and Tom addressed themselves to sleep. It was some time before "69" ventured to come forth from his hiding-place; and when at last he stole out into the hall, he felt so elated with his success, that he could not find it in his heart to return soberly to his own lair. It was rare sport. He must try just one more taste, at the risk of his skin. But to return to Ned's room, that would not do, the repetition of the trick there might lead to discovery. So our prowler steals into a room on the opposite side of the hall.

The bed under which he crept was occupied by a boy of a quick, excitable temperament, who easily lost his self-possession, and when "69" gave his toe a severe pinch, he started up in great affright, crying,

"Rats! Rats! A light! My toe!"

"Hush! hush!" said one of his less excitable roommates, "you have been dreaming, and you'll get reported." The caution was too late; the footsteps of Mr. Weston were heard, and the order, "Report this room!" at once followed.

On this occasion, however, the suspicions of the teacher were aroused. There was some mischief going on. He paced up and down the hall several times, considering, probably, whether it would be worth while setting a watch for the possible offender, or better to wait for further confirmation of his suspicions.

Before, however, he had fully decided how to act,

"69" drew himself stealthily from under the bed that had protected him, and thrust his head out at the curtained door-way, in order to make an inspection of the hall. An ill-timed movement, for he was quietly seized by the watchful sentinel, and hurried away to an interview beneath the gas-light of the teacher's room.

It was here decided to give the lad the use of Mr. Weston's arm-chair, as a couch, on which he could either pass into a troubled sleep, or, being wakeful, reflect during the remainder of the night upon the good old proverb, "The way of the transgressor is hard." And thus it was.

CHAPTER XI.

RATS! RATS!

The next morning there was much talk among the boys concerning the events of the preceding night. "69's" adventure, however, with the telling incidents with which it was rounded off, was not known to them, for the sound sleep of boyhood is not easily disturbed, and "69" kept his own counsel. But the two boys, whose toes had been, as they thought, bitten so badly, were of course full of wonder, and had much to say about it. It was agreed that it was no rat who had thus disturbed their slumbers, and that some other sort of animal had been prowling about. Then some one had a dream of a witch riding on a broom-stick, who had come in at the open window and had galloped "like mad" up and down the hall, and some thought that she had bitten the toes of the two boys, and that it was a sign of ill-luck to them. Others said that they had heard strange noises like the flapping of wings by a bird of prey. "69" still "kept dark." But Ned and Tom, and the three or four other boys who had been reported, submitted quietly to their marks; there would be no use in seeking to palm off stories of witchcraft upon the principals.

The remainder of the school week passed off very quietly. The juniors in general, having the delights of Paradise Island in anticipation, were careful of their conduct, and attentive to their studies. "69," since the night of his adventure, was considerably sobered down, and did not feel inclined to run any extraordinary hazards for the present. Ned did not, it is true, come to the standard of perfection necessary to qualify him for the intended expedition, but had reconciled himself to his disappointment; besides his Wednesday holiday would remain unbroken, for only those boys had to expiate their offenses in the "jug" on that day, who had received over ten marks in the course of the week.

But Tom also, having received a bedroom mark, would be denied the privilege of accompanying the expedition, though he did not seem much troubled about it. But this restraint on Tom's enjoyment weighed more heavily on Ned's mind than his own misfortunes, for he considered himself as the cause of it and as, therefore, alone worthy of blame. He secretly made up his mind that Tom should not be the sufferer, if he could help it.

On Wednesday morning it was the custom to call the boys together in the school-room at an early hour after breakfast. Then the Principal took his seat on the platform at the head of the room and examined the reports of the week, previously transcribed and summed up in a book kept for the purpose, and having ascertained who had rendered themselves liable to detention, and the period of time to be allotted to each, he read aloud their names, or rather their numbers. Then if there were any explanations to be made, he was ready to listen to them. The appellant, however, had to take care not to offer a frivolous, or dishonest excuse, at the risk of increasing the period of his confinement.

The much longed-for Wednesday morning having at last arrived, the boys were assembled in the school-room at an earlier hour than usual, so that the expedition to Paradise Island might have an early start. The report-book had been examined, and the names of those who were not entitled to the full holiday had been read off, and finally the fortunate boys were designated who should have the privilege of joining in the expedition.

Now was Ned's time to speak for his friend Tom, or never. Having obtained permission to come forward, he advanced to the Principal's desk, and explained in a low voice what had happened to him on the night of the bedroom mark, and ended by saying that he was willing to take all the blame, since he was the first to speak, and that Tom had received no other mark but that one to debar him from joining the expedition. The Major was evidently pleased with Ned's pleading for his friend rather than in his own behalf. He put to him a few questions, and mused a little. It was evident he began to have his suspicions. On the same night that Ned's toe had been attacked in that singular manner, "69" had been caught prowling. In short, the Principal smelt a rat. "69" was called up, and a few pointed questions soon elicited the fact that the rat stood before him. And very demure did the rat look, thus entrapped.

Thereupon the other boy, whose toe had also suffered on that eventful night, rose and claimed exemption from the penalty of the mark he had received, since, suddenly awakened, he had only called out, "Rats! Rats!"

At this declaration, which was made in a very comical manner, all the boys laughed, and some one at a distance—for on such occasions a little liberty was allowed,—cried out "Rat!" pointing to poor "69." The cry was caught up on all sides, "Rat! Rat! Rat!" till "69" was fain to slink unforbidden to his seat.

When the general laughter had subsided, the Major said, that of course the bedroom marks of which "69" had been the occasion would be stricken off, and that consequently "35,"—that was Tom's numerical name,—would be permitted to go on the excursion, as there were no other marks against him.

The Principal went on to say that he was sorry that "25's" (Ned's) other marks prevented his being one of the party; but it would be paying "25" a poor compliment to suppose that in generously pleading for his friend, he was seeking favor for himself; and that the gift of a holiday excursion would only confuse and belittle the far higher reward he would receive in the approval of his own conscience.

These words were followed by a profound silence. It was broken at last by Ned, who rose in his place, and with a tremor in his voice, but with a look of noble pride in his bearing, declared that he was quite willing, indeed preferred, to suffer the penalty due his marks; he wanted to pay his debts.

At this honorable speech involuntary applause broke out from all parts of the room, and for the moment all Ned's school-fellows shared in Ned's sentiments, and in a manner identified themselves with him, though few, perhaps, would have imitated his heroism.

When the applause had ceased, Tom took the floor. He said, addressing the Principal, that he, for his part, had a selfish request to make; it was that he might be allowed to remain at home with "25," and he was, he added, asked by "20" to prefer the same request on his behalf.

There was again silence throughout the school-room. The boys were evidently struck with wonder at this new instance of self-sacrifice. Renunciation seemed to be the spirit of the time. The Major, after a few moments' reflection, turned toward Tom, and said, "that of course he should not be obliged to accompany the expedition. But," he added, addressing the school, "if this goes on, the expedition will have to be abandoned for lack of troops. There is such a fine magnetism in the noble conduct of these friends, that I fear you will all be drawn to keep them company. I see no help for those of us who desire to go on this expedition—and I am of that number—no help but to take the magnets along with us." At this suggestion he was interrupted by a furious clapping of hands.

"But," he continued, "Ned will not accept a pardon which will place him on a different footing from other offenders, he will not accept any favoritism." "Yet," resuming after a profound silence, "there is one way of getting over the difficulty; it is one which I gladly avail myself of, as the only way opened to me of duly honoring the noble example of friendship, which you have witnessed. The plan I speak of is described in two words—*universal amnesty*." At this there arose a wild shouting and clapping of hands from all sides.

"Except it be," he again added, doubtingly, as the noise quieted, "in the case of '69.' How say you? I shall put it to vote. All those in favor of '69's' being allowed to accompany us, will signify it by saying—'Rat.'"

At once "Rat!" "Rat!" "Rat!" arose everywhere.

The merriment had scarcely ceased, when suddenly it swelled up again louder than ever. The innocent occasion of its renewal was a couple of Scotch terriers belonging to the establishment. These vivacious little animals, on hearing their hereditary foes so vociferously invoked, bounded into the room, in a high state of excitement, and with ears pricked up and nostrils distended, darted about under the desks and into every corner, and did not rest till they had thoroughly satisfied themselves that the alarm was false. To add to our amusement they smelt about "69" for some time, with an evident look of suspicion.

CHAPTER XII.

THE EXPEDITION.

For the next quarter of an hour there was much bustling and confusion in the dormitories of the Junior department. In the midst of merry talk about the events of the morning and frequent outbursts of laughter at the expense of "69," rapid preparations were made for the intended expedition.

At length the ringing of the bell summoned us all to the open space in the rear of the school-building, and, a muster of our forces being made, it was found that not one of the juniors was on the sick list or absent for any other cause; those who were ailing on Tuesday were full of spirit and vigor this morning.

With the Major at the head of the column and Mr. Ellery, closing up the line, we marched, two by two, with a steady, even pace through the village. When, however, we had reached the open road leading toward the river, there arose an evident impatience of military restraint, and, the expected signal being given, the column quickly broke into fragments, and there ensued a wild chase down the hill. On reaching the more level road, our first fury of freedom being spent, we sauntered along in groups of three or four, Mr. Ellery joining the Major.

The day was a delightful one. A light autumn

haze hung like a veil over the river, and lay folded among the hills on the opposite side. The foliage had awakened from its summer sleep, and renewed somewhat of its early freshness, and the birds that started up before us from the meadows on the road-side, or concealed themselves in the trees and thickets that lined our way, had hardly slackened the spring and exultation of their early morning carols. All things conspired to make our journey a pleasant one; and this morning of nature, with its life and freedom, its glow and its sparkle, was hailed and embraced by a like morning in our young hearts.

Paradise Island does not lie, as the reader may suppose, in the midst of the frequented waters of the Hudson; its shore is not touched by the great steamboat, puffing and blowing with much self-confidence from the tumultuous city; it has no public wharf upon which travelers are landed, with little trouble on their part, and their baggage delivered to them "with promptness and dispatch." The tourist must turn aside from the thronged way, and, taking some little boat, which he can propel with his own arms, enter the solitary waters of the Croton.

Rowing a mile or more up this stream, if he meanwhile retain a quiet frame of mind, having thrown off his burden of cares to be washed away in the limpid waters, meditating no longer on things of this world, but yielding himself freely to the influences of the day, he will, after having passed several low flats, which are not islands of Paradise, but rather sloughs of despond, come in view at last of the "Quaker's" bridge, and there, between him and this bridge of peace, as the name may be interpreted, Paradise Island will greet his eye, lying low on the bosom of the water, and shut in on all sides by high hills—a world of its own. Let him steer his boat within the shadow of the vine that overhangs the water, and, landing, stray whithersoever the spirit of the hour and the place lead him; and, though the island is a small one, yet he may wander about interminably into new coverts—surprises of delight hitherto hidden from him, such enchantment precedes and attends his steps.

We, however, were to get to the island from a different direction, for while it is only by the one internal path, the one preparation of heart, that this favored spot can be really visited, and its beauties seen; it is accessible externally by various approaches. We followed the road leading to the Croton, to where a branch verges off to the left, just opposite an old, weather-stained, lonely house, which has the reputation of being haunted. Here, descending a gentle slope, it enters the gloom of a primitive wood, where the tree trunks and gnarled roots are coated thick with moss, and a stream rumbles somewhere unseen at its side. It is not, however, by this dark twilight way, haunted by vapors that take form, and fright the lonely wayfarer, that Paradise Island may be best reached; yet it, too, may be followed, for as—thus it is said—all roads lead to Rome, so every beaten way of this region has a turn-off which brings the wanderer at last to Paradise Island.

We, however, guided by the Major, who knew well the roads, and "many a time and oft" had visited Paradise Island, took the main road that verges to the right and upward. This brought us to the top of a bluff, looking off from which we saw Croton Point, stretching out into the broad waters of the Hudson, and beyond it, in the distance, the slumbrous Highlands, among whose folds the river mysteriously loses itself. Below us, imperfectly seen through the trees, that, often half-fallen and caught in the boughs of one another, grew in wild confusion upon the steep declivity which pitched down before us and which was furrowed by frequent spring torrents, lay the Croton. At this point the road took a turn to the right and followed the line of the river, still keeping on the high grounds. We were bid by the Major to follow the road till we reached Quaker's bridge, whither we were all to rendezvous within an hour; we were not, however, forbidden to make in the mean time little excursions from the direct course into the wilds that fringed the river, or to climb the loftier heights on our right, whence could be seen a richer and more wide-reaching view of river and hill and mountain, intermingling and separating, infolding and unfolding and sweeping round into a mysterious unity forever,—a grand choral earth-hymn.

Some of us climbed the heights. Others of us, in parties of three or four, dived down the hill-side, scrambling from rock to rock and clutching the roots in our descent. Among these were my friends, Ned and Tom, and myself.

There was just risk enough in the descent to give it the spice of adventure. We were not content to reach Paradise Island, without asserting the youth's sense of personal power, of originative will; we must diverge from the beaten path, and dare the devil a little. So down the hill we precipitated ourselves, not mindful of a few bruises or a few rents, more or less. Here and there in our course we perched on one and another bold projection of rock, and grasping the stem of some tree that sprung from its cleft, leaned forward to look upon the stream that flowed below us. Its waters were black and deep, as if hiding some unknown fate, and yet this was the sacred stream in which Paradise Island lay; well—perhaps the "dark river" and the "river of life" are one and the same.

We were not long in making the descent, and then found that, after all, the stream flowed along at some distance from the base of the hill, a marshy meadow intervening, which had so treacherous a look that we dared not set foot upon it. We strayed along at the base of the hill, extricating ourselves from one tangle, only to find ourselves confronted by another, pausing in the clearer spaces to pluck some flower, or to snuff the odor of the sweet fern, or to bury the foot in some bed of moss, stuffed between the twisted roots of an old tree, or anon to catch in the open palm the water that dripped from the crevices of an overhanging rock.

By and by we came upon a brook that with much turbulence dashed over and among the rocks in this its last leap down the hill-side. It might have been named the stream of "self-will," with such headiness it pitched this way and that, seeming to go out of its course to butt against the rocks or overleap them, knowing not that its waters would soon be merged and lost in those of the dark-flowing river. We determined to make our way to the top of the hill by following this stream; in that hey-day of life, we found it a companion whose devious courses suited our own bent; its self-asserting clamor, filling the woods, was echoed in our bosoms; and then it was ever speeding from us, yet ever with us,—a mysterious associate.

We found the ascent difficult and slow. The pathway of the brook was hidden from us by rocks and woods, and we followed it blindly, and our wilful guide so turned us about by his strange windings, that we became quite bewildered. In fact, as we afterward discovered, the brook, instead of having cut its way down the hill which we had descended, was flowing in a tortuous ravine or cleft between two hills. At last, however, after having missed many a step on the slippery stones of the water-course, and splashing into eddying pools, after having had to creep on our hands and feet beneath the thick tangles of underwood that frequently overhung the bed of the stream, we found ourselves standing, much spent of breath, beneath a bridge spanning the stream. We climbed the rocks upon which the bridge rested, and planted our feet once more on the open road.

Much time had passed in this escapade, and, sobered down by our hard scrambling, we were content to follow the beaten way, and ere long arrived at the "bridge of peace," which the Major had appointed as our place of rendezvous. We were the last to reach it, and the Major after chiding us brusquely for our delay, at once led the way over the bridge.

The bridge abutted on sheer precipices of rock. Through the chinks of the planks with which it was floored we caught gleams of the river flowing far below; through the crevices of the roof we saw here and there the clear open sky; but our view up and down the river was shut off by the closely boarded sides, and about us there was the dusk of twilight. When we emerged again into the full light, we paused to draw in full breaths and to survey our position. Turning, we looked upon the river, and there, as pointed out by the Major, lay the goal of our journey,—Paradise Island. It was separated from our side of the river by a channel of but little width, and indeed filled up the greater part of the space between the two banks.

We stood quietly gazing upon the promised land which had been so much in our dreams for the past week. It lay low on the water, but was seemingly full of rocky inequalities,—sheltered nooks and hiding-places, such as the early Greeks would have made the haunt of nymphs and demi-gods, but which modern thought fills only with a divine impalpable presence. The rocks that indented the shore were often gracefully draped with running vines, which sometimes hung in festoons from the trees, and wove a net-work of cool shadows over some recess in the shore, where the waters, undisturbed by the current, lay smooth and still. Here and there, through the trees that covered the island, we caught snatches of open spaces deliciously green with moss and turf, across which the sunlight fell with a soft, liquid splendor, and the whole island, though it lay so near us, was folded and swathed in that tender October haze, which seemed, as we looked, almost to lift it from the surface of the river and float it off to an ideal remoteness.

Following the Major a little distance to where the hill sloped off gradually to the water's edge, we rushed down it, as if we expected to leap at once across the intervening channel upon the shore of the Island. But we were brought to a stand on the hither side, for its width was greater than it seemed from the hill.

How to get across. A little way off, near the river, we descried a hut; and it was suggested that perhaps some Charon or other lived there who would ferry us over for a petty coin apiece. Others thought we might collect some of the logs and sticks along the shore, brought down by freshets from, doubtless, a remote region,—even as the fragments of ancient beliefs and systems are strewn along the shores of the present,— and with these construct a bridge for ourselves. But Tom, who meanwhile had strayed down the river bank, by his loud calls gathered us all to his side, and pointed out a willow-tree which hung over the water, and along which, he said, we could climb and then swing ourselves upon the opposite shore, and he immediately illustrated his words by deftly performing the feat.

We all followed Tom's lead, and landed successfully on the shore of Paradise Island,—with one exception; it was "69," who, when his turn came, eager to show his dexterity, proceeded without due circumspection, and, slipping his hold, fell splash into the middle of the channel. But the water was not deep, and the Major, who had armed himself with a stout pole to meet any emergency, or rather immergency, of this kind, and who, withal, was an accomplished fisherman, skillfully twisted the forked end into the pantaloons of "69," as he lay sprawled on the bed of the stream, and raised him up in the air, his head, legs, and arms hanging slimpsily below him, and dripping at every extremity. We could not help laughing loudly, as we stood on the shore of Paradise Island, at the ridiculous plight of poor "69." He was, however, deposited safely on land, where he was obliged to strip himself and hang up his habiliments to dry, and was thus enabled to realize more perfectly than the rest of us the conception of primitive life in Paradise Island.

We meanwhile had dispersed ourselves in groups of three or more, according to our likings, among the coverts of the island, that, with their nooks of sunlight and shadow, their wildness of foliage and rock, stole and broke into one another, and enticed us on and on through a labyrinth of beauty. But to depict all the delights of the brief hours of our sojourn in this spot, so favored of nature, is not in my power; they were so delicate, so evanescent, so impalpable to the grosser sense, so intermingled and blent into one luxury of enjoyment, that all incident eludes the memory, and only a golden halo remains.

We lunched, however— I remember that. It was in a grove near the center of the island, where a clear, cool spring bubbled up from the earth at the foot of a rock; its waters doubtless found their way thither through the interstices of the rock that formed the bed of the river, and had their origin in some remote region; they may have been a rill from that fountain of life, that *elixir vitæ*, which has been sought by the enthusiasts of every age,—so delightful was a draught from them caught to the lips in the hollow of the hand. I have heard that this spring has since dried, and, indeed, that the enchanting features of the island are in these later days much impaired, the river having undermined and cut away considerable portions of it; thus it is that nature, appearing for the moment in all her witchery, ducks and dives from the pursuit of man.

Lunch over, some of us, contrary to our wont, were strangely overtaken by slumber, and, awakening, spoke of soft visitations of dreams, in which the delightful experiences of the time seemed to blossom and expand into a higher life. Was it the waters of the spring that wrought this enchantment in us?

The allotted time of our sojourn in this beautiful haunt quickly passed. Yet ere it had drawn to a close, notwithstanding our serene, unalloyed enjoyment of the brief hours, I surprised Ned, who had in the beginning of the week looked forward to this occasion with such eager anticipation, standing on the shore of the island, and looking wistfully with a slight air of melancholy up the stream, the current of which eddied at his feet; he was thinking of other Paradise islands that lay in the bends of the river, far up in the distant mountain land; for thus the human heart never rests, but images to itself islands of bliss lying beyond its present ken, hidden behind the promontories that jut into the stream of life.

CHAPTER XIII.

THE RETURN.

In returning from Paradise Island we took the road down the right bank of the Croton, with the intention of crossing by the lower, or "long" bridge.

It was a pleasant road, leading along the hill-side and for a great part of the distance through the woods, giving picturesque snatches of the river and the opposite bank between and beneath the opening and closing curtains of leaves. But Tom, Ned, and myself, and one other of my school-mates, impatient of the narrow restraints of the beaten way, took a turn over the hills upon our right, purposing to rejoin our comrades in good season at the bridge, and in the mean time to get a look at the region beyond.

When we had attained the point at which we had aimed, and were satisfying our eyes with a good look, we observed with surprise that the aspect of the day had greatly changed, that the mistiness of the air was gone, and that the clouds, which had hitherto floated lightly far above us, were gathering in dark and lowering volumes. Nevertheless, with the carelessness and dilatoriness of boyhood, we loitered till a few heavy drops, here and there, warned us of what was to follow. Taking at once to our heels, we scudded across the hills at full sail, steering as directly as we could for the long bridge.

Emerging from a grove of trees that stood in our course, we suddenly found ourselves involved in the ornamented grounds surrounding a house; and, fearing to intrude, we were about to beat a retreat and make a circuit of them, when just at that moment the rain burst upon us with full force. Tom, bolder than the rest, led the way under the shelter of a tree, whose wide-reaching arms and matted foliage promised, at least a present shelter. We did not, however, remain long to test the sufficiency of our leafy roof, for we stood in full view from the house, and a lady who had descried us from the window appeared upon the broad raised piazza and beckoned us to enter. We of course could not decline; on the contrary, we were forced to throw aside all appearance of decorous hesitancy, or even of dignity, and run at full speed across the intervening space and up the high steps; and when we reached the presence of the lady, we panted and puffed so, that we were unable to articulate our apologies. The lady, however, led us at once into the house, and though she could not repress her smiles, made us understand by her words and her manner, that we were welcome guests. She knew by our " uniform " whence we were, and therefore would not, as she said, make strangers of us.

The hospitable lady soon succeeded in placing us at our ease and in engaging us in conversation. Our curiosity was awakened by the remarkable portraits that hung on the wall, which our hostess perceiving, she indicated one of them as the head of Joseph Brant, the famous Indian warrior. The picture was somewhat blurred by time, but the strong features of the chief, thus seen, as it were, through the gloomy shadows with which the imagination invests the life of those children of the forest, were all the more impressive.

In the course of the inquiries to which the contemplation of this picture led, and which the *naïveté* of boyhood excused, our hostess informed us that the house which then sheltered us from the rain, was built long before the Revolutionary days, while yet the region about it was an untamed wilderness—the hunting-grounds of the red men; that the walls were originally constructed to serve the double purpose of a fort and a dwelling-place, having been provided with embrasures for cannon, which could still be seen. And many other things she told us which carried the mind back to those early days, when civilization and barbarism met, to that border life which is so interesting to the imagination of boyhood,—here a little settlement, a point of civilization, and around it the unexplored wilderness, within whose glooms lurks the tawny savage. There were also to be seen on the walls the heads of well-known Revolutionary patriots, the memory of whose lives linked that remoter, shadowy past with the prosaic present.

The rain still continuing to pour, our gracious hostess sought to vary our entertainment, and to gratify our curiosity, which her words had still farther excited, by showing us the library and other portions of the time-honored house; and while pointing out the mementoes of the past, she narrated one and another interesting tradition linked with them. But there was one apartment which, she remarked, as she led us back to the reception-room, she had purposely refrained from showing. It was one that was seldom opened; a few faint rays only found entrance through the crevices of the window-shutters and dimly lit the faded hangings, the antique bedstead and the few other pieces of furniture with which the room was supplied, and there was in the air a dry, musty odor of decay. It was the haunted room.

"Every old house has, doubtless," said our hostess, "its haunted room, which is, one may say, the soul of the house. The imagination is prone to people old places with the ghosts of past life. It is, perhaps, the instinct of immortality in the human heart,—that will not let the dead die.

"But be this as it may," the lady continued, "this room is kept locked, and it has been the custom of the family never to permit a guest to spend the night in it, never, at least, since—"

Here the lady, interrupting herself, paused a few moments, thoughtfully. "But, perhaps," she resumed, looking up and smiling a little, "you would like to hear the story of 'the haunted room.'"

No proposition could have been more agreeable to our boyish appetite for the marvelous, and we were accordingly not slow to manifest and express in words our eagerness to listen.

CHAPTER XIV.

THE HAUNTED ROOM.

As the storm now broke forth with renewed violence, beating heavily upon the window-panes and throwing dark shadows into the room, while the creaking of the branches, and the roll and rumble of the thunder were only momentarily intermitted, we drew our chairs in a closer circle around our hostess, without waiting to be bidden,—partly to hear the better, partly from that instinctive sense of fear which prompts the fowl in the barn-yard and the cattle in the open field to huddle together when the storm threatens.

You have heard, perhaps, began the lady, that, at the time when the first settlements were made in this country, the region stretching along the north bank of the Croton formed the hunting-grounds of the Kitchawans, a famous tribe of warriors, who were the terror of the Sint Sinks, Weekquaskeks, and other tribes living south, of them, into whose lands they sometimes made stealthy incursions after the manner of the savage. They were themselves, however, destined to become the prey of their more numerous and more powerful neighbors on the north. These they by their valor and address for a long time successfully resisted; but, feeling their strength begin to wane, and forewarned by the doleful prognostications of their medicine-men, they built a strong palisade upon the neck of land which is now known as Croton Point. This point, by the way, was a sacred region with the Kitchawans. Here, far out on the bosom of the water, they held their great assemblages, and celebrated the weird, uncouth rites of their religion; here, with wild outcries and ringing chants, that disturbed the composure of the hills on either shore, they danced their wild war-dances; and here the fires, kindled to prepare the feast, startled the night with their hissing flames, and flung ghost-like reflections upon the water, at which times, as may often have happened, the captive bound to the stake heightened with his tortures the interest of the savage throng. On this neck of land, within a dark ravine, was situated the ancient burial-ground of the tribe, where lay the ashes of many a famous hero, whose spirit now roamed the happy hunting-grounds. It was finally here, behind the palisade which they had constructed, that the brave remnant of the tribe were forced to retire with their women and children; and here, as tradition reports, was waged a protracted fight, which resulted in the extermination of the Kitchawans to the last of the race, and the fact that a great abundance of arrow-heads are still found or dug up on the spot, is proof that, in this instance, tradition does not lie.

On the last day of this struggle, when the Kitchawans no longer hoped for victory, but fought on with the ferocity of despair, they were headed, as is said, by an old chief of the tribe, who had long ago been compelled by age to withdraw from the war-path and the chase, but in whom, at the hour of this death-struggle of his tribe, life flickered up anew and animated him with a semblance of youthful fire. This was that famous warrior and sachem, Croton,—the chief from whom the stream that flows before our door gets its name. The tradition is, that when all his tribe had fallen, and the palisade was now wrapped in flames, the aged warrior, as the flames and smoke swayed aside, was seen standing on the most towering part of the wooden wall, arrayed in all the bravery of his youth; with one hand he draws the folds of his blanket about him, and raising the other aloft, pronounces the imprecation of the Great Spirit upon his foes, or perhaps foretells their speedy expulsion from the hunting-grounds of the Kitchawans by a pale-faced tribe from the sea,—let us, at least, fill out the outlines of the tradition by something like this. We may conceive, too, that the throng of swarthy savages confronting the fort are struck with awe and stay their hands from the barbed arrow, while the awful form of the aged chief, grows more and more indistinct amid the smoke and the darkening night, and his words break forth in broken gusts of sound, until at last a sudden wind wraps the whole structure in flames, and it falls in with a crash; not till then does the loud, shrill yell of victory escape the savage host, upon whose painted faces the flashing fires throw a demoniac light.

But it was not long thereafter, when, as the dying sachem may have predicted, the pale-face came, in his winged boats, to take possession of the land. A century and more before the Revolution, the ancestor of the family which still occupies this house, sailed up the Hudson in his sloop and established himself on this spot; and here, in a little plot of ground that lies yonder, on the brow of the hill, not far from the ancient Indian burial-ground which I have mentioned, the forefathers of the family have been laid to rest. The dust of the two races almost mingles, and if, as some think, the spirits of the dead are wont to revisit fondly those places where their skeletons lie inhumed, what solemn councils may we not conceive to be held on that lonely hill-top, or in that deserted glen, between the grim sachems of the Kitchawans and the stately fathers of our race, by the light of the waning moon? Certain it is that these old chiefs of the Kitchawans do often haunt the glen in which their bones lie; that is, if the word of the rustics of the region can be trusted, who assert that they have often seen them,—at times, in the dusk of sultry summer evenings, disappearing amid the shadows of the foliage which thickly covers the sides of the glen, and even sometimes when the light of day is fullest, standing with the drawn bow, in the attitude of shooting at some visionary deer. And a half-crazed youth there was, who asserted that, one dark evening, just before moonrise, he saw the shadowy image of the burning fort with the stately form of the aged sachem standing on it, encircled with ghostly wreaths of smoke and flame, while in front, under the shadow of the trees, gleamed the red faces of the savages,—in fact, the very scene we have already described, save that it seemed like a transparency, the somber outlines of nature being visible through all. But such ghostly visions have become exceedingly rare in these later days; perhaps the whistle of the steam-engine and the roar of the passing train have driven the startled ghosts from their beloved hunting-grounds.

But I have not yet come to the ghost of my story,— the ghost of the haunted room. It is in times of trouble and anxiety, when men are looking forward to some serious change, the weal or woe of which is uncertain, that ghosts are most frequent and communicative. Of such nature were the early days of the Revolution. Then men were called upon to decide between duty to king and duty to country, between old memories and ivy-mantled associations on the one part, and the bald claims of the dawning era on the other; between safety and ease, and the uncertain issues of war. And in this their dilemma, did not the spirits of the dead come at their bidding to advise, to threaten, and command?

But the ghost! the ghost! the ghost of the haunted room! You begin to fear he is so ghostly as not to be visible in my story. Ghosts must not be approached too suddenly. An advance somewhat overbold often shatters and prostrates their delicate organizations.

The owner of the estate, of which this house was the manor-hall,—the lord of the manor, as he was called,—a man of deep, serious mind, governed in all things by a severe sense of duty, though fully decided to espouse the cause of the colonies, nevertheless painfully felt the rupture of old ties, the violation of time-hallowed obligations. Many an hour did he walk his garden, under the shadow of trees already grown old and stately, or along the river-bank, deeply moved by this internal conflict between the old and the new. It was while he was thus exercised in mind, that Governor Tryon and a general of the royal army, one day sailed up the Hudson, and disembarking at this point, became the guests of the house. The object of this visit soon became apparent; it was to tempt the lord of the manor (so let us call him) to forsake the cause of the colonists and cast his great influence on the royal side, a high commission in the king's army—tendered to his son, a man already conspicuous in the councils of his country

—being used as the bribe. The offer was rejected with a quiet, stately scorn, and the crest-fallen visitors did not prolong their stay.

But on the evening following their departure, the lord of the manor sat up long in his room, deeply moved. The midnight hour had come. A profound silence had settled upon the house. The troubled patriot, upon whose brow the finger-marks of time were already apparent, sat with bowed head in his large oaken chair. A book lay in his lap, in which from time to time he had made pretense of reading, but which had now dropped from his relaxed grasp. The candles had burnt low in their sockets, and now one and another flickered up and went out, and only the embers on the hearth—for a fire had been kindled to dispel the chill of a late September evening—lit the room with their fitful red glare. The breast of the absorbed thinker rose and fell with almost the regularity of a sleeper's. His thoughts, as the long hours of the night had worn on, had wandered from the present critical condition of his country to its early history, the hardships of the first settlers, their contact with the untamed wilderness and its savage possessors, and from this to the memory of his own progenitor, who had built the solid walls of the present manor-house, and had extended his sway over the hunting-grounds of the Kitchawans; and thence his dreamy meditations lost themselves in the somber shadows of the primitive forest, which had for unnumbered ages overspread this region.

Suddenly he moved in his chair with an uneasy, perturbed manner, as if his reverie were interrupted by some strange thought or unbidden presence; he soon, however, became composed, and drew deep, full breaths as before. But not long after he roused himself with a sudden start, and sat upright. There, on the opposite side of the fire-place, in a chair which was the mate of the one he himself occupied, sat in haughty state the person, or phantom, or,—be it what it may,—of an old Indian, whose ornamented blanket, plumes, and general bearing betokened a chief of the tribe. The flickering light of the embers on the hearth heightened, while it disturbed, the stern, hard-set features of the apparition, and deepened the hollows which age had dug in its cheeks. The lord of the manor gazed fixedly at him,—or it,—gazed without moving, without, perhaps, the power of moving. The ghost, if such it were, returned the gaze. And so the two sat in the light of that uncertain fire.

At last the lord of the manor seemed to hear a sound that shaped itself into words, though so deep was the shadow about the mouth of the apparition, that he could see no movement of the lips. The words, if such they were, were pronounced in a monotone, and with a deep guttural accent that gave them almost a sepulchral effect. They seemed like the echoes of some Indian dialect, and yet, strange to say, the lord of the manor took in their meaning as clearly, word for word, as if they were spoken in familiar English.

"Son of the pale-face," said the voice, "Croton, the chief of the Kitchawans, speaks to you."

With this brief utterance the voice relapsed into silence—a silence so fixed and deep that it bound the soul of the lord of the manor as in the grasp of a stony hand.

"Let us smoke the calumet of peace," said the ghost.

Whereupon the aged warrior raised slowly to his lips

a pipe which seemed to light without the aid of the burning coal. With a deliberate, measured manner he blew forth copious whiffs of blue smoke, which seemed to issue more from the nostrils than the mouth, and then handed the pipe to the lord of the manor, who, unexpectedly to himself, and as if compelled by some power other than his own, put forth his hand to receive it, and then, with a certain nervous energy, smoked several minutes in silence, and returned the glowing pipe to his ghostly visitor.

The smoke, which now floated around them in thick clouds, so obscured the outlines of the ghost, that at times he seemed to melt into its substance, as into a congenial element; but then again, as the smoky cloud rolled aside, he would momentarily loom out with a grimness that would have alarmed even this doughty grandsire of the family, but that the spell of the ghostly presence seemed to render him incapable of fear; besides the tobacco, if tobacco it was which they smoked, had an effect upon him so peculiarly soothing and insinuating, that he hardly felt conscious of mortal existence, and was ready to hob-nob with his ghostship, as one ghost may with another.

"Son of the pale-face," began the ghost, this time, as it seemed to the lord of the manor, in tones no longer distant and sepulchral, "Son of the pale-face, Croton, chief of the Kitchawans, greets you. Be not surprised that I am here. Where your house of stone now stands, once stood my hut of logs. Why should I not make this house mine; why shall I not haunt it?" And a grim smile seemed to hover over the stern features of the ghost; but anon a cloud settled upon them as he added:—

"Do you think you have driven us from our hunting-grounds? No; my beloved Kitchawans still roam the woods that border my beloved river. Your little farm-yards are to us but the vision of a dream. To us, children of the forest, there is still everywhere the unhewn woods; our foot-paths thread it; the bear and the panther and the deer haunt it; it is still our hunting-ground. A ghostly land, do you call it? I tell you, child of the rising sun, yours is the realm of shadows; you pale-faces are the ghosts, and tread a ghostly soil. Do you think you have driven us from our hunting-grounds? 'Tis a lie. The land is ours." Saying which, the visage of the old chief loomed fiercely out from the darkness, and his fingers felt for the handle of his tomahawk.

"Nay," said the lord of the manor, undaunted, "perchance we are both but shadows, and walk amid shadows. Let us not darken our council with angry words. 'Tis fitting, rather, that we smoke again the calumet of peace."

"'Tis well," said the ghost.

Whereupon they smoked by turns from the same pipe, and the smoke thereof floated throughout the room, and hung like a cloudy pall above them. The silence was again long and intense; and meantime the gaze of the lord of the manor was held fixed upon the features of the ghost, which seemed momentarily to mingle with the surrounding darkness, and then again, as the embers on the hearth flashed up anew, to start forth with fearful distinctness. At last, the voice of the old chief broke out, huskily at first, but yet with a certain kindliness and even sadness of tone.

"Yes, 'tis true; I do but delude myself. To you

pale-faces belongs the world; we red men have dissolved from it like a mist, like an exhalation of the dewy morning. You have cut down my forests, you have turned up my lands with the plow, you have bridged my streams, and here, where my cabin once stood, you have built a house of stone. Still changed as it all is, shorn, tamed, despoiled, I shall cling to it, I shall haunt its woods and its dark ravines, and here, where my cabin once stood, I shall often come. Thou shalt share with me your room, my noble pale-face. Here, in the still hours of the night, we shall hold council together. Take heart. The invaders shall not prevail against you. The land is yours. Go forth on the war-path. The victory shall be yours. Croton, chief of the Kitchawans, declares it."

The ghost rose and extended his hand to the lord of the manor, who, as if under the influence of a spell, rose simultaneously and touched the shadowy fingers of the ghost. A cold chill ran through him, and he sank back in his chair unconscious. Deep sleep settled upon him, and it was late in the morning before the stir of household life awakened him.

As the lady ended, a sudden burst of sunlight flooded the room. The storm had cleared. Thanking our hostess for her kind hospitality and the entertainment she had afforded us, we took our leave and soon rejoined our companions, who meantime had found shelter from the storm in the old ferry-house near the bridge.

CHAPTER XV.

THE FOX-HUNT.

One Wednesday morning of December, Ned and Tom and myself, with two or three other of my schoolmates, were roused long before daybreak. We were to be favored with a special treat. The Major at this season of the year was in the habit, every fair Wednesday, of going out with his well-trained hounds on a fox-hunt. A few of the boys were always selected to accompany him, and on the present occasion my friends and I were the fortunate ones.

We needed no second wakening, and dressing was an act of miraculous celerity. We groped our way by the dim gas-light down to the kitchen, in which we found hot coffee and sandwiches already prepared, to fortify us against the December airs. These are quickly dispatched. We tumble into the wagon; a light crack of the whip, and the horses, which have been fretting and pulling under the rein, are off on the jump. The air is sharp and frosty, and the stars shine with almost preternatural brightness. But the rapid riding soon gives brisk flow to the blood, and in half or three-quarters of an hour, we reach our destination.

It is a small, old house, or hut, before which we pull up. A friendly hand has already grasped our horses' heads, and we leap out with alacrity and stamp the ground friskily, for after all our feet are a little cold at the toes.

But we are straightway led by the Major into the hut. A bright fire illuminates the room, and lo! a table laid out with coffee, and rolls, and ham,—all steaming hot; an anticipatory delight penetrates our nostrils. The Major, after rubbing his hands over the fire, takes his seat at the table; we follow quickly, and—but my object is not to commemorate our breakfast, though after our early ride in the sharp morning air, that breakfast was something to remember, it was a new sensation. Meantime, as we ate, our hostess,—Aunt Heddy the boys called her,—a negro woman, fat and jolly-looking, busied herself in attendance, and as she crossed and recrossed before the fire-place, and momentarily hung over it to move the kettle, the gleam of the fire played fantastic tricks with her brown-black features, and kindled a new glory in her wide-rolling eyes.

Our situation affected us strangely. We wondered if we were not in the hut of some enchantress with whom the Major was in league. Were these viands real? We tried them. They certainly were. In fact, it was only the Major's foresight which had provided all this. There was some magic, however, in the rapidity with which the hot rolls vanished. When we rose from the table and bathed our faces again in the cool air, we found that the day had broken; there was a sensible lifting of the load of night, and in the east a red glow emerged above the horizon, and even as we look, the dawn came on apace, and over the frost that whitened the ground crept a silver luster.

We were in a desolate region,—they called it "Alaparthus," or some such heathenish name, which a Christian ought not to spell correctly. On all sides of us were low, rambling, scraggy hills, covered with wood of a stunted growth, or with low bushes. Not a farm-house with ample barns and well-stocked barn-yards, was to be seen; only here and there, from the lone chimney of some poor hut, like that in which we had breakfasted, a column of blue smoke wreathed up in the still, frosty air, and in the neighborhood of it, perhaps, a few lean and lank cattle browsed among the rocks. It was the haunt of the foxes; hence, nightly they descended upon the rich, farming country lying southward,—the land of ye Sleepy Hollow, breeder of fowl; and many a good housewife, as she gathered her chickens about the kitchen-door in the morning, counted them over and over again in vain.

But there is no time to spare. We must unleash the hounds, while the frost is on the ground, for it is then the scent is keenest. See, how the pack look and leap toward their master!—they are loaded and primed for the sport. "Juno," "Brontes," "Bellona," "Bonny-belle,"—they are classic hounds these, whose ancestors, doubtless, shared in the great Cretan boar hunt, while they, forsooth, must chase with loud yelpings some miserable modern fox. But there they go, snuffing everywhere the ground, as yet with only low whimpering barks, expressive of an almost painful eagerness for their prey. They beat every leafless bush, send along every hill-side, while we, eager as they, follow them up, not like the English hunters, on fleet horses, but on legs something less fleet of our own.

Hurry-skurry we go, down into the hollow, splash into the brook, splash through the mire, now on the upland, skirting the wood, headlong down the hill again, panting and puffing, keeping the hounds all the time in sight, for they are not yet on the trail, and beat about in various directions with noses to the ground. Hark! hear that clear, sharp bark from Juno, a ring of exultation in it; she has scented the prey; in a moment her mates are by her side; the whole pack are on the trail, and now from one hill and another away off, even in the remote distance, the echoes of their fierce, quick barking are heard; and the frosty morning rings like a bell. We too, we dogs of boys, can scarcely restrain our shouts.

Follow them! No! Follow the wind! Do not be concerned, Ned; Sir Reynard has a way of his own; he will not leave that hill, but will lead the hounds many a turn, perhaps, around it, before he suffers himself to be caught. Here, from this height, we can overlook the country round for a mile or more, for the trees have taken in their green sails and stand with bare poles.

There they go in full chase along the hill-side! Hark! with what measured cadences their barking sobers down in the distance, and with what mocking, silvery sweetness the echoes are returned, fainter and fainter, from the hills of the Croton! Ah, how the all-charitable nature takes up into her bosom the discordant cries of these yelping hounds and turns them into music!

Now the clear, low ringing of their bark almost dies away. They have turned the hill, and on the farther side, Sir Reynard leads them, still doubtless far ahead, for what he lacks in speed he supplies by ingenious devices, which throw his pursuers momentarily off the scent. Let us descend the hill from which we have watched the chase and cross the intervening hollow, for it is now time for us to take part in this little tragedy. These dogs and the echoes that bounded from every covert, have alone shared in the play, while we have stood inactive aside. But this is not a classic drama, nor are we the mere moralizing chorus. We must be in at the death. Are your guns in order? Look to the priming. Press the caps well down.

All ready? Then do you, "20," take your stand by this clump of trees; yours, as Sir Reynard leaps along the hill-side, shall be the first shot. Watch well your chance, bide your time, and be prompt to the occasion. You, "25," take your place behind that rock yonder, over which the grape-vine droops from the elm-tree; that is a capital covert; yours shall be the second shot. We others shall find hiding-places at suitable distances beyond. Let us on to our posts.

Hark again! the bark of the hounds grows louder, fiercer; and again troops of echoes start forth from the distant hollows, as if packs of hounds were doubling every hill and converging to the chase. Suddenly the hounds and echo-hounds are silent. Have they overtaken their prey, and is the tragedy ended with our parts left out. No; Sir Reynard has played them a cunning trick and eluded their pursuit. But, alas for him! 'tis only for a moment; a single quick yelp is heard, and at once all the hounds break forth anew, fierce, exultant. On, on they come, nearer, nearer. The whole air is filled with the discordant resonance; and the few withered leaves that cling to the swarthy limbs of the old oak-trees quiver and rattle as when a ripple of wind stirs them, or as when they feel the keen morning light breaking through.

Ha! I see something bounding low along the hill-side; something red and tawny. 'Tis Reynard's self. Yonder he comes around the base of that rock, with gaping mouth and panting sides. Now! Now! Quick, ere he passes. Bang goes "20's" gun!

Much smoke, and a green sportsman picking himself up from the leaves, while there goes Reynard with unabated speed; he looks over his shoulder for an instant, with a quick, frightened glance, and vanishes behind that clump of trees. Let him go. 'Tis better to contemplate the wild fox-grapes that hang from this vine, still plump, unshriveled by the biting frost.

Ah! how one's peace is disturbed this calm December morning! There come those dreadful hounds. A rushing, tearing sound among the dry, fallen leaves, and now they turn the rock in the track of the fox. They stream past the trees, fierce, eager, with outstretched necks, overlapping one another. Juno a head and neck in advance,—a compact body, a Cerberus let loose.

Bang from "25"! Another shot follows, and soon again another! Hurry-skurry in the track of the hounds! To be in at the death!

Reynard has sped unharmed past Ned. But Tom's shot has crippled him, and the Major has brought him to the earth, and with the butt of his gun intercepts the dogs, as they are about to wet their teeth in the blood of the victim.

The tragedy is nearly concluded. Poor Reynard lies in his death-throes. We stand round leaning on our guns, while the hounds lie crouched to the earth, with lolling tongues, and eyes that look up for their master's approval.

All is over. The morning sun floods the sky; the white frost is fading from the hill-sides; the snow-birds pipe quietly among the undermost branches of the trees,

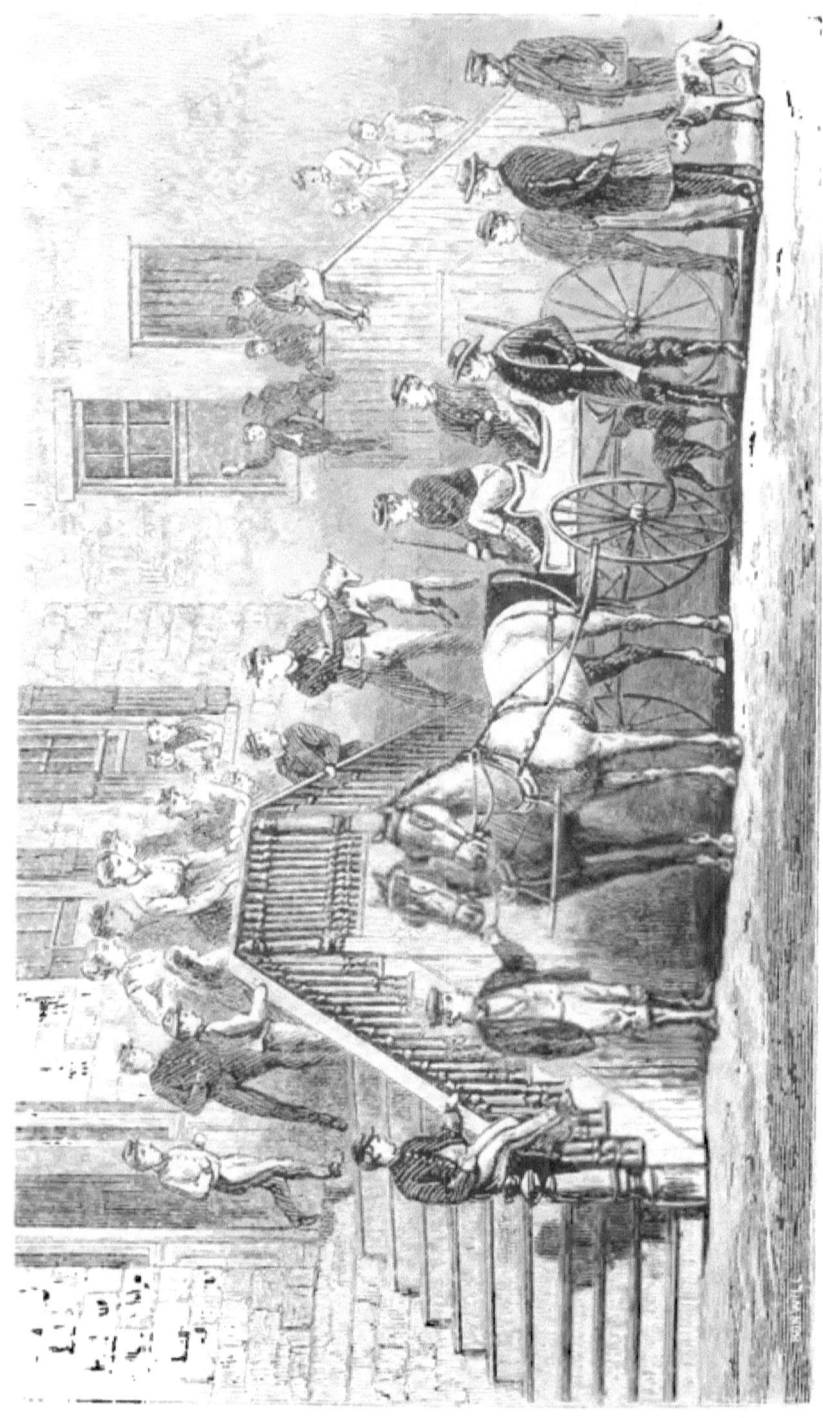

and the red squirrel frisks along the mossy sides of the fallen trunk, and stops to stare at us. Infinite peace wells up from the bosom of nature.

We take up the corse of the poor fugitive, and march in procession back to the hut, the dogs lagging behind with drooping tails.

CHAPTER XVI

THE EXAMINATION.

Though so many of the foregoing pages have been devoted to a narrative of some of our expeditions, they occupied in fact but a fraction of our time. We were, meanwhile, held closely to our studies, and our excursions only formed the brief and bright interludes, scattered through our more serious work, which then, indeed, often seemed to weigh oppressively upon us; it is only in memory that the golden days of freedom stand forth with a brightness which throws all the long intervals into oblivion.

But we were now approaching the Christmas holidays, and the anticipation of them began to infuse among us a more than wonted animation. If with the man "coming events cast their shadows before," with the boy it is more frequently the case that coming events fling upon the present a precurrent glory, leaving their shadowy side out of sight; coming events are, it may more truly be said, but the satellites of radiant boyhood, and, therefore, always turn toward it their illuminated face.

There were, however, it must be confessed, certain spots upon the brightness of the approaching holiday period, for, before being dismissed to our homes, it was necessary to pass through the trying ordeal of a public examination, the report of which would accompany us on our way homeward, and serve as our letter of introduction into the delights of the home circle, or as a pursuing fate, following close on our steps, to scourge us for our misdoings and short-comings. Accordingly, in the midst of our hilarity, there was an element of trepidation and uncertainty. Meantime, with the exception of the few incorrigible do-nothings, we worked like beavers, and strove to repair our former waste of the waters of knowledge by damming up what remained of the stream.

As the fatal days which were to precede the festal days drew nearer, our anxiety became intense. Even those who had studied hard and seldom failed in their daily recitations, began to be preyed upon by secret doubts. What if at the last moment their memory should fail them? What if some sudden terror should surprise them, and a dark cloud should settle upon their vision, and all their laboriously acquired knowledge become transformed into misty, mocking shapes?

Another source of anxiety respected the order in which the classes were to be examined. Until this were ascertained, until we knew where to find the head and front of our enemy, it was an aiming of blows at random, it was carrying on a campaign in the enemy's country without a plan. Strange to say, or, rather, not strange to say—since other equally momentous civil wars have furnished the precedent—it was the custom of the enemy to divulge the position of his forces several days in advance of the projected battle. The enterprising editors of the "Réveillé"—a monthly newspaper issuing from the senior department of the school—were not slow to avail themselves of the information thus freely given, and to promulgate it in an extra edition of that wide-awake sheet. Then it was that the stir and bustle in our camp was carried to the highest pitch. There was hurrying to and fro, and marshaling of forces in this direction and that. Each young soldier inspected his arms anew and furbished them on this side and that to the last touch of brilliancy, that the most gallant show might be made. And it was even said that some of the less hopeful ones, to whose prophetic souls sad visions of impending doom ever presented themselves, were busily engaged making their wills, leaving to one and another comrade the torn and battered relics of their military career.

The place selected for the battle was the library. Here, on elevated ground of their own choosing, behind a well-constructed breastwork of tables and desks, were ranged a formidable corps of principals and professors, with some volunteer forces drawn from the clergy and magnates of the town. The main body of our forces were massed in the school-room, though detachments were to be seen upon the parade-ground, exercising themselves for the fray, and bands of foragers often wandered as far off as Main Street, and made dashes upon the supplies of Mammy Robinson, the confectioner, or upon the tempting stores of some other unfortunate matron, while scouting-parties sometimes ventured as far as the library-door and made reconnoissances of the enemy,—an exposed position from which they always retreated in dismay, for a dark and lowering cloud hung over the brows of the foe, and their nostrils were dilated with martial ardor. Meantime aids and messengers, with visages fraught with the importance of their several missions, were flying to and fro; so that, taken altogether, the scene was an animated and exciting one.

The roll of the drums at last announced that the hour for the opening of the contest had arrived. There was a moment of breathless expectancy, in the midst of which the adjutant, who was our highest officer in command, entered the school-room and called out the division which was first to be led to the attack. The plan of the battle was to throw division after division upon the works of the enemy; in fact, situated as they were, so that neither their right nor left flank could be turned, this was the only strategy that was open to us. In pursuance of the plan thus formed, it was wisely decided to open the contest by a charge of our heavy-armed troops—our *hoplita*—with the view of making a good impression in the beginning, and of feeling the strength of the enemy. This was to be followed by the attacks of our light-armed forces—our *peltasta*—who should worry the enemy with their penetrating darts, and prevent them from reorganizing. Finally, as good generalship demanded, the heaviest blows were reserved to the last, and these, it was hoped, would complete the enemy's discomfiture.

Accordingly, the first division in the order of attack consisted of a band of seniors,—the class in rhetoric. Veterans as they were, they knew no fear. Then, eftsoons, was to be heard the din of arms. The rhetoricians threw at the foe such formidable missiles as metonymy, paragoge, parabole, hyperbole, and many another *bole*, with crashing force, and thereby succeeded in producing not a little consternation in the opposing ranks, so that indeed frequent glances were cast toward the means of retreat, and one or two of the enemy, before the onset ceased, were seen to retire limping from the field.

The enemy employed a missile of a peculiar character. It had very much the shape of an interrogation-mark. Its point was exceedingly sharp, and its snaky look, as it came whizzing through the air, was such as to make the stoutest heart recoil. Flung with a skillful hand, it was well fitted, if not as skillfully rebutted, to produce that irritating, lacerating wound, which, when often repeated, puts the victim *hors de combat*. Not a few of the rhetoricians showed the marks of this weapon, and one or two, whose defensive armor was poor and weak, had to be borne from the field in a bad condition.

The attack, however, was, on the whole, eminently successful, and an inroad had evidently been made upon the strength of the enemy. The next division was drawn from our light-armed forces, and consisted of a band of beginners in Algebra. They were a gallant set of little fellows, and advanced to the front with enthusiasm, though many of them had never been under fire, and doubtless, notwithstanding their outward show of pluck, experienced much secret trepidation. Their armor, however, was well-wrought and well-fitted, and left but few points exposed to the darts of the enemy, and they showered upon him in such profusion all the most irritating letters of the alphabet linked together so intricately by plus and minus signs, that his annoyance and distress was extreme. The enemy's breastworks stood him in very little stead, for our little band of Algebraists adopted the device of flinging their weapons with great force upon the blackboards in their rear, from which they rebounded at an angle that lodged them right in the midst of the enemy. When the favorable moment arrived, our adjutant led off his sturdy little band in triumph, and almost unscathed, so perfect was their armor, and so alert had they been in the exercise of all the arts of defense. Many, indeed, were the weapons of the enemy,—those sly interrogation marks, as I have described them,—which were dexterously caught in the angles of a plus or multiplication sign, or on the end of a minus, and thus hung useless, objects of derision to our gallant fellows.

On the retirement of this valorous body, a force of heavy Algebraists marched to the front with measured, firm step, and deployed before the works of the enemy. Their mode of attack, as befitted the heavier character of their arms, differed from that which I have just described. While, indeed, they sought to divert the attention of the enemy by a similar use of small-arms of the plus and minus order, their sappers and miners industriously aimed to undermine the works of the enemy by means of ingeniously combined and interlinked radicals. Many of these were sprung with telling effect in the very bosom of the enemy, so that distracted and dismayed, they seemed for the moment on the point of abandoning the field, and some of the less hardy were compelled to withdraw temporarily from the contest.

On the other hand, the muse of history—who leans over me as I write—wills it that I record the fact that several countermines were worked by the enemy, and were exploded with terrible effect at the very moment often, when we were looking for the assured success of our own subterranean labors, and, as a consequence, several of our men were borne to the rear in a shattered condition.

But it is not my purpose to go consecutively through all the incidents in this protracted contest, lasting as it did from morning to night for three days. Our boys behaved in the main with great bravery, and made a stout fight; many indeed, by their intrepidity and address, compelled the admiration of the enemy themselves on the very field of battle. Nevertheless, as I have already sorrowfully related, not a few, who made but a clumsy use of their weapons, or, in culpable ignorance of the arts of war, exposed themselves to attack, were led off pale and stricken things, objects of pity alike to their comrades and their foes; over these let History cast her veil, nor ruthlessly expose their after-fate. For them, I fear, on their return home, were no victors' wreaths, twined by fair hands, no approving paternal smiles, no cake abounding in plums, no loose cash for the open hand.

But to return. On the last day of the contest, when the enemy began to show signs of inability to hold out much longer, several bands of Latins and Greeks were marched gallantly to the attack. The light-armed of these were provided with slings, and they had a peculiar mode of attack. Selecting from their well-filled pouches a missile adapted to the special occasion, they hurled it at the head of the foe and caught it again on the rebound, and giving it a peculiar turn sent it whizzing back upon him; thus they often kept the same missile flying to-and-fro dozens of times, so that the ear was stunned with the reverberations. In this mode of warfare, the success of the fighter depended upon his readiness in giving just the right turn to the weapon at each rebound. It was in the use of these antique slings that my friends, Ned and Tom, particularly distinguished themselves.

The protracted contest was brought to a close by a body of *hoplita*—a brawny set of fellows whose very presence was fitted to inspire terror. These, confident that they were about to deal the decisive blow, and sure of their ability to carry the works, began the attack with admirable spirit. They rolled huge Ciceronian periods over the enemy's defenses, well-stocked with explosive epithets. They plied him with saddle-bags of well wrought antitheses, well linked together, and replete with combustible matter. They scaled his works with many a towering climax, and from the height thus gained hurled upon him, with crushing effect, words a foot and a half long. Anon they threw whole parasangs of Xenophon over him, and flung into his ranks frequent jets of Greek fire. Then one might almost see the gods themselves mingling in the fray— Apollo, with his clanging bow; Mars raging with dactyls and spondees; Minerva, full-armed as when she sprang from the head of Jove, and Neptune surging in on the topmost wave of a resounding hexameter. Need I say that the success was complete. The enemy abandoned his works. The field was won. The sun of that fearful December day set in peace.

The enemy, having retired, sent forth a flag of truce, under the cover of which amicable relations were reestablished and an alliance formed. The *débris* of the battle having been cleared away, the victors and the vanquished prepared to celebrate the return of peace by mutual rejoicing, which should obtain expression in the festivities of a ball, wherein the contending parties could join on an equal footing.

And thus gayly, after the ardors of the fight, and the long and sometimes, as it seemed, monotonous antecedent labors, was our life at school brought temporarily to a close. In that concluding festal scene, we young fellows participated more with our eyes than with light fantastic toes. Notwithstanding the kindly efforts of Mrs. Blaisdell to draw us out, we nestled closely into the corners of the rooms. Unused to the dazzling array of beauty, which had been gathered from the neighboring villas to grace the occasion, we were fain to shrink from view into nooks, where, from a safe distance we could behold the gorgeous pageantry, meantime cuddling in our hearts the darling thought that on the morrow night we should be sitting by the firesides of our own homes. But those seniors, those sesquipedalian fellows—even those of them who, in the contests of the three preceding days, had more than once shown the white feather, now walked up to their gentler but far more dangerous foes with inimitable pluck, and the pale faces which they bore from the earlier encounters, were now, in heraldic phraseology, a field upon which beaming sunrise flashes were emblazoned.

But I must make an end. I perceive these memories are overpowering me. For myself, I felt that the few preceding months, were but an introduction; the real story of my life at the military school was yet to come.

CHAPTER XVII.

THE FIRST SNOW.

It was a genuine winter's day on which the school re-opened after the brief play-spell of the Christmas holidays. The season thus far had been an uncommonly mild and open one, permitting us, up to the very day when the school broke up, to carry on the customary autumn sports. We had looked in vain for a good fall of snow, or for a hard field of ice; only now and then a thin snow-veil had covered the earth, or a light frost had clad the waters with a fragile coat of mail, which the sun's darts easily pierced. At last, we said, winter has come. The hale, hearty old gentleman had put on his thick white coat; but his face, to us boys, was red with the warm flush of life, and his eyes twinkled with fun and jollity.

The snow began to fall about midday, and the sky seemed to have settled itself, as we expressed it, for an old-fashioned snow-storm, for though we counted up but few years, yet to us, as to our elders, close, snow-bound winters seemed to belong to the merry olden times; your degenerate slip-slop "season," with its draggling, mud-bedaubed skirts, was an innovation of the modern fashionable world; we boys liked rather the old Knickerbocker time, with its short petticoats and red stockings, its great open fire-places, its generous supply of hickory nuts, and great knots of wood to crack them on.

In the afternoon, the boys began to arrive in little flocks of ten or fifteen; every train from the North or South brought fresh additions. I was among the earliest to reach the school, where I was kindly welcomed by the principals and such of my school-mates as had preceded me. Among these was Tom Manning, No. 35. Tom received me with great *empressement*, and ushered me at once, wrapped up as I was in frosted great-coat and furs, into the great room directly off the hall, which I have already described as "the old school-room," where a generous fire was burning, not in a huge open fireplace, but in the great stove, from the windowed sides of which a rich red light illuminated the ceiling and near walls, while elsewhere in the room the dusk of the storm and of the early winter evening already hovered.

The old school-room was becoming more and more animated with the eager talk and busy movement of boyhood. There was not much rough play, for we all had a great deal to say to each other about the holiday times now brought to a close, many amusing and wonderful things to relate, many anticipations to indulge concerning the winter sports in store for us.

Some of us stood by the windows, watching in the midst of our talk the thick-falling flakes of snow, which seemed to flit for a moment out of the gray twilight to be again swallowed up and lost. We saw the night come on silent and sad, with head bowed low and veiled; but our hearts danced merrily within us, as if they felt the light cool touches of the snow-flakes.

Others of us huddled affectionately about the stove, as about some common friend, whose great warm heart kindles all other hearts into a blaze. Elsewhere throughout the room there was a constant moving about, an intermingling of threads of life spun into a web that here gathered into knots, there again unraveled into loose skeins.

The door into the library stood open, and the burning coals heaped up in the ample grate shed a warm glow throughout the room, touched by which, the long rows of books on the walls lost the venerable look of age and dry learning, and assumed the rosy tint of romance. Peering into the quiet room from the open door, it was not difficult to imagine that the heroes of ancient story sometimes escaped from the book-caskets in which they had been confined by the spells of the magician, and moved about in high state, though invisible to our eyes, and talked proudly as of old, and perchance fought over again their old battles. We were, however, in no mood just now for the stillness of the library; the happiness which the recollection of holiday pleasures and pranks inspired, and that satisfaction which the sight of old faces and exchange of greetings afforded, as well as the anticipation of a new line of amusements—this past, present, and future aspect of the moment demanded nothing else than a free and abundant talk; so the stream of articulate noise ran high.

A ringing of the bells was ere long heard in the courtyard, followed by the outcries of merry voices, as the sleigh drew up at the door. A new batch of boys had arrived, perhaps the last. We flocked to the windows and the hall-door, and hailed the new-comers with loud shouts of welcome, to which a few snow-balls were added as an earnest of our good wishes; the driver of the sleigh, as he whipped up his horses to escape from the court-yard, was most liberally honored with testimonials of the latter character, which, however, he literally received with a great deal of coolness; we heard, nevertheless, as he drove off into the darkness, some wrathful sounds which mingled wildly with the mutterings of the storm.

Among those who ascended the steps, Tom and I easily distinguished our common friend, Ned Eldridge. We hailed him with many exclamations of pleasure, and taking from him his valise, helped him to shake off the snow which whitened his overcoat, and led him at once to the glowing fire in the old school-room. Ned's eyes beamed with pleasure, and showed that if, when the school broke up for the holidays, he was the gayest of the gay at the prospect of seeing home and its loved ones, he was hardly less pleased with the return to the scene of his toils, and to the sight of the familiar faces of his comrades.

The old school-room now presented an animated spectacle. Everywhere was life and commotion, and a confluence of voices in every boyish key, in the midst of which the gas was suddenly lit.

"Well, Ned," said Tom, "how do you like coming back to the old prison walls, to sing-sing the old tune?"

"The old tune suits me well," said Ned, "while yours and Ralph's voices join in;" and he turned with a look of boyish candor from the one to the other.

"And we are willing captives in your society," said I.

"And if we make you captives now," said the well-known voice of Mr. Ellery, who unobserved by us had approached and overheard our conversation, "if we make you captives now, it is only that you may forge the instruments with which you may make for yourselves hereafter a large liberty in the fields of knowledge. Therefore work well at the anvil, my boys, and keep the iron glowing."

At this moment the bell rang for supper, and at the command "Fall in," we ranged ourselves in our respective divisions on each side of the room, and waited for the seniors to pass through.

Presently their measured tread was heard in the hall communicating with their department. As they marched between our ranks, each of them in turn saluted the principals. As the last of the seniors reached the middle of the apartment, the juniors, each division under the command of its chief officer, took up the line of march to the supper-table.

Thus did our military school discipline begin anew.

CHAPTER XVIII.

THE BATTLE OF THE SNOWS.

The morning dawned cold, crisp, and clear. The air seemed to have a crystalline sparkle; and there was in it that tonic and exhilarating quality which is always noticeable after a considerable fall of snow. Awakened at the first flash of light by the morning drum, on descending to "the old school-room" we gazed with unmeasured delight, through the windows overlooking the court-yard, upon the clean pure surface of snow, unbroken as yet save by the tracks of "Juno," the hound, which extended in a straight line from the kennel under the eaves of the gymnasium to the kitchen door. There were among us various and conflicting opinions as to the depth of the snow, but all agreed that it was certainly not less than eighteen inches.

The first day of school was not marked by a devotion to hard study; a day or two was needed to break us anew to the traces; our spirits ran too high as yet for settled and dogged work. But we required no preparation for a hearty participation in the sports of the season; accordingly, as soon as the bell announced the morning recess, we hastened out of the school-room, without much regard to decorum, and having reached the parade-ground, worked off our first ardor by a general *mêlée*, in which the snow-balls flew thick and fast in all directions, and one knew not from what unexpected quarter the cool salute might reach him.

In one part of the field, our friend Tom seemed to be receiving especial attention; from a wide circle the balls were aimed at him, compelling him to exert all his agility in dodging, and leaving him no time to return any of the numerous compliments of which he was the recipient. With such skill, however, did he bow his thanks, that only now and then, amid the shouts of his comrades, did a well-directed ball leave its white impress upon some unguarded part.

At length, one of the thick flying missiles was seen to shiver into fragments upon the very boss of Tom's facial buckler—the nose itself, and a few drops of blood tinged the pure white of the snow; whereupon Tom held out his handkerchief as the white flag of truce, and asked for a parley. He was willing, he said, to stand as a target, for his friends to practice on, if each of them in turn would take the same position; but he was of the opinion that before we had gone the rounds, the sport would become very dull, and he was for a partition of forces and a more equal contest.

The proposal was at once acceded to and immediately acted upon, and Tom soon found himself the captain of a considerable force, to which a body equal in number was opposed under the leadership of Ned, for these two friends, in consequence of the events already narrated, had become the heroes of the juniors. It was arranged that whenever any one on either side was hit above the knee, he should retire from action in order that the contest might be decided in favor of the one or the other party.

Tom having gone back with his men to a little distance, drew the greater part up in line, at intervals of four or five feet, and at the same time,—determining to bring his military science to bear,—he effected a partition of the line into three divisions, constituting a right, left, and center. The remainder formed a fourth division, and were drawn up in the rear. Tom instructed his troops not to fire except at the word of command, and to be careful to throw no random balls.

The enemy, under Ned, were not drawn up with any special care, but were left in that disorderly array usual with boys in such contests. Ned, indeed, perceived Tom's arrangements and would have imitated them, but there was little time to spare. All preparations being completed, Ned began the action on his side by himself throwing the first ball, an example which was at once followed by his entire force; but as his men stood much in each other's way, as too, inspired by Ned's ardor, they threw with great precipitation and haste as well as without regularity, their balls generally flew wide of the mark, or were easily dodged.

It was now Tom's turn. He gave his orders with great deliberation, taking up a central position in the rear, and not personally engaging in the contest.

"Load,"—whereat each boy supplied himself with a well-compacted ball, taking care all the while to watch the enemy, and dodge his missiles.

"Aim,"—each boy selected his opponent.

"Fire,"—the air between the two armies was for a moment whitened with the thick flight of balls, confusing the sight of the enemy and incapacitating them for a successful effort at dodging.

At the moment that the order to fire had been given, the fourth division, obeying instructions previously imparted, and taking advantage of the confusion of the enemy, marched at double-quick, under the order of a subordinate commander, and took up an advanced position on the right, flanking Ned's left, and immediately, before the enemy had yet recovered, poured an enfilading fire into his ranks, which proved very destructive; many of Ned's bravest were placed *hors de combat*, and he himself narrowly missed several well-directed balls.

Ned seeing the disadvantage under which he was placed, endeavored to withdraw his men to a new position, but the attempt, in the absence of any organization in his ranks, only served to throw them into greater confusion. In the mean time, volley after volley was poured into them, to which they could oppose but an ineffectual, straggling fire in return. Tom, meantime, perceiving that his enemy had become massed on his right to meet the attack in that quarter, ordered forward the division constituting his left wing, to an advanced position on the right flank of the enemy. The movement was executed with rapidity and precision, while the attention of the enemy was occupied by a vigorous fire. Ned's forces were now assailed from three sides, and as the volleys were often poured in simultaneously, his men knew not to which side to look for the coming ball. They were consequently fast becoming demoralized.

Tom, seeing his enemy begin to waver, conceived that the moment was come for the final blow. He accordingly ordered one of the two divisions which still occupied their original position, to load, advance at double-quick and charge the enemy's center, firing at will. The remaining division he kept back as a reserve, to render support wherever it should be needed. The two flanking parties were also ordered forward to advanced positions, to intercept or harass the enemy's retreat. The attack executed, as it was, with great *élan*, was completely successful. The enemy were driven back some distance, and finally broke and fled ignominiously. Ned sought in vain to give encouragement to his men by word or example, and at length disdaining to flee, surrounded by his foes, fell, struck by a dozen balls. The small remnant of his followers were, in accordance with Tom's orders, pursued by his two advanced corps, and being prevented from scattering in all directions, were driven to the wall, and forced to surrender.

Tom's victory was complete, and beautifully illustrated the advantages of organization and military science over undisciplined valor. Tom, however, did not yet relinquish the reins of discipline. He caused his forces to be drawn up in good order to await the pursuing parties, who were now approaching, marching in hollow square with their prisoners in the center.

The majority of the prisoners Tom released on parole, but there were three whom he pointed out, who, as he said, forgetful of honor and good faith as soldiers, though repeatedly shot, in fact killed outright, persisted in fighting on.

"These men," he said, with a severe voice, and frowning like a cloud of war, "must be thoroughly convinced of their ghostly condition. Let them be covered with a pall of snow." Tom's entire forces were formed in a hollow square about the doomed men. The successive orders were then given to load and fire. The poor fellows shrunk and dodged in vain from the balls that showered upon them. After the third such volley, the offending trio were found rolling and writhing in the snow, and completely enveloped with its fleece-like shroud.

At this moment the school-bell rang. Tom, in a brief speech, applauded his men for the valor they had exhibited, and for their ready subjection to military discipline, and congratulated them on their victory as the result, and in honor of this victory he proposed three rousing cheers. These having been given with a will, he pronounced the order, " Break ranks—march," which was immediately followed by a rapid scampering toward the school-room door.

Of the three fellows who had been so ruthlessly snow-balled, two, one of whom was our old friend " 69," rose and shook the snow from their coats with evident good humor, recognizing the punishment as a legitimate part of the sport; but the third skulked off with an angry, sullen expression, casting many invidious glances toward Tom, and muttering something between his teeth.

CHAPTER XIX.

REMOTE STARS—NEBULÆ.

That portion of the year extending from the winter holidays to Easter, at which time a vacation of ten or twelve days was granted, constituted a period, when we were the most vigorously pushed in our studies, and when the greatest advancement was expected of us. The military training, to which in the spring and the fall of the year, several hours of the day were devoted, was at this season, in consequence of the shortness of the days and the frequent inclemency of the weather, necessarily omitted; nor for the same reason could so much time be given to out-door sports. At this season, then, in particular, our preceptors sought to inspire us with a quickened zeal in our studies.

It is doubtful in the opinion of the writer, whether the methods, ordinarily pursued in schools to excite effort, are not productive of more harm than good. The few pupils of talent carry off the prizes, while the many, —consisting in part of those who are industrious but dull, in part of those capable of apprehending, but of slow memory, and of still others whose only fault is immaturity of powers,—seeing success beyond their reach, put forth even less exertion than if no prizes, tangible or intangible, were held up before them. Oppressed with a secret sense of comparative disgrace, they lose whatever interest they would naturally take in their studies, and even look upon them with distaste as being the cause of their unhonored position. On the other hand, the few successful ones are puffed up with a vain conceit of themselves, or nourish a secret pride which vitiates all their future efforts.

Happily for me, the method of encouragement adopted at Mount Pleasant did not appeal to a spirit of rivalry, for though ambitious of honorable distinction, my retiring nature was ill-fitted to participate in the embittered personal contests which this spirit excites.

At Mount Pleasant all who were not physically too indolent or morally perverse,—and such are generally very few in number in any school,—could attain an honorable mention, sufficiently flattering to keep alive their self-respect; no one was allowed to wander into the slough of despond. A record was kept of the daily proficiency of each pupil, and at the close of every month a reckoning was made, and every one who did not fall below a certain standard of excellence was placed in the roll of honor. Nor was this an idle distinction, for the list of honored names was not only hung up in the school-room, but was published, and sent home to parents and friends.

The medium through which this publicity was effected, was the "Réveillé"—a paper edited by three of the more literary members of the Senior department, who were yearly selected for the work. This paper, which was issued monthly, contained lucubrations which, emanating from the more advanced pupils, were both witty and wise, at least in the estimation of the writers themselves. But the feature of the publication which was always looked forward to with most interest and anxiety, was this "Merit Roll," and with great delight did the happy youth, who found his name there enrolled, do up the valuable sheet in a clean envelope, and inscribe thereon, in bold characters, the address of a beloved parent or a respected aunt, uncle, cousin, or friend, always taking care to underscore his own name in the list of the honored.

Of course among the great number of those who were allowed a place upon the "Merit Roll," there were many degrees of excellence. No one, however, was assigned a precedence; the names were placed in alphabetic order. Thus the few were not encouraged at the expense of the many, nor was the vanity of any one appealed to, or a proud sense of superiority excited and inflamed.

At times, however, in order to enkindle a renewed spirit of enterprise in study, some special inducement was held forth, such as an unusual holiday, an expedition to some hitherto unvisited locality, and the like. At the present time, as the season was not favorable to excursions, and as unusual holidays would prove an interruption to the continuous effort demanded of us, the principals had sought an incitement to activity, of an extraordinary nature.

On the evening of our first day at school, when the study hour had drawn to a close, Mr. Ellery entered the school-room, and taking his seat at the desk, after a few words of pleasant talk on the holidays that we had enjoyed, said he did not doubt that, refreshed as we were by the sight of our homes and the endearments of our friends, we had returned with a determination to apply ourselves vigorously to the work of study. He reminded us that the period of time intervening between the New-Year and the Easter holidays was the one most favorable to a laborious delving in the field of knowledge. We were a company of gardeners; the school was the conservatory in which we labored; it was in our minds that we must sow the seeds and plant the roots which he and his associates—the head-gardeners—would furnish us. Now was our season of hardest work; by and by, when the warm weather came, the windows of our conservatory would be thrown open, and nature's sunlight and air would, with but little help of ours, if we worked well now, vitalize and nourish the germs we had made our own.

It is doubtful whether we seized upon the meaning of these words, in its fullest extent; but we caught from them a sense which animated us with a decided relish for the horticultural labors pointed out. We began to look upon ourselves as the assistants and co-operators of nature.

But our respected Principal knew that with boys such feelings were of an evanescent character; he accordingly went on to say, that he proposed to bestow on all those who succeeded in winning, every month till Easter, a place upon the "Merit Roll" a special mark of distinction; their names should be published in the "Réveillé" as the stars of the school, and they should have the privilege of wearing temporarily, while on their visit to their friends during the Easter vacation, a star of silver tissue, fastened to the left breast of the coat. This distinction, he said, was open to the attainment of all, and he hoped that the constellation would be a full one, and that none of his pupils would be content to remain in the merely nebulous condition.

He proposed, still further, to decorate the five of the seniors, and as many of the juniors, whose record showed the most persevering and successful effort, with a double star. Though all, he said, could not attain this highest honor, all should aspire to it. Aim at the highest, should be our motto, and he pleasantly referred us to the Alpine hero, with his proud device, "Excelsior!"

As to those who showed a determined disposition to shirk their duties, even these should not go unhonored,—they, too, should "see stars," such at least as are reflected in the waters of "salt river."

With this briny allusion he left us. The drum soon beating the tattoo, we were marched off to bed, and in our dreams, if those of my comrades resembled in any respect my own,—we sailed up a stream, whose waters were chilling to the view and bitter to the taste, and as we sailed, the stars danced down from the heavens and frisked before us, yet always dodged as we clutched at them, every time flinging a spiteful sparkle into our eyes; on either side rose steep mountains, whose sides were loaded with the weight of many snows, and far off, upon the loftiest peak, struggled ever upward a noble youth, and his banner wore the strange device, "Get up! Get up!" Anon the roll of a drum seemed to reverberate among the hills. I turned around and saw Ned standing by my side in the dusk of the morning. I was awake. The night had passed like a fleeing shadow.

CHAPTER XX.

THE SPOILED CHILD.

Among the listeners of the preceding night to the Principal's words of exhortation and encouragement, there was one upon whom they did not have the effect intended. It was the youth, who, having been well peppered with snow-balls, for his bad faith in the mock-contest of the morning, accepted his punishment with so ill a grace. While all around him there were frank bright faces beaming with interest in what was said, and animated with at least a momentary determination to win the sparkling honors held up before them, his own countenance wore an assumed expression of contempt; his lip was forced into a cynical sneer, which ill became one so young, and showed a premature experience of evil.

The pale face of the youth had the marks of a quick intelligence, apt to apprehend and distinguish, but crossed by a look of cunning, which was at times almost malignant. He was a boy of lively sensibilities, which seemed to have been perverted by some ill management in his early training. He was not incapable of generous emotions, but his jealous self-love soon overmastered them. I have heard that he was an only son, and that, his father dying in his early childhood, his early education devolved wholly on the mother, who, a woman without much mind, but of a passionate disposition, devoted herself to her child, without, however, gaining his respect. She not only herself submitted to all his caprices and gratified every passing humor, but compelled all her attendants to the same course. The little master fed upon these flatteries and caresses as his daily food. He constantly craved and received the homage of love, without being called upon to render a return in kind. The sensibilities of his heart were thus aroused without being led to that free and healthy outward flow which nature designed; they were allowed to revolve about his own self-consciousness, which was thus constantly absorbing the attentions and caresses of those around him in the whirlpool of a morbid self-love.

When he had reached his twelfth year, his mother died, leaving him under the guardianship of an uncle. The treatment he now received was of a kind for which his previous life had ill prepared him. His uncle was a strict disciplinarian, who saw in his nephew the plain evidence, as he supposed, of a heart naturally depraved. His plan of education was simple, and easy of execution. It was, to whip the depravity out of the boy, never slipping by a favorable occasion. Under this treatment, so conscientiously pursued, his nephew's moral nature, strange to say, did not thrive and expand. The sensibilities of his heart were still more compressed and beaten, so to speak, into themselves. What was before passive self-love now became active hate; and the lively intelligence, with which he was gifted by nature, was turned to the uses of a petty subterfuge, to which he resorted in order to circumvent the tyranny of his guardian. The latter, finally, not finding his educational methods productive of the best success, determined on sending the boy to the school in which the reader now finds him. It was to be feared that the mischief of his education was already irreparable.

"Seventeen," for that was the number by which he was designated, was glad enough to escape for the time from the rigid grasp of his uncle; still, he did not find his life at the school agreeable to his inclinations. There were restrictions to which he must necessarily submit, but the enforced submission secretly angered him; he looked upon the school, represented by its principals and corps of teachers, as in league against him. He did not receive the personal favor he coveted; he was only one among many. Ambitious of popularity and applause, his personal qualities were yet not such as to attract the good-will of his fellow-pupils; he accordingly stood aside and looked with a jealous eye upon the happiness of his comrades, or if he shared with them in their sports, it was with a sullen, dissatisfied air. In particular did my two friends, Ned and Tom, in consequence of the high favor in which they stood, both with teachers and pupils, call forth his secret enmity.

"Seventeen" did not return to school, when the winter holidays had ended, with a disposition at all softened or cheered by the interchange of those domestic charities which around most hearths sanctify and illumine that season of the year. His uncle, the disciplinarian, was not a believer in holidays. His theory of life did not embrace the element of play, and the plan of life which was built upon his theory did not leave much room for it. Accordingly, "17" was not much benefited by holidays. Whatever germs of good were hid in him were certainly not then warmed into life. His uncle knew well that the devil finds work for idle hands to do, and took care that the nephew should be well employed and kept under strict surveillance.

As I have said, Ned and Tom were special objects of "17's" secret enmity, and when, shaking himself clear of the snow after the contest which I have described, he saw the two friends going off together in gay mood, without heeding his ill-concealed anger, he secretly determined to seek out some way of revenging himself, as he called it. It was, however, against Tom rather than Ned that his ill-will was most particularly directed. Tom, with his air of calm self-reliance, compelled his fear, which feeling only contributed to the intensity of his spite; Ned, with his volatile, flexible nature, he affected to despise.

Ned, it must be confessed, had also in a slight way the air of a spoiled child. He was accustomed from childhood to being much fondled and caressed. Very little restriction was openly placed upon the gratification of his desires. His mother was as fully devoted to her child as had been "17's" to him; but the difference was that of an intelligent and an unintelligent spirit of sacrifice. Ned's mother, while she put forth but little restraining power, seized every occasion and used every little device to call forth her son's affection, to give them a healthful flow out of himself. Thus in those early years, when the youthful imagination seems almost to assign an actual life to external things, instead of seeking to remove this illusion, she took advantage of it, and if the child accidentally, in the midst of its play, hurt itself in contact with some inanimate object, she did not, as foolish nurses do, seek to soothe it by scolding and beating the inoffensive cause of its pain, but rather diverted it from a regard of its own ill-luck by pretending to pity the poor table-leg or chair, or what not, against which he may have fallen. By skillfully availing herself of innumerable opportunities of this kind, she fostered in her son a genial sympathetic disposition, which did not limit itself to a regard for persons, but overflowed upon natural objects, and expressed itself in a sentiment of universal kindness.

But his education, refined as it was, cultivated more exclusively the emotional nature; accordingly Ned was as yet too plastic and pliable, too open to impressions and influences from every quarter, too much dependent upon the affection, sympathy, and applause of others. He needed a little of the toughening and hardening which life at a great school is calculated to give—a preparatory discipline for the school of the world.

"Seventeen" was not slow to perceive the weaker side of Ned's character, though he did not clearly state to himself in what that weakness consisted. With Tom as the definite object of his spite, he determined to use Ned as his first means of gratifying this feeling. With what success we shall see.

CHAPTER XXI.

VAPORS.

The Principal's encouraging exhortations, and the anticipation of a triumphant return to their homes, covered with glory, produced among nearly all the pupils, at least for the first few weeks, a close attention to study, and a careful observance of the rules of the school. Of course, after the first ardor of the attack, there were many that relapsed, and some that fell away altogether. Still the greater part worked on with a commendable degree of zeal, for every one knew that his success depended, not on his merit as compared with his fellows, but on his individually reaching a certain fixed standard; the faithful student, therefore, though slow at learning, and sensible of his incapacity to contend in rivalry with others, might still hope by hard work to attain the coveted honor.

But the highest prize, the "double star," called forth a zealous competition among those pupils who were fitted by nature to take the lead, as well as among those who, having fair capacity, hoped by the aid of close application to rank with the former. It is hardly necessary to say that both Ned and Tom had set their hearts upon the "double star;" and certainly they had good reason to expect success, for among the juniors there were, perhaps, none of superior general powers, and they had therefore only to bring to the aid of these a determined purpose.

It must not be supposed, however, that we did not take advantage of every hour devoted to our out-door recreation. We were boys, and we irreverently snapped our fingers in the face of old Winter; we were not to be housed by his whistling winds or drifting snows. The snow-balling contests, such as I have described in a previous chapter, were of frequent occurrence, so long as the snow remained soft and light. Ned, chagrined at his easy defeat on the first occasion, sought to redeem his reputation. Ambitious of leadership and applause, his affection for his friend Tom did not prevent him from disliking to come off second best; he was full of ardor in his desire that the party he led should be victorious. However, it generally happened that Tom, by his superior strategy, won the field.

It was after a fresh fall of snow, near the close of the second week of school, that the fourth or fifth of these contests had occurred. In the evening of the same day, we juniors had gathered as usual in little groups in different parts of the school-room, and were spending the half hour that remained between study hour and bed-time in gossiping about the events of the day. The seniors had withdrawn to the dignified retirement of their own rooms. Mr. Homans, our teacher of mathematics, remained with us as a check upon the spirits of youth, which uncurbed are apt to run too high.

Mr. Homans held the boys in control, not by an ostentatious display of authority, but by a quiet, self-contained manner that impressed us with the sense of a reserved power, which a suitable occasion might call forth. There was, beside, in his expression and bearing, notwithstanding the masculine decisiveness of his features, an element of almost feminine delicacy which made him very attractive to the boys and easy of approach; it was a common sight to see a knot of boys gathered about him, chatting with him in the most familiar manner. It is rare that great force of will and a certain sweetness of temper, a certain feminine *finesse*, are centered in the same person.

Ned was one of those who were especially drawn to Mr. Homans, and he was frequently to be seen among the gayest of the gay circle of boys that formed about that teacher. On the present evening, however, Ned did not mingle in the lively talk of his comrades. He kept his place at his desk, and occupied himself with his books; he had "Cæsar's Commentaries" before him, and seemed to be intently studying the plan of a battle, with which the book was illustrated. The truth is, he was deeply annoyed at the repeated defeats which the party he led had suffered in the recent contests, and in particular at the unsuccessful issue of the fight that morning, and he hid himself behind his books to avoid hearing any disparaging remarks that might be made by his fellow-pupils.

Tom missing Ned's company would have sought his friend, but he himself had become the center of a group in a remote part of the room, from which he could not politely break away, nor could he succeed in catching Ned's eye with the view of beckoning him to join his circle. Ned, in short, was in the dumps, and did not wish to be drawn out. "Seventeen," who had been moving about the room from one group to another, finally, with an air of the greatest nonchalance, took his seat at his own desk, which was immediately in front of Ned's, and began occupying himself for the moment with his papers.

This jealous, envious youth had recently displayed an unusual gayety of mood; he seemed suddenly to have acquired the power of putting himself upon easy terms with his fellows, and though he did not win their hearts, he seemed to be acquiring a certain kind of popularity. In truth, the secret purpose he had conceived, had given him a vivacity of spirit which he had not before evinced, and was developing in him that power of evil fascination which is frequently the characteristic of natures at once intelligent, passionate, and intensely selfish.

The designing youth did not sit long before finding a means of breaking in upon Ned's meditations, without seeming to have an object in view. As if by accident he let his pen fall in such a manner that it rolled out of his own reach and under Ned's feet. Of course Ned picked it up and handed it to him. "Seventeen," as he politely expressed his thanks, added: "You are very studious to-night, '25.'"

"Yes," said Ned, who had substituted an exercise-book for his Cæsar, "I am a little behind in my French. 'Mush' (school-boy for *Monsieur*) will trip me up to-morrow with that lingo of his."

"Ha! ha! When 'Mush' gets a little excited he trips it on the light fantastic tongue as nimbly as our dancing-master trips it on a toe of the like kind." After a little pause he added in a casual way: "Those fellows over there are having a merry time—talking over the affair of the morning, of course. Indeed it is the talk all over the school. Tom and his set are very gay about it."

Ned could not help showing an interest, though the expression "Tom and his set" grated harshly on his ear. But "17" had turned about to his own desk, as if the subject was ended; but he was pretty sure that Ned would not let the matter pass without a few more words.

Ned held his peace for some time, though he could not help dwelling in his thoughts upon the invidious words to which he had listened. *"Tom and his set."* Was then Tom glorying over him, and making him the object of his witticisms? It was a suspicion which he sought at once to expel from his mind. Nevertheless, in an awkward, hurried manner, with none of the ease usual with him, he put the question: "What was Tom saying about it when you were over there?" But the words had hardly passed his lips when he blushed at the jealous suspicion which they concealed, and wished them recalled. But "17" was ready with his response.

"Oh, Tom was joking a little about your silence this evening. He said he saw you had your Cæsar before you; he guessed you were studying a plan for your next campaign; if you invoked the spirit of Cæsar to your aid, he should tremble for his military reputation. You know what a dry way Tom has of saying such things. The boys were very much amused, I assure you."

These words, uttered in the light, off-hand way of a passing conversation, as if they contained nothing of much import to either the speaker or the hearer, stung Ned to the quick. It was true, then, that Tom—his best friend, as he supposed—had turned from him, and was making him the laughing-stock of his comrades. The venomed shaft had taken hold with its hooked barb. The unjust suspicion which Ned had too easily admitted had already begun to fester. His distorted fancy now put a bad construction upon many an innocent speech of his friend; and even Tom's silence, and the abstraction which his devotion to study sometimes occasioned, were interpreted as an evidence of failing regard. With his sensitive, sympathetic nature, nothing so touched Ned as an apparent coldness in a friend, or the least mark of ridicule. That his friend Tom was not only slighting his affection, but, in school-boy parlance, was making fun of him, wounded him more deeply than he cared to express. He returned no answer to "17's" wily speeches.

Quick and impulsive in all his feelings, with Ned what was at first mere suspicion, rapidly became an undoubted truth. And when, the tattoo having been beaten, Ned and Tom had reached their rooms,—it will be remembered that they were occupants of the same apartment,—and Tom had addressed his friend in his usual pleasant strain, the latter hardly paid any heed, and pretended to be very much occupied in setting in order the contents of his trunk.

CHAPTER XXII.

THE VAPORS THICKEN.

The course of events seemed to favor "17" in his primary design of creating an estrangement between Ned and Tom. Yet it may more truly be said that in such cases the alienating cause more frequently lies in the feelings of the heart that give their coloring and interpretation to the accident of circumstance; a secret jealousy, once conceived and encouraged, will feed itself upon the most innocent actions and sayings of its object.

Ned continued for several days in a very moody frame of mind. He declined participating again in the snowball war, and seemed to be devoting himself wholly to his studies. Tom attributed this unsociable turn to the recent lack of his usual success in his recitations, and attempted occasionally to rally him on his low spirits, alluding playfully to the late battles; but in Ned's present mood these references though uttered in the kindest manner and without the least particle of self-glorification, only fanned the smoldering fire which he was concealing. Tom, after one or two unsuccessful efforts, left Ned very much to himself, trusting that his naturally joyous and overflowing nature would soon reassert itself; besides Tom's own pursuits necessarily occupied most of his attention.

Ned studied hard; he sought in his books a refuge

from the disagreeable feelings which pursued him. He was compelled by this experience to learn that a certain freedom and buoyancy of spirit is necessary to genuine progress in study; failing in this, he was slow to perceive and understand, committed to memory with much labor and difficulty, and in the class-room often gave his answers and explanations in a confused, uncertain manner, which left an unsatisfactory impression upon the teacher of the hour. Ned, therefore, began to lose ground. At the same time the wily "Seventeen," perceiving with a malicious pleasure the success of his first attempts, took pains by some insidious word, addressed directly to Ned or intended to come to his hearing through the mediation of others, to increase the jealous suspicion which was gnawing at Ned's heart.

Ned, Tom, "Seventeen," and myself belonged to the same grade in mathematics, and recited with five or six others at the same hour. Our instructor was Mr. Homans, whose character and manner I have already attempted to bring before the reader. Mr. Homans was particularly respected and loved by Ned, and though Ned was not gifted with a special aptitude for mathematics, he always exerted himself to the utmost, and generally with success, to appear to good advantage in Mr. Homans' room. Great then was his mortification, when, a few days after his jealous mood had taken possession of him, he was publicly, though gently, reprimanded for his seeming want of due preparation of late, and was required to remain after school, and " make up lost time."

On this occasion the class was reviewing a subject which they had recently gone over, and which had necessitated a great deal of explanation on the part of their instructor, who now trusted it was well understood by all who had given due attention. Ned was called upon to work out on the board a problem of average difficulty under this head. To the astonishment of Mr. Homans, Ned proceeded in a confused, laborious manner, explained himself with difficulty, made several bad mistakes in computation, which excited the smile of the teacher and the ill-suppressed merriment of the boys, and finally stopped short altogether. A link was missing; after groping about for it for some time in vain, while the mental darkness kept momentarily increasing, Ned threw up the chalk in despair, and returned to his seat. Tom, being then called to the board, worked the problem in a clear and admirable manner, and explained the different processes of his solution with a logical precision, for which, on resuming his place, he was highly complimented.

Mr. Homans made no remark on Ned's failure till the close of the hour, evidently not wishing to add to his discomfiture. But then, on dismissing the class, he was glad, he said, to have it in his power to express himself highly satisfied with the performances of the entire class with the exception of one member, and in his instance, while he was willing to make allowance for a momentary confusion of mind, he was pained to notice that there had been a great falling off of late; that the best safeguard against attacks of mental aberration was a thorough preparation; nothing would so fortify the mind as this. Perhaps he added significantly, a little study after school would have a decidedly tonic effect.

Mr. Homans' quiet ironical way gave a sting to his

reproofs, which made them far more dreaded than the severest reprimands of others. Ned hung his head in shame, and could with difficulty repress his tears.

That afternoon, as he sat at his desk, after most of his comrades had been dismissed, a few others only in like situation as himself being seated here and there throughout the room, Ned's thoughts and emotions were of the most tumultuous character. He blamed every one but himself. Mr. Homans was unjust. He had no right to insinuate in his mean way that he— Ned—was lazy and careless in his preparation—he ought to know better. He studied as much as the others—more too. Mr. Homans tried to confuse him by his mean questions, he wanted to show off Tom—Mr. Homans wasn't impartial at all—never was—of course not! He—Ned—wouldn't study any more; it was no use—if this was the way he was to be treated. Then there was Tom—a selfish, cold-hearted fellow, who was making fun of him behind his back with his silly jokes, and turning the boys against him. After all, "17" was the best fellow of them all, whatever Tom thought. But here Ned repented a little of his hard thoughts against his old friend, and as the memories of the many pleasant hours and days they had spent together thronged upon his mind, he suddenly burst into tears, which dripping plentifully upon the problem open before him effected a more perfect solution of it than was required.

The "jug" having been at last uncorked, and its contents, which had been undergoing a silent fermentation, having effervesced, Ned betook himself to the library and there met, as the sole other occupant, his evil genius—"17".

"Seventeen" was careful not to approach Ned in his present dejected mood too precipitately; he knew that an officious manifestation of sympathy would offend Ned's pride; it is a delicate matter to offer consolation to a sensitive spirit, suffering under any disgrace. "17" waited patiently while Ned sat quiescent, at times gazing out of the window upon the gray wintery sky, which seemed draped in a veil of snow that might at any moment hover and glide to the earth, at times with his eyes vacantly wandering over the paper which he held in his hand. "17" hoped that Ned would of his own accord speak of the subject which he knew to be uppermost in his mind. But as Ned kept silent, "17" at last ventured to say, in a quiet tone expressive of unobtrusive concern—

"Homans was rather hard on you to-day, '25'?" to which Ned replied with a monosyllabic "yes," as if not inclined to encourage conversation on the subject.

But "17" was not disposed to lose the advantage of a favorable opportunity. He knew Ned was in the right condition to be worked upon. After a few moments of silence, he suddenly broke out, as if the conviction were forced upon him:—

"In my opinion, Homans doesn't mean to be impartial. He is trying to bring out Tom and make him his 'double-star.' I do believe he took pains to confuse you this morning, that Tom might show off to advantage; he wants him to be the cock of the walk."

This chimed in with what Ned had been saying to himself, but when he heard it from other lips than his own, he felt at heart that it was all wrong; yet such was his angry and jealous mood that he assented to "17's" utterances. His conscience smote him, but he determined to smite back, and therefore even added the opprobrious words :—

"Yes, he's a mean sneak."

A glance of malicious pleasure shot across the face of "17." "I almost think so myself," said he. "Did you notice how confidential he has been with Tom of late?"

Mr. Homans actually had taken occasion to call Tom to his room two or three times of late. Having a great respect for the manliness of Tom's character, as well as for his intelligence, he sought by occasional conversation to draw out and give direction to the best tendencies of his nature. This was at times his practice with all those pupils whom he thought he could benefit in this way—Ned himself had frequently been favored with interviews of such a character. But in his present jaundiced mood, this fact did not occur to him. In truth Ned was under the influence of an evil eye.

Said "17"—"I don't know that I blame Tom for taking advantage of this favoritism. We should all perhaps do the same thing in his place. One must look out for himself, and the devil take the hindmost. Still," he drawled out, after a little seeming reflection, "I—don't—altogether—like Tom's manner about it. Do you know, he said to me this afternoon, while you were in the 'jug,'—in his laughing way,—'Ned's numerous defeats of late in our snow-ball fights, have had, I fear, a confusing effect upon his brain. Cold snow is almost as bad as cold steel.'" There was a glitter as of cold steel in the eye of "17" as he made up this lie, and watched its effect upon his victim.

"Did Tom talk in that way?" said Ned, with a voice a little faint and slightly tremulous.

8*

"Those were his words," said "17" in a careless, indifferent manner, as if he was tired of the subject.

Ned turned away to hide his emotion. It really then was true, and no mere moodish fancy of his, that Tom no longer cared for him, was tired of him, jealous or—what he knew not. His first feeling was one of deep dejection, but his pride soon came to his rescue, and he determined to resent Tom's conduct in what he considered a manly manner. He, accordingly, on the impulse of the moment, sat down before the library table, and indited the following note:—

"THOMAS MANNING,—

"As you have chosen your part, I mean now to choose mine; but it shall not be a double part. I don't want your easy, jaunty kind of friendship, and I haven't any skill in the make-believe kind. In a word I don't care to have any further conversation with you.

"EDWARD ELDRIDGE."

Ned spoiled several sheets in this effort. He read over the last amended copy with great satisfaction, and having carefully folded and addressed it, he turned to "17," who had patiently waited, easily surmising what business Ned had in hand, and requested him to deliver it.

"Seventeen" was ready enough to undertake this little office, but Ned stopped him, as he was about to set out in search of Tom, and said that on second thought he would like to delay the delivery of the note till the next morning; "17," however, could keep it in his possession till then.

Ned had suddenly bethought him of the fact that he and Tom occupied the same apartment. If this note were delivered now, their position would be a very awkward one; besides Tom might call for an explanation, and he—Ned—might after all be cheated out of his independence, for that was Ned's feeling. His pride took the alarm at the possibility of this easy subjection, and he determined to avoid meeting Tom. But how to do it? Ned finally, though with a little lingering aversion, made a confidant of "17."

He had determined, he turned and said, to break with "35;" he didn't mean to acknowledge him any longer as a friend; he didn't wish to remain his roommate. Couldn't "17" help him to make a change at once.

"Seventeen" pretended to be sorry to hear that Ned was going to break with "35." Couldn't he do anything to bring about a reconciliation. No! Well then, if Ned was determined to change his room, he must consent to be his—"17's"—room-mate. He thought he could manage it—There was "20"—the present writer —in his room; perhaps he would change with Ned: this "20" seemed, too, a sort of a satellite of Tom's, and would be glad enough to get nearer his luminary.

To cut the narration short, Ned consented to become "17's" room-mate, and I was soon sought out and buttonholed by this artful fellow. I would not have been loath to change my room, as my present associates, particularly "17," were not altogether to my mind, but this proposition coming as it did from Ned astonished me; it did not seem possible that such friends as Ned and Tom could actually have fallen out,—or could this "17" have actually supplanted Tom in Ned's esteem? And Ned had not taken me into his confidence at all in this matter.

I felt, I confess, a little aggrieved. I do not now, however, find Ned's reticence at all surprising; Ned was yielding to motives and impulses which he instinctively felt to be unworthy of him; he was ashamed therefore to reveal his state of mind to those whom he really esteemed, and was ready the rather to seek the confidence of those whom he at heart despised.

Having seen Ned and found him set upon it, I consented to the proposed change, but merely as a temporary arrangement, which Ned could at any time terminate. Of course the consent of the principals had to be obtained; this, however, was effected without much difficulty.

We went up to the dormitories to make the necessary transposition of trunks, etc. I tried to get Ned away from "17," hoping to receive his wonted confidence, but the wily youth remained near his new friend, nor did Ned show any desire to be communicative; and presently all further opportunity of explanation was cut off by the ringing of the bell, which announced the evening roll-call.

CHAPTER XXIII.

ASTRAY IN THE DARKNESS.

I seized the first favorable opportunity that evening to tell Tom of the change of rooms that had been made, and of the conditions upon which I had consented to it. Tom was astounded. He knew not what to think about it. Was Ned really offended, or was this a mere wayward freak of his? He had confidence in Ned's frank, open nature, and did not believe that he would covertly and without explanation surrender himself to some misconception, and "cut" his best friend. Nevertheless, he called to mind, with alarm, Ned's strange manner of late, and resolved at once to seek his friend, and if any thing was wrong, set it right. He was polite enough to add, that, if Ned really changed rooms with any one, I would be his next choice.

Tom was prevented, however, from immediately executing this intention by the approach of "17" with the note which Ned had commissioned him to deliver; for now that the change of quarters was effected, there was no longer any reason, as "17" suggested to Ned, for delay in its delivery. Besides, Ned wished it all over with as soon as possible; in truth, he had already begun to experience some qualms of repentance, which he thought to repress by this final act.

"Seventeen" left us at once, knowing that no reply was wanted; but I saw him look back over his shoulder, with a glance and smile of keen satisfaction, as he watched the effect of the note on Tom.

Poor Tom! he was utterly bewildered; he seemed at first to suspect the affair was a joke. He could not at once persuade himself that his best friend would thus curtly cut loose from him; and when at last the serious nature of the affair impressed itself upon him, he appeared quite prostrated for the moment, but presently recovered a little.

"Poh! poh!" said he, "it will amount to nothing. Somebody has been lying; shouldn't be surprised if that fellow, '17,' was at the bottom of the mischief; he seems to be a sly, wily sort of a dog, and looks as if he might perpetrate some little villainy for the mere love of it. Yet stop, perhaps I'm wrong. We must wait a little and see. I hardly know whether to laugh at Ned or be angry with him. However, I must just let him take his own course for a day or two, perhaps he will come around himself by that time, and clear it all up. At any rate, it will not do to run after him at once, that would spoil him altogether, and he's always had to be humored a good deal. Yes, yes! we'll consult *our* dignity *too*, and wait a little. He has chosen his part! has he? well, perhaps then he had better play his part out without interruption,—at least for the present."

Ah, Tom! you made a mistake there, when you consulted your "dignity," as you called your pride. Granted, Ned had acted hastily, inconsiderately, petulantly, contrary to that frankness natural to him, still you should have gone at once to your friend's side, and sought an explanation; you should—so to speak—have disinfected him of the foul vapors that may for the moment, have clouded his heart and brain. Delays are dangerous when friendship is under a shadow; that shadow may deepen, and in the darkness the travelers may wander forever apart.

Pride is a dangerous counselor; how many a pure bright friendship, that might have been the consolation and ornament of a life-time, has a gloomy reticence at important crises obscured or destroyed! Friendship should be single-eyed. Where there is substantial congeniality, all momentary aberrations on the one side or the other, all capricious humors, and all those nameless vapors, that rise from we know not what Avernus in the human heart, should be overlooked, pardoned, chased away by a generous and confiding love.

So Tom went his way, and Ned his. Both held proudly aloof. On the playground, in the school-room, everywhere, they avoided each other as much as possible, or, if they chanced to meet, passed with unseeing eyes. Thus, on the one side, baseless suspicion springing from a momentary jealous humor which misinterpreted every thing, and easily submitted itself a prey to deceit, and on the other, a haughty pride, were rendering these two youthful souls unhappy. A warm breath of love, a little of the sunshine of mutual confidence, would have swept away these chilling vapors, and shown them to each other in their true relation,— that of a substantial and beautiful friendship.

A week or more thus passed on. Ned was evidently very unhappy. At heart he repented his hasty action, and if he had been left to the direction of his own impulses, I do not doubt that he would very soon have got the mastery of his wayward mood, and have freely unburdened himself to Tom, and have asked his forgiveness. But "17" was ever by his side with his insidious suggestions, skillful at throwing a false light over appearances.

"Why," he would say, "does not Tom answer your note? Why does he not seek to explain his treatment of you? He seems to have pocketed the note and accepted the situation. Well, well, I can not, for my part, see how any one can so easily give up a friend. But some fellows are incapable of a true friendship; they pick up a friend and let him drop, without caring much about it. Your cool witty fellows are generally of that sort. I don't see that you can do any thing toward a reconciliation, unless you mean to be a vassal of Tom's, a follower, satellite, humble-pie-man, or—what you will."

Ned was not proof against the wiles of this new associate,—friend he called himself,—whose smooth accents always enveloped a half-concealed sneer. Ned held out on the path he had marked out for himself, though with a certain faintness of heart.

Tom, on the other hand, wrapped himself up in a cloak of gloomy pride. At first, daily expecting his friend would resume his old frankness, and give some explanation of the course he had taken, and thus open the way for a reconciliation, he pursued the customary routine of school duties without much loss of spirit; but as the days passed on, and Ned made no advances, the crust of Tom's pride thickened and hardened. It would have been now much harder to break the ice, than to have yielded in the outset to a warm melting impulse. He did not make the attempt. Thus they stood apart, a dark tide flowing between them, the shadow upon whose waters seemed to deepen daily.

CHAPTER XXIV.

DERISIVE ECHOES.

Tom, since the rupture with his friend, devoted himself to study with even greater assiduity than before, and his success in the class-rooms was unsurpassed. His sorrow at the loss of his friend, so far from weakening or dissipating the action of his mind, seemed rather to add force and intensity to it. He was serious, but not cast down. There was in Tom a many-sided capacity for thought, a native recognition of vital ideas, which transmuted all personal experiences into springs of power, enlarging the sphere of life.

It was otherwise with Ned. Ned's was a receptive, impressionable nature. He was more dependent upon the sympathies of others; from these,—so to speak,—he in a great measure drew his life. A friendship lost was a spring broken, and consequently so much power as was therein represented, destroyed.

Let not this peculiarity of Ned's nature be too greatly deplored. If this lively susceptibility to the influence of men and things often opens dangerous pitfalls, it is capable also of leading to the highest attainment. Nor is mere accident the determining power. There is always a secret plastic force which eventually molds the evil experience of such natures into good, for their errors are not those of too little, but, if that may be, of too much love. In the end, the very aberrations of a soul thus constituted, as the character comes forth and matures, supply the elements of the richest life—rich in varied sympathies, and rich, therefore, in the multiplication of its insights.

Ned, in losing the friendship of Tom, was much undermined and demoralized. He lost heart in his studies, and often manifested a slovenly and imperfect preparation. All the while the influence of "17" over him kept increasing; and he was thus gradually drawn into a circle of boys from whom formerly he had kept himself aloof. Among these "17" had of late constituted himself the leader.

They were boys,—such as are found in every school,—who have, for the most part, a physical inaptitude for study, and a mental aptitude for mischief. They are not always evil-disposed, yet rarely are they well disposed. They labor hard and overcome many difficulties, and endure many hardships, to avoid performing their school-duties. They can not then be called lazy; they do not lack energy and vigor; but their tastes do not lead them to study. They have their proper field, but it is not the field of abstract science or of classic letters. With proclivities such as theirs, they form a discordant element in a school. But their warfare is generally of a desultory guerrilla sort; their incapacity for study is also an incapacity for organization in mischief. But let a youth of a more positive character appear among them, one who does not seek in mischievous doings an escape for superabundant animality, but who acts under the direction of an envious and malicious spirit, and let such a one have a faculty to control and lead, and this nondescript class may become an element dangerous to the peace and harmony of school-life. Such a youth was "17."

These boys, who had hitherto only obeyed, individually, their impatience of restraint, or gratified their love of fun, "17" had gradually infected with his own determined spirit of evil. They formed, under his influence, if not leadership, an organized band of evil-doers, who were the torment of all the well-disposed and studious. They not only would not join in the caravan of pilgrims on the march to the Mecca of science, but hung on the flanks of these and harassed them in every possible way,—abstracted and hid their text-books, interrupted their studies, distracted their attention in the midst of recitations, involved them in their own mischief, so that the innocent were confounded with the guilty, and suffered like disgrace and punishment. All this was carried on for some time, unsuspected by the teachers. The principles of honor among school-boys did not permit of any "blabbing." The persecuted must fight their own battles, endure or resist in silence.

Ned's relation to these boys was at first peculiar. Without himself taking an active part in their doings, he yet by associating with them, gave them the advantage of at least a negative approval. Naturally, however, it was a difficult matter for him to retain this dubious position any length of time. His former associates, finding him always in an alliance, though of a passive character, with their foes, day by day grew cold toward him. Ned, then, to show, as he thought, his indifference to their esteem, began to put on something of an air of swagger which, however, was in reality only a vain effort to hide his sense of shame. He was fast becoming a boon companion of his evil associates, and was "cheek by jowl" with them in the conclaves where deeds of mischief were planned.

The poor fellow was becoming very mirthful; he laughed loud and long, whenever one of their number reported the accomplishment of any cruel trick. But there was always something hollow in his mirth, and after his laugh, one listened, as it were, to hear the derisive echo.

Ned did not, however, wholly neglect his studies. After he had become somewhat accustomed to his changed mode of life; after the distraction which the struggle with his better nature produced, had passed, he was able to apply himself with tolerable success, and thus present a fair seeming in the presence of his teachers. His pride would not suffer him to submit tamely to disgrace; it was this, and not as formerly, a desire to gain the approbation of his parents and instructors, that sustained him.

The guerrilla band, with which Ned was thus connected, had not interfered, as yet, in any open manner with Tom, in part because Ned had sufficient influence to dissuade them from carrying into execution any device against his former friend, but in particular because there was in Tom an air of quiet resolution, and a certain grave reserve of character which had grown upon him since his recent experience, that intimidated these unruly spirits, whose courage, where it existed at all, was of the purely animal kind.

The bold and somewhat haughty position which Tom assumed toward this set, and in the undisturbed possession of which he was left, only increased the hatred of "17," and his determination to find some way of reaching its object. Besides, Tom did not hesitate to show a marked contempt for "17," whenever the occasion permitted. Though he could not adduce any positive proof, he nevertheless considered "17" as the real cause of the alienation of his friend, and more than suspected him of some foul play. At any rate, "17's" influence over Ned was very evident, and Tom, while he felt nothing but pity for his old companion, and regret for his lost friendship, was disposed to visit upon his wily seducer whatever indignation and anger this unhappy event excited in him.

"Seventeen," on his side, however much he assumed an air of indifference, secretly winced under the open contempt with which Tom treated him, and while not personally daring to cope with his enemy, he set his heart all the more upon finding some underhand method of reaching him.

CHAPTER XXV.

CHIROGRAPHIC STUDIES.

The change for the worse which Ned had recently undergone, and his affiliation with the less worthy element of the school, had not escaped the observation of the principals, and Mr. Ellery set about an investigation of the causes which led to the unwelcome state of affairs. He took pains to learn the origin of this deterioration in Ned, and, having ascertained that a coolness had grown up between him and Tom, he naturally inferred that there was some connection between this change in relation between the two youths and Ned's new line of conduct.

It was decided, however, that no direct interference should be made at present. Long experience in school management had taught him that it was unwise to control by an exercise of authority the varying relations of boys with each other. The little drama or dramas of school-life should be allowed to develop naturally to their proper denouement, and only in the case of some very dangerous complication should the *deus ex machina* appear. Still, a watchful eye must be preserved, and guiding influences may be often indirectly introduced.

Since the rupture between Ned and Tom was accompanied, only in the case of the former, with a manifest relaxation of tone in the performance of school duties, while Tom was even more faithful than ever, and with his increased seriousness gave a still stronger impression of high-minded rectitude, the Major and Mr. Ellery inferred that in Ned lay the hidden cause of their unhappy change of relation. Keeping, therefore, a careful but unseen watch over Ned, lest his new associations should lead him too far in the wrong path, they trusted that his own better nature would regain the mastery of him, knowing well that an unaided victory in such an internal contest would bring him an accession of strength, which would prove his best defense in future trials. They saw clearly that Ned's character needed more of that power of resistance which the experience he was passing through, if not prematurely interrupted, if left to its natural evolution, was calculated to give.

When nearly three weeks had passed by in this way, Tom's magnanimity and affection for Ned at last so far conquered his pride as to impel him to take the initiative in an effort to bring about a reconciliation. He began to think that by his long silence he had sufficiently asserted his dignity. Hitherto he had requested me as a particular favor in my intercourse with his former friend not to mention his name in any connection, or seek at all to effect a reunion; he felt sure, he said, that Ned would of himself return to his old affection, and he, for his part, would feel better satisfied if Ned acted spontaneously in the matter; besides, Ned would think that I was acting under his suggestion in any advance that was made, and, as Ned deserted him without any ostensible cause, and without condescending in the least to give any reason for his conduct, he, for his part, did not feel as if he ought to do any thing about it. Ned had "chosen his own part," he added with a bitterness mingled with haughty regret.

To this request I assented with great reluctance. At last, however, when time had softened the hardness of Ned's note, Tom's pride, as I have said, yielded a little, and he in turn wrote a note, couched in the following terms:—

"If Ned Eldridge still retains any affection for his former friend, and will consent to explain his treatment of him, the latter, who still recollects with pleasure the old days, would be glad of an opportunity of reconciliation.

"TOM MANNING."

Tom did not show me this generous note, or inform me at all of his intention to write to Ned. Though he had overcome his scruples so far as to make the first advance, Tom's pride, which was his besetting fault of character, induced him to be as secret about it as possible,—or was it a noble magnanimity prompting him to conceal his action, that Ned might appear to have himself been the first to seek a reconciliation? Let Tom have the benefit of this doubt.

Tom carried this note with him all the following day seeking a favorable opportunity to put it in Ned's way. At last, having been sent by the teacher having the general charge for the day, to light the gas in the school-room in preparation for the hour of the evening study, Tom, having performed the duty, being alone in the school-room, hurriedly seized the opportunity to place the note in Ned's "Cæsar," which was lying on his desk, and which Tom knew would certainly be brought into requisition by Ned in the course of the evening. He was careful to insert the note between those leaves which included the lesson for the morrow.

It turned out, however, very unluckily; for, when the juniors entered, "17," who, in consequence of his superior height, had a place among the first of the line, in passing Ned's desk accidently brushed the "Cæsar" off upon the chair in front; in the concussion the note escaped from the leaves and was wafted under "17's" own desk. "17" at once replaced the book on Ned's desk, and quickly taking his own seat, covered the note with his foot, till he had an opportunity of picking it up unobserved, partly prompted, perhaps, by a presentiment of its source and object, partly because, in certain natures, there is a craving to finger forbidden fruit.

A moment or two afterward, Ned, whose place was near the middle of the column, reached his desk and became seated. Tom, who, as I have failed to mention, had been recently promoted to the rank of sergeant, formed the closing file of the division which was last to enter. He observed with satisfaction, as he seated himself at his desk, that Ned's hand was already placed upon his "Cæsar," as if about to open it, and that with his other hand he was arranging his lexicon so as to be convenient for reference. Tom, therefore, congratulated himself that his note was safe, and turned his attention to his own studies. The next moment the silver tinkle of the school-room bell gave warning that the work of the hour must now begin, and immediately everywhere studious heads were bent over the desks.

"Seventeen" devoted his attention to the study of chirography. He was not slow to perceive that the note in his possession was directed in the handwriting of Tom, and having established himself as the friend and protector of Ned, he deemed it his duty to break it open.

"Ah, ha! so, so!" he muttered to himself, as he read the carefully worded lines. "What a dignified fellow we are! How grandly we write! How magnanimous we are, how forgiving! Truly we must take good care of this curiosity of literature," and therewith he slipped the note into an inner pocket.

"So, so! Mr. Tom," he said to himself, looking up with a triumphant smile, in the direction of Tom's desk, "you mean to circumvent us, do you? Well, let us see! We took the loan this morning of Ned's French exercise-book! Yes, here it is; with its help we will do our exercise. Certainly we shall not be so rude as to leave our friend's polite note unanswered."

With these words, he set himself to the task of composing, in Ned's name, a reply to the note. With Ned's exercise-book open before him, and his own natural aptitude for the work, he did not find it difficult to make a successful imitation of the handwriting of his victim. The note briefly ran thus,—

"Ned Eldridge begs to express his appreciation of Tom Manning's polite condescension, but must positively decline any renewal of acquaintance."

"Seventeen" could not avoid infusing some of his own feeling into this note, for it was Tom's calm and self-possessed superiority, having to inferior souls the air of condescension, which in particular excited "17's" hatred.

After the study hour was concluded, when conversation and some freedom of movement was permitted, "17" took a favorable opportunity, at a moment when

Ned was shut in by a circle of boys, and Tom and I were conversing apart in one corner of the room, to deliver this note. On this occasion, as before, he retired at once, to avoid being questioned. But again, when he had reached a distant stand-point, I saw him glance aside at Tom's face, while a singular smile played momentarily about his lips, and his dark eyes gleamed with a strange satisfaction. Standing, as he was, almost directly under the gas-light, which threw across his face strange shadows, there was something startling, and almost demoniac in his expression.

Turning toward Tom, I saw he could with difficulty repress his agitation on the perusal of this note. At last, with a deep-drawn sigh, which one might give, in whom a sad experience had taken deep root, he hastily placed the letter in his pocket, and asking me rather by a gesture than by word, to excuse him, walked away. Presently I saw him, after seeking permission from the teacher in charge, leave the room.

Under the circumstances it was not difficult for me to conjecture whence the note proceeded, and what was the nature of its contents. I did not, however, seek Tom's confidence, and it was not till some time after that I was made acquainted with the details of the transaction. Tom evidently shunned the topic; he seemed to be making a strong effort to shut down the lid on this coffer in his memory.

"Seventeen's" triumph was complete.

CHAPTER XXVI.

COASTING.

Thus the days passed on with their round of duties and their allotment of good and evil. We had now reached the middle of February. In the interval since the first great storm, several light falls of snow had added fresh layers of this wintery fleece to the snow-mantle that covered the hills of Ossining, ever bringing fresh delight to the hearts of "us boys."

Our chief sport at this time was what is known, among boys at least, as "coasting." Coasting—if there be those who do not know it under that name, and fallaciously associate it with river or lake margins and pleasant June breezes—is an amusement, let all such learn, which is carried on upon the "firm land" and at a season when the keen nor'westers do blow.

The apparatus, with which those who engage in this sport must supply themselves, consists of a good long, steep hill, the longer and steeper the better, though one of gentle descent and moderate length will do; in addition to this a hand-sleigh, not more than eighteen inches wide, but from two to ten feet long, according to the number of persons it is designed to "accommodate." Having now with slow steps and much expenditure of breath, which congeals in icicles upon your tippet, if you are a boy, your beard if you are a man, having thus climbed the hill, occasionally slipping by the way and leaving the print of your face in the soft snow by the way-side, having, I say, in this pleasant manner, and with such pleasant interruptions, gained the top of the hill,—of course a circumstance I had nearly omitted, you have dragged your sleigh up behind you,—you then either seat yourself astride the sleigh, legs spread wide apart, heels prepared to skim the polished surface of snow, or you stretch yourself upon it longitudinally in the attitude described in the picturesque language of boys as " belly-gutters."

If asked which is the preferable of these two methods, I should say that *in the long run* and when the air is quiet, the first is the more comfortable, to say nothing of its greater dignity, but if a sharp wind is blowing in your face, then sacrifice your dignity—and "lie low." When you have chosen your favorite position, a slight push from a friendly hand, if you are seated, or, if you are procumbent, a frog-like movement of the legs, the toes touching the snow, will give the sleigh a sufficient start ; the law of gravity will do the rest, and you will at once offer a practical illustration of this law in its application to the inclined plane.

The momentum, according to the well-ascertained principles of science will, as you descend, keep increasing, at a fixed mathematical rate, governed by the inclination of the plane. Now this steady acceleration of velocity has a strange effect upon your nervous system. The motion with its measured increase affects you as if a serpent were winding you in its coils. As you go down, your sensations go up in a giddy whirl; at last you experience a strange sinking away in the pit of the stomach; you feel that you have left this portion of your body behind you, or that it is dispersed in the winds, which now blow clean through you; you see your legs making an angle before you, and you are conscious of head and shoulders, but the connection between the upper and lower members, seems for the time quite apocryphal.

Let it not be supposed that this splendid sport is open to the uninitiated, and that it is only necessary to get astride the sleigh and push off. A tyro with inexperienced legs would probably, before one-quarter of the descent were made, exhibit a headlong movement into the adjoining snow-bank. I say *with inexperienced legs*, because it is by a skillful use of these members that the sleigh is guided in its course; and amid the tumult and whir of emotions, which your rapid flight excites, this requires no little experience.

On the southern border of the village, Broad Avenue, leading down the hill, which rises with steep sides back of the academy, afforded an excellent opportunity to the boys for this, their favorite sport, of coasting. Every clear afternoon the greater portion of the school-boys thronged thither; and a gay turnout they presented with their variously painted and fancifully constructed sleighs, their silver buttons, their round, red faces and bright eyes. On such occasions there was a copious flow of youthful blood; down the hill it coursed in a fleet, uninterrupted, motley-specked current; up the hill it streamed slowly, but ever on and on;—a venous and arterial circulation, at the foot of the hill spread out in a capillary net-work, at the top, collected into a pulsating heart. There were not wanting abundant lungs that shot up shrill, exultant cries into the frosty air, and gave forth intermittent clouds of vapor, which the wintery air with its keen appetite quickly quaffed out of sight.

With few exceptions, each boy had his own sleigh, of which he was at once pilot and passenger. There was, however, one long sleigh capable of seating ten or twelve boys one behind the other, which belonged to the establishment; its name, familiar to many successive generations of Mount Pleasant boys, was the "'76." This sleigh was much sought after, for in youth as in advancing age we like to go down the hill in company. The "'76" was not long enough for the whole school to fasten on, even though the boys sometimes clung to it as swarming bees to the apple-bough. It therefore was necessary to assign it in turn to one and another group of boys, that there might be no dispute over it.

On one afternoon, unusually quiet and genial for the season, the boys turned out in full force, and actively plied their gay craft in the coasting trade. The "76" this afternoon had fallen to the set of boys who were associated with "17." Ned, however, was not among them; he had brought out his own sleigh, upon which, sometimes alone, sometimes with a comrade, he sped along, in the midst of the noisy fleet, down the frozen stream. At one time, however, he was urged by "17" and his associates to take a place on the "76" for the trip it was then about to make; at first he declined, but seeing Tom standing near by, and fancying that he observed in his face a certain air of covert contempt, he strove to throw off the uneasiness which he felt, by putting on a gay defiant carriage, and accepting the invitation. Before the party had fairly got seated and ready, Tom, with myself as his companion, had pushed off in our own sleigh. The "'76" soon followed. We had accomplished about one-half the descent and had gained the steepest part of the hill, before our formidable pursuer, going at a much more rapid rate, had come close upon us. The road was broad and there was ample room to pass. But "17," who sat in the front part of the long sleigh, obeying a malicious impulse, pressed his left heel upon the snow, so as to give the sleigh a direction toward us; one and another of his companions, either perceiving the movement, or animated by a like spirit of evil, did the same. The "76" came swiftly on and grazed against us with sufficient force to throw our sleigh from its course and drive it down a bank which there bordered the road. Tom, who was seated before me, was precipitated with great violence into the snow, I falling over him.

I rose at once, feeling no injury, beyond a mere momentary shock—Tom too struggled up, but, after staggering blindly for a moment, fell bleeding and senseless at my feet; he had struck, head foremost, against the sharp edge of a rock, which was hidden beneath the snow. I endeavored to raise him up and at the same time called loudly for assistance. The boys at the top of the hill, among them many seniors, came running down as fast as it was possible over the slippery snow. In the mean time the "76's" company had reached the foot of the hill, and stood collected in a knot, alarmed at what they had done. Ned had walked apart much agitated, and stood looking with trembling glance up the hill, without power to move, or ascertain the extent of the mischief he seemed to have been instrumental in causing.

Among the youths gathered about poor Tom there

was happily one,—the adjutant of the school,—who had sufficient self-possession to know what to do. Acting under his orders, some of the boys proceeded hastily to the foot of the hill after the long sleigh; Ned, having recovered himself a little, attempted to assist them in drawing the sleigh up; but he was rudely and almost violently jostled and thrust on one side,—they did not want *his* help.

These jealous friends of Tom were not long in bringing up the sleigh; Tom was then gently lifted upon it, and one of the larger boys seated himself behind him and supported him in his arms; others took off their overcoats and tenderly placed them over the still insensible youth. Then as many as could, ranged themselves on each side of the sleigh, and checked a too rapid descent of the hill. Thus the wounded hero was borne from the field.

And how was it meantime with Ned? While these preparations were in progress, he looked on in silence from the foot of the hill, not daring to approach: when the sleigh had descended and was now turning the corner of the road, near which Ned stood, he caught, through the crowd of boys that thronged about it, a single glimpse of the bleeding face of his old friend. He did not stay to look again; he had not the courage to ask any questions; deeply agitated, he silently stole out from the crowd of boys, who were too much occupied to observe him, and walked rapidly away, in what direction he knew not, as if he sought only to escape from himself and the recollections that pursued him.

CHAPTER XXVII.

PHANTOM HILLS.

Ned unconsciously followed a road, which in summer was a favorite walk of his, and which led to an eminence that commanded a wide view of the river and of the western hills. On the north the Highlands, sweeping southwestward and meeting, as seemed from that point of view, with the precipitous trap rock of the High Torn range, formed with the latter a spacious and noble amphitheater, while on the south the view was terminated by a bold but comparatively low bluff, which jutted out in the Tappan Zee.

By this time the sun had already set. An orange sky was dying low in the west; a few scattering stars had come out in the dark blue overhead; and on that border region between the fading hues of the west and the overarching blue, in the midst of a pale remote light floated the crescent moon, holding up the orb of the old moon in her arms as some new consciousness supports the dim and unreal shadow of the past. In the water glimmered in confusion the last reflections of the sun, the shivered light of the out-coming stars, and the silver radiance of the moon. The snow-clad earth, shadowy and pale, lay below like something remote and unreal.

Ned climbed the hill slowly and wearily; he no longer strove as it were to escape from himself; sadly, with a sense of utter self-abasement, he was now looking his sin and shame full in the face. When he had gained the summit, actuated by an instinct derived from his old habit of resting at that spot, he stopped full short, and, turning, suddenly raised his eyes.

At once the whole magnificent spectacle flashed upon him; he saw, as it seemed to him, not so much with the sensual faculty of vision as with the soul itself. At that moment his warmed and softened inner consciousness was laid bare, and this fading day and luminous night, the stars, and the shimmering river, and the pale phantom hills in their shroud of snow—all as one, swept with swift and silent march into his soul, and yet at the same time all seemed to recede from him in an unending flight, leaving him there alone, self-accused, self-convicted.

Ned hung his head in shame, as if he actually heard a sad and solemn voice rebuking him, and the hot tears streamed from his eyes. He stood thus for some time.

When, at last, he directed his steps homeward, a serene but sad composure seemed to have settled upon him. He uttered no word to himself; he was scarcely conscious of definite thought; yet from that moment he was changed, converted; he had risen to a higher, stronger nature, and his old self was, as it were, sloughed; it seemed to belong to a remote past.

In this mood, deeply sad, but full of consolation, in which, however, were mingled anxious thoughts of Tom's present condition, Ned reached the school. The evening roll-call had not yet been made, and his absence had therefore passed unnoticed.

CHAPTER XXVIII.

THE OFFICE.

In the mean time Tom had been tenderly cared for. He was carried up to the sick-room, as it was called, and the physician of the school was sent for. But before the arrival of the latter, Mrs. Blaisdell, and the other ladies of the house, hearing of what had happened, immediately hastened to the bedside of the sufferer, and, by applying the proper restoratives, recalled him to a state of consciousness. The doctor, who arrived soon after, found Tom in a very weak condition; having examined and dressed his wound,—for Tom was cut badly across the forehead,—he left strict orders that he should be kept perfectly quiet, and should receive careful nursing; his external injuries were not great, but there was danger of fever setting in.

Tom's misfortune excited universal interest among the boys, for he was a great favorite with the better sort. At the same time their indignation against those who perpetrated this wrong was intense, and they would not place any faith in the stout asseverations of the latter, that the collision was accidental; there was even some talk among the more impetuous spirits of executing upon them some kind of Lynch law.

These clamors, however, were checked for the moment, when, soon after supper, an order came for all those to whom the long sleigh had been assigned that afternoon, to present themselves at the office. Verbally, Ned was not included in this order, since he only participated, by special invitation, in that last trip of the "'76"; yet, much as he loathed the company in which he found himself, Ned determined to face his disgrace, and, accordingly, with cheeks and brow reddened with shame, he marched off with the rest. As they left the old school-room, in which the boys were then assembled, some one hissed, then another followed with a like demonstration, and, before the culprits had reached the door, hisses loud and prolonged proceeded from all parts of the room.

The Principal had ascertained by previous inquiry that none of the boys who were out coasting on the hill that afternoon, were, at the time of the collision, sufficiently near to make their evidence of any value; he had also privately questioned me, and found that I could not positively assert that the "'76" had been purposely steered against the sleigh upon which Tom and I were riding. He had, therefore, to form his conclusions concerning the guilt or innocence of the boys, from a personal examination of them.

In carrying on this examination, he was careful not in any way to tempt one boy to inform upon another; no boy was ever permitted to do this except in his own defense. To each boy in turn, on this occasion, the question was put:—

"Did you steer or aid in steering the long sleigh against '35's' sleigh?"

To this all answered in the negative. Some, as they replied, looked the Major in the face and tried hard not to seem in the least disconcerted; others glanced fixedly down on the one side or the other, till they were rather sternly bid look up. But in the replies of all there lurked a sense of guilt, which did not escape the keen eye of the Principal,—save Ned alone, who answered sadly, but with the sincere accents of truth. The question that next followed was:—

"Did you seek to steer the long sleigh clear of '35's' sleigh?"

This question was first put to Ned, who answered, both with truth and truthfulness, that he did. The other boys, in their haste to exculpate themselves, answered in turn that they also sought to avoid the collision, till the question reached, last of all, "17," who was too wily to make this reply, and said that he, for his part, did not attempt to steer the sleigh off, because he was not expecting a collision; he thought the "'76" would pass by without touching—and in making this declaration he was successful in assuming an air of candor.

When this question had thus gone the rounds, the Principal, changing his tone, which before had been low and measured, exclaimed, with great severity of accent and manner,—

"You shameless fellows! Here are seven of you, all of you, indeed, but one, who profess to have tried to steer the sleigh clear of '35's,' and yet you expect me to believe that you could not succeed. You all exert yourselves to steer the sleigh to the right, and yet it goes to the left. It is very evident, in fact, that you have spoken falsely in answer not only to the last question, but also to the first. You are guilty of this injury to '35,' and shall be punished accordingly. You, '17,' alone have saved yourself for the present, but the question of your guilt is still reserved. You have either truth or superior cunning on your side; which of the two we shall yet find means of ascertaining."

After a short pause, he turned to Ned, and resumed: "As for you, Edward Eldridge, I am pained to find you in this company, under an accusation of intentional wrong against one whom you seemed once to cherish as your friend—I can with difficulty believe that you have allowed the coolness which has sprung up between you to be carried to a degree of positive enmity; I can hardly think you would take pleasure in seeing your old friend suffer any injury. Besides, your previous good character and your present air of truthfulness are in your favor. I am disposed, therefore, to except you for the present from punishment."

Ned, all the time, had held his head down, oppressed equally by a sense of shame, and by the weight of his repentant sorrow. There needed only this reference to his former relations to Tom, as well as to the happy innocence of his former life, to touch the full fountain of his heart. He burst into a flood of tears. His grief lasted for some time, during which there was a profound silence in the room. At last he found words to say, interrupted by sobs, that he deserved punishment for having treated Tom so badly, though he did not try to steer the sleigh against him and never intended him any harm.

"I can believe you," said the Principal, affected by Ned's tears and his repentance, "and I exculpate you from all blame in the affair of this afternoon. As to the other matter"—meaning his recent relations to Tom—"let us talk that over in private. For the present, sit down and compose yourself. As for you," he added, turning to the others, "with the exception of '17,' you are not permitted to leave the grounds from this prescut hour till the Easter holidays; and bear in mind, that your footing in the school is very insecure; every disorder at all marked shall be visited with severe punishment. '17's' case will yet be held in consideration; in the mean time he, also, is not to leave the grounds. Beware! every one of you shall be watched. If this order is infringed, the offender shall be at once dismissed from the school. You can now go."

Ned was left alone with the Principal. The latter's manner instantly changed, and, calling Ned to him, he with great gentleness bade him explain all about his relations to Tom. Ned needed no encouragement, for the consciousness of his ingratitude to his friend oppressed him continually, and the opportunity to unburden his heart was seized with eagerness. The true nature of the jealous, suspicious sentiments which he had allowed to take possession of him, was now made plain to his conscience. His recent experience affected him as some incubus, some dark dream, which he was struggling to throw off.

In his narration of the minute circumstances which were connected with the growth of Ned's unworthy mood, the Principal did not fail to observe the covert influence that "17" had exerted, and made some allowance for Ned on that account. In the end, as he dismissed him, he consoled him by saying that he was glad that Ned had at last recovered a right way of thinking, and sentiments worthy of his better nature; all that remained was to make amends to Tom as soon as Tom had sufficiently recovered to bear the interview, and all would be well.

CHAPTER XXIX.

THE SICK-ROOM.—MILK-SOP.

That night, as the doctor evidently feared, notwithstanding the intelligent care which he received, Tom was attacked with a fever, which by morning so increased in intensity, that the sufferer lost all consciousness of his present situation, and, as it were, groped blindly about amid the images and memories of the past. At first he seemed to think himself at home, and talked with the charming ignorance of childhood, now to his father or mother, now to a brother or sister. Afterward he appeared to be living over again his earlier school-days at Mount Pleasant, roaming over the hills on some holiday trip, with Ned by his side, to whom he was constantly addressing the most endearing epithets, and to whom he talked as if they were walking together, arm over neck, in school-boy fashion. Then he seemed to be alone and to have lost his friend, upon whom he called repeatedly in saddest tones.

The doctor, who came early in the morning, inquired of Mrs. Blaisdell who this Ned was, to whom the sufferer was so much attached. On being told that he was one of the school-boys, he requested that he should be sent for, and that he should remain by the bedside of his patient; his presence might have a quieting effect, and recall him sooner to a rational consciousness.

Thus Ned was permitted to enter the room of the friend whom he had wronged, but whom he now loved with the fervor of a humiliated yet renewed and expanded nature. To have the privilege of sitting by the bedside of his friend, and of applying the cooling bandages to his brow, and of moistening his parched lips, was what he most desired, but dared not ask. The request was delivered by Mrs. Blaisdell herself, who had learned Ned's recent history, and was desirous of offering him, by her manner at least, that consolation which only a woman has the art to manifest by a glance. Ned could only express his gratitude both for the privilege that was granted him, and the unspoken yet not the less certain sympathy which accompanied it, by his tearful eyes and the speechless trembling of his lip.

Thus he was installed by the bedside of his friend, and no tender and sympathetic girl could have been more quick to understand the wants of the sufferer, and more ready in administering to them. In the afternoon the fever momentarily subsided, and Tom became conscious again of his situation, and recognized his attendants. He manifested no surprise at seeing Ned; and, indeed, to judge from occasional remarks, his recent life up to the time of that last sleigh-ride was blotted from his memory, and Ned's presence and devotion to him seemed only like a continuation of the old days. Ned, on his side, had been cautioned not to say any thing to Tom calculated to recall recent occurrences; indeed, any lengthened conversation was forbidden.

In the evening the fever again set in with greater violence than before; again Tom's mind strayed to the past, and his speech brought up fragmentary yet charmingly-pictured bits of his early life,—his home and its surroundings, his first playmates, the district school, the lake, the grove. The name of his mother was oftenest on his lips. But yet in the midst of these visions of home, was now and then mingled some fragment of his life at Mount Pleasant, and Ned would hear his own name pronounced in connection with some pleasant incident of their companionship. Ned could not listen to these reminiscences, accompanied as they were by so many evidences of Tom's affection, without his eyes filling with tears.

However, the medicines which were administered seemed to have a favorable effect, and in the morning when the doctor again called, his experienced eye at once recognized a change for the better. He announced the crisis as passed, and that careful nursing and quiet were all that was needed to bring about a speedy convalescence. Ned instinctively grasped the doctor's hand, as he said this, and looked up to him with eyes of tearful gratitude. The kind doctor smiled at the enthusiasm of the boy, and seeing he was worn as much by emotion as by his constant watching—for Ned had insisted on remaining all night by the bedside of his friend—he prepared some simple, quieting drink for him, and bade him, with a certain gruffness of manner, —which benevolent nature had given him, as she gives a protecting husk to her sweetest fruits,—to swallow the dose, and go to bed. Ned obeyed, and slept more soundly and sweetly than he had done for many a day.

The next morning, for Ned was not admitted again till then, he found Tom much improved. Tom manifested a quiet satisfaction in seeing his friend, though as before, it was accompanied with no surprise. He still was oblivious of his recent life. Ned, of course, made no reference calculated to arouse unpleasant memories; he said, indeed, but little, yet as he moved quietly about in attendance upon the patient, he showed by a certain gayety of manner, which like the veins of the marble, played through his sadder mien, that a fountain of life had been touched within him, capable of nourishing the native flowers of his heart.

Ned continued his constant attentions for several days; he could not be persuaded to leave his friend, except to take needed rest, or for a short walk in the open air, at times when the boys were not at play, for the wild freedom of their ways conflicted for the present with his quiet yet not unhappy mood. He frequently had occasion to pass by "17," but occupied by his own thoughts, and his solicitude for his friend, he paid no heed to his recent associate, nor did the latter, perceiving the change that had come upon Ned, and fearful of repulse, seek to force himself upon his notice. Yet Ned at that time was sensible of no positive feeling of resentment against "17," for he was too conscious of his own fault, and of the self-humiliation which it brought, to seek to transfer the blame to another.

"Seventeen" saw clearly that Ned had escaped him, that Ned and Tom were friends again, that in fact by that last maneuver—that cruise, as he called it, of the "76"—he had overshot the mark. Conscious of defeat, he was consumed with a passion he dared no longer express. Only on one occasion did an expressive syllable escape him. He was standing, together with some of his chosen associates, near the door between the old school-room and the library, which Ned then had occasion to enter. "17," as Ned approached, assumed the most intense sneer he could command, and as Ned passed, hissed into his ear the word—

"Milk-sop."

Ned started, not with resentment, but as if a serpent had sprung up in his path; he, however, passed on without even turning a glance upon the intruder, or paying any heed to the low derisive laugh of "17's" associates.

CHAPTER XXX.

THE ENCOUNTER.

One morning, after Tom had passed three or four days in that feverish condition which accompanies the first stage of convalescence, Ned entered and found his friend still asleep. Pleased with this sign of improvement, he walked on tiptoe about the room, arranging the curtains of the window and the movables in such a way as, he thought, would make the effect the most agreeable to his friend. As he was putting on the last touches, Tom suddenly awoke, with a low cry, and a look of alarm, which was at once dispelled by the sight of his friend.

"Oh, Ned," said he, "what an ugly dream I have had. I thought we two were walking out in some rocky region, and when I turned about in our path to speak to you, I saw that a serpent had coiled himself around you and was dragging you down a steep shelving rock. I reached out my hand to pull you away, but you slipped from my grasp, and left me standing on the edge of an abyss, trembling with fear and horror, when happily I awoke and found it—all a dream."

Ned stood still in the center of the room, scarce able to move,—overtaken with a poignant feeling of remorse, —the dream tallied so with the reality of his life.

Meantime, Tom was passing his hand anxiously across

his forehead, as if striving to remove some confusion of thought. All at once his whole recent life seemed to flash upon him. He cast toward his friend a look of deep reproach, which, however, was so quickly blended with an expression of gratitude at his return, that its sting was lost. Tom fell back upon his pillow, extending his hand toward Ned; the latter hastened forward, grasped it and buried his head in the bed-clothes at Tom's side. Tears found their way to the eyes of both. No words were spoken, and none were needed; their mutual understanding was complete.

At last Tom broke the silence: "Ned, let us bury or burn all memorials of these recent affairs. We have both awaked from an unpleasant dream. Please look in my writing-desk,—you know where it is, in our room,—and you will find there the two notes you sent; then, if you have preserved it, bring that note of mine. Let us touch a lighted match to them, and so make an end of the matter; amid the bright days to come we shall easily forget it; it will seem to float away and disappear like a cloud."

Ned shook his head, and said he did not wish to forget his part in the affair; he deserved the punishment which the recollection of it would inflict, and would like to keep all the memorials of it as a warning against falling again into mean jealousies.

"But what," he added, "is that you say about two notes of mine? I sent but one, nor did I receive any from you."

"You received none from me!" exclaimed Tom, rapidly, and looking anxiously at Ned.

"No."

"Then that villainous '17,'" he cried with great

heat, "has made a dupe of us both. Did you not find a sealed note between the leaves of your 'Cæsar'?"

"No," said Ned, with great astonishment.

"Then that base fellow stole it, and opened it, and subscribed your name to a reply of his own. Ah, how could he, how could he do it? What harm have I done him?"

These last words were not heard by Ned, who with all his old impetuosity had rushed from the room, and was hastening to search in Tom's secretary for the evidence of the crime which had been perpetrated against them. And when at last he had torn open with trembling hand the forged note, and saw with his own eyes how he had been practiced upon, he could scarcely contain his excitement; but when, seeking further for the first and genuine note, he found in the same envelope what was evidently a copy of the note Tom had written him, and when he had read its generous and conciliatory phrases, he was no longer master of himself, and without returning to Tom's room rushed down-stairs and out upon the play-ground, where the boys were then enjoying their morning recess.

He was not long in finding "17," and hastening, forward, he seemed about obeying his first impulse to throw himself upon him. He, however, controlled himself; the very sight of his betrayer, near at hand, seemed to have the effect of diverting his rage into the most intense scorn. He shook open the forged letter, which he had in his right hand and holding it up, while he pointed to it with the left, he at last found voice to ejaculate:—

"There! you miserable fellow! You viper! see that picture of yourself. Look at those writhing, snaky lines, to which you have dared to add my name. Bah! they are written with a slimy finger."

"Seventeen" turned deadly pale. Meantime, Ned's school-fellows, attracted by his singular and excited action, had thronged around the two youths in great numbers. Pausing in his speech, but continuing for a few moments to direct upon "17" a look of deep contempt mingled with an expression of aversion and disgust, Ned suddenly turned to the silent circle of auditors around him and said:—

"Look you, my school-mates! Do you see that base cringing fellow there? See here, what he has done. You all know that '35' and I had broken with each other, and did not speak for a long time. Well, it was all that base fellow's work! See, here is the way he did it,"—continuing to hold up the note,—"he intercepted our letters and forged replies of his own. Look at him, the snake swelling with venom."

The simile was not without application, "17's" paleness seemed to grow more and more deadly, while his dark eyes gleamed with a fixed glare, and his shoulders seemed to rise, and his neck to swell with contained wrath, till the tension was at last snapped, and he rather hissed than spoke,—

"He lies!"

Ned made a sudden movement, as if about to precipitate himself upon his enemy; but before he had time to do so, if that was his intention, his excited school-mates animated with one mind, had rushed upon "17" with cries of "Thrash him, maul him."

In the *mêlée* that followed, "17" might have suffered serious injury, such was the excitement of the boys, if two or three of the seniors, who held positions as officers, had not felt it their duty to interfere. They only succeeded in allaying the disturbance, by proposing that "17" should be led at once before the Major. This proposition was at once adopted, and "17," pale, but determined, collared by the officers, and surrounded by an agitated crowd of his school-fellows, was ushered into the presence of the astonished Principal. Ned followed after, the forged letter still in his hand, and his cheek flushed with an unnatural glow. As he entered the room, way was made for him to the front.

The older boys had already explained why they had brought "17" in this summary manner, and Ned was now called upon to state his case, which he did as calmly as was possible under the circumstances. He concluded by submitting the letter which he held in his hand.

The Principal, on listening to this exposure of a premature villainy, with difficulty preserved the calmness of his manner; he briefly asked "17," in a low voice, in which it was doubtful whether there was more of anger or of sorrow,—

"Is this handwriting yours?"

The question was followed by an intense silence. "Seventeen," pale but resolute still, seeing that all evasion was useless, knowing well that Tom could corroborate Ned's account, at last, without lowering his eye, uttered the monosyllable,—

"Yes."

The Principal, in a case of so much importance, determined to proceed with great deliberation, and, accordingly, simply placed "17" for the present under a guard, consisting of two or three of the seniors, and isolated him altogether from his school-fellows. He was apprehensive that he would attempt to escape from the school; besides he knew not what mischief a boy of his evil nature and ungoverned will might seek to perpetrate, now that he found himself unmasked.

Ned's school-fellows, on leaving the room, forced and almost carried Ned to the play-ground, where they gathered about him and rent the air with cheers in his honor. He was now fully restored to their confidence; indeed, the scene which they had witnessed a few moments before,—his noble indignation and impulsive scorn,—had completely captivated them; he was again their hero. Ned, however, escaped as quickly as he could, pleading that Tom was needing his attentions.

On his return to his friend he found him much agitated and alarmed, for Tom had heard the unusual noise on the parade-ground, and the shuffling of many feet in the hall, and he feared that Ned's impulsiveness had brought him into some difficulty. The cheers that he afterward heard had, however, somewhat reassured him.

On hearing Ned's report of what had occurred, he manifested much pleasure in his friend's perfect restoration to the good opinion of his school-mates, yet, when Ned had ended, he looked a little sad.

"Ah, Ned! impulsive as ever! I am glad on your account, and yet, perhaps, it would have been better to have kept the matter to ourselves about these notes. Now, I suppose, he will be expelled, and he might perhaps have changed for the better. Who knows?"

Tom's fever, in awakening a sense of human weakness and dependence, had softened his heart and made him incapable of lasting resentment; it had burned away that husk of false pride, and left him in a condition to feel and see that the essential elements of all hearts are the same, and that all rebound toward the good, when at last the right spring is touched.

Ned felt and acknowledged the justice of the gentle rebuke which Tom's words rather suggested than expressed.

CHAPTER XXXI.

AN OPEN SKY.

Tom now recovered his strength so rapidly that he was able, the week following the occurrence I have just related, to resume his old routine of school duties. His first appearance among the boys was hailed with great acclamations; his face, still pale and bearing the mark of his fall, appealed to their naturally warm sympathies. Indeed, he received a real ovation.

During the latter part of Tom's convalescence, arrangements had been made for Ned to resume his former place in Tom's dormitory, without, however, disturbing me, to which Ned would not at all consent. Thus at last we all found ourselves situated to our liking, and the winter's term, which had gone so early under a cloud, promised to end brightly and happily.

"Seventeen," after all, contrary to the expectation of every one, was not dismissed from the school. If I were writing a fiction, and looked to artistic effect in the construction of my story, I should straightway dismiss this youth from the drama; both as artist and theologian, I should consign him at once to the bottomless pit, and proceed with entire self-satisfaction on my predetermined course. A fiction, being designed, as is right, to please the artistic sense, having brought out its lights and thrown in its shadows, must keep these substantially fixed; all the rest is but a lightening of the lights and a deepening of the shadows. The only difference between the fiction-maker and the artist is, that the former spreads out his canvas and paints the picture before your eyes, the latter exhibits only his completed work. But nature and life can not be confined in the prescribed limits of art. In nature shadow is nowhere permanent; the evil of the darkest soul is not a part of its element, and may yet be cloven by a sudden ray coming we know not whence.

The first impulse of the principals was to dismiss "17" at once from the school. The boy's fault, or rather crime, was of so grave a nature, that his expulsion seemed to be the only course open to them; no ordinary punishment would be an adequate *mark of reprobation*. Still they had always hitherto resorted to expulsion rather as an act of self-defense, than as a punishment; and on further consideration the necessity for it in this case did not seem absolute. "17's" claws were cut; he could do no further harm. And, perhaps, for the boy's sake it would be better that he should remain in the presence of his disgrace, and be made, if possible, to feel the true character of his offense, by seeing its dark colors reflected in the faces of those around him.

They considered that "17" was not one of those brutish natures with which nothing can be done, and against which no other protection is possible but that of physical compulsion. On the contrary, they thought that his was in a certain sense a refined nature; for his moral perceptions were not lacking; they were, in fact, very acute; it was by the stress of an unfortunate education, that he had been diverted from a love of the good he saw,—or rather, having been taught to see the good as beyond his own reach, he had come to hate those who seemed to be privileged to possess and enjoy it. This is not the mark of a low and coarse nature, but of one acutely sensitive. Such natures must not be thrown aside as worthless. Education has undone them; education must seek to repair the wrong. They thought, therefore, that "17" should be allowed to remain; indeed, that the circumstances under which he would now find himself, might conduce to a change in him for the better.

Tom also had a little influence in determining the matter; for when Mr. Ellery, the morning after "17's" exposure, made him a little visit of inquiry, Tom ventured to hope that "17" would not be dismissed; he thought that Ned and he would feel as if they were in some sort the cause of his dismissal, if he should be sent away.

The result was that "17" was let remain. The Major, after this decision had been made, partially explained the reasons for not dealing more severely with him, and bespoke for the offender a freedom from all insult; we were not expected to take him to our hearts, as one who deserved well of us, but neither were we to fling his fault in his face; only mean spirits would take advantage of his disgrace to heap contumely upon him.

"Seventeen" thereafter moved about among us as one not of us. It seemed to be his own wish to remain isolated from us all, and, on the other hand, few seemed inclined to penetrate this isolation. His old companions indeed, when the freshness of his and their disgrace was past, its edge a little blunted, when they thought they might dare to hold up their heads again, sought to renew their alliance; but "17" treated their approaches with a keen contempt, and made them feel at once, that if he had consorted with them before, it was not as one of themselves. In this gloomy isolation he occupied himself busily with his studies, in which, aided by a quick intelligence, he made rapid progress.

As the days past on, the better class of "17's" school-mates—for boys easily forgive and forget—would willingly have readmitted him to more friendly relations; they even, seeing his loneliness, began to feel a degree of compassion for him; but they found it impossible to entice him from the moral and social seclusion now as much self-imposed as enforced. Tom, in particular, frequently felt an impulse to make some friendly advance toward his old enemy, to whom originally he had experienced no affinity; but he found no means of doing so without running the risk of offending "17's" proud sensibilities by a seeming air of magnanimity.

How was it then with "17"? Was he gathering up hate in his heart? was he wreathing coil upon coil to spring it with the more force, whenever occasion favored?. I think not—his exposure, his disgrace, his sense of defeat, his isolation shattered his moral world, left him confused and uncertain, and, notwithstanding his proud mien, had shaken his confidence in the power of evil. From a ground thus prepared may there not spring forth some good?

CHAPTER XXXII.

TINGLING VEINS.

The remainder of the winter passed without any change in our relations to one another.

Soon after Tom's recovery, a few mild days, followed by a warm rain, had pretty well cleared the ground of snow, leaving only a patch here and there in the hollows and under the cover of the fences. These days were followed early in March by an interval of clear, cold weather, which coated all those recesses of the river, lying out of the line of the channel, with a shield of that hard, transparent ice, whose glistening surface, yet untouched by the steel of the skater, looks so alluring, and withal so treacherous.

But such ice, in the vicinity of Mount Pleasant, was not long allowed to retain its original gloss; its fair face was soon marked and cut in all directions by the ruthless steel of an army of audacious youths, and ere long loose crystals of ice lay like a light snow or a hoar frost all over it. Skating at that season became our sole amusement. Every afternoon saw a long line of boys, with skates swinging from their shoulders, wending toward the river, gamboling and curveting by the way like unbroken colts.

How the young blood tingled in our veins as we passed and repassed each other on the ice; now describing many a curious curve, then cleaving the wind in straight course like arrows shot from the bow. Now we are massed like some ocean fleet bearing down upon the shore, then of a sudden we break and flee in all directions, as if some adverse wind had blown upon us; or we advance in long line, like a wave which anon breaks and recedes and disappears in the midst of foam beneath that which follows. Now we speed on in silence,—a silence relieved only by the hiss and crush of the steel upon the ice; anon we raise a combined and prolonged shout, whose echoes come back like weird cries from the hills that border the Croton, as if they were the voices of the river-spirits held in icy chains,—and in the long after-pause, as we stood motionless on our skates, one fancied that he heard a faint repetition of the shout from the hills of Rockland.

Thus occupied, evening fell upon us as a surprise, and the first stars were out before we were warned of the hour of roll-call.

Oh, the glow and sparkle of those days! In the heat of our blood the sunset hues seemed but the sympathetic flush of nature, and the winter's sky lay near and warm, and its stars throbbed with our own heart-beats.

CHAPTER XXXIII.

ON THE WING.

Winter, long in coming, was long in leaving; he extended his sway far down into March, breathing white frost upon the hill-sides and keeping his icy hand upon the streams, to the great delight of "us boys." At last, however, almost in a single night, he broke up his encampment and fled through the passes of the Highlands. We woke up in the morning to the din of rushing waters, and found that the Sint Sinck Run and the more distant Croton had escaped from their long icy bondage, and swollen with the pride of new-regained power, were precipitating themselves with all their force into the Hudson, and that even this majestic river had risen in his might and was shaking loose the ice that fretted his sides.

Spring was near at hand. Already she had sent warm breathings from the south, entering the opened cottage-windows; and we seemed to see in the distance her light blue robes floating over the hills. With the spring came the promise of a larger freedom. We began to cast longing glances upon the surrounding country, and to surmise what wonders lay beyond the heights that bounded our vision, for the "faery" touch of spring awakens in every fresh heart the dreams and promptings of romance.

One afternoon, having of my own will remained in

the school-room a little beyond the hour of dismissal, on going out I turned my steps for the moment toward the library. Here I found a group of boys, among whom were my two especial friends, Ned and Tom, gathered about Mr. Ellery, who was leaning over a table and inspecting a map which lay before him. Ned made room for me and called me to his side, telling me in a low voice that the map was one of Westchester County, and that they were planning out expeditions and examining the routes. His eyes beamed with delight at the prospect, for, with the advent of spring, Ned seemed to be regaining all his old elasticity and lightness of heart.

While the Principal continued his survey of the map, we waited quietly and expectantly about him eager to catch the words from his mouth. At last he broke the silence,—

"Here, my young friends, you have spread out before you the map of a noble region,—one abounding in picturesque scenery, and dotted all over with localities that are hallowed in the memory by legendary or historical associations. We can not, of course, traverse it all in our brief holiday intervals, but with this map before us we can in imagination set out from our pleasant mount, and make rapid journeys over the whole ground, which will afford us a good preparation for our less ambitious pedestrian excursions.

"And first, I shall bid you follow me to a high point nearly due east from Sing Sing. Here it is. It is called Whip-poor-will Hill. We are now, for the journey is already performed, on the highest ground in the county south of the Croton reservoir. How do I know this? Easily. South of this hill the streams all flow in a southerly direction; north of it, in a northerly direction,—and water, I believe, always flows downward. From this point, then, we can survey the land in all directions,—northward to the Croton, westward to our own Hudson, and eastward and southward to the Spuyten Duyvil Creek and the Sound, and a splendid view we have with our far-reaching vision.

"Do you see that little spring almost at our feet, and the rill that issues from it? Follow its line of light southward, and you will see that it takes a middle course between the Hudson and the Sound, and empties into the latter not far from Hell Gate, dividing this neck of land nearly equally. That is the famed Bronx river. Now observe, that on the east of this river, the streams all flow into the Sound, while on the west they empty into the Hudson: we know, therefore, that the Bronx river follows the line of highest elevation traversing the lower part of the county. Parallel with this stream there runs a ridge of hills which constitute the backbone of the county, or rather we will call them the vertebræ of this neck of land, and, to carry out the analogy, New York shall be the great nervous center— the brain,—while the vast back country forms the body of our gigantic State.

"Observe, too, that west of the Bronx the streams, for the greater part of their course, run parallel with this so-called river; now as the direction of the lesser streams generally defines the line of the hills, we know that the region between the Bronx and the Hudson consists of parallel ridges. Looking, from our height of Whip-poor-will, southward over this region, we see only a medley of hills, as if they danced and skipped together; we are unable to discern their trend; but follow those glistening threads that begin up here on our right, and with rapid windings glimmer here and there, yet after all are never widely divergent from a straight course, and you will soon get the lay of the land, for the hills do not affect the mazes of your modern fashionable hops, they remain faithful to the old country dances, in which the long lines of revelers are only slightly confused by the graceful yet dignified coquetting of one dancer toward another.

" But now let us cast our eyes over the region lying east of the Bronx. Here we observe that the streams do not flow in the same direction with the Bronx, but rising in the hills, that run along east of this stream, flow in a southeasterly direction. It is evident, therefore, that from the line of the Bronx the land descends by a gentle southeasterly slope toward the Sound.

" Look down the north slope of our Whip-poor-will hill, we shall see—for we are endowed for the time with a vision that passes right through such intervening obstacles as rocks or woods—another little spring, the waters of which, gathering as they flow, empty into the Croton, not far above the reservoir. You perceive that the sources of this stream and the Bronx are perhaps not a mile apart, and that both flow along the same range of hills, though in opposite directions.

" If, setting out from the Whip-poor-will, we travel northwesterly toward the Quaker's bridge on the Croton, we shall first have to mount the Chappaqua hills; here we shall have, on our right, the sources of some little streams that flow into the Croton, but, looking southward, we shall easily trace with our gifted vision the course of two streams that run parallel with the Bronx, and which, with the Bronx and the Croton, constitute the sacred streams of the county.

"The greater of these two, rising within a stone's throw of us, is known among the country people by the not very classic name of Saw-Mill river, but it has also retained the old Indian designation, Neperan. Saw-mills are often picturesque additions to the scenery of a water-course, and the popular name therefore is suggestive; but, unfortunately, there are hundreds of saw-mill rivers—so called—in the country, and we should be unwilling to permit our beautiful Neperan to be confounded with the common run of streams. The Neperan empties into the Hudson at Yonkers.

"If we go on and descend the western slope of these Chappaqua hills, we shall perhaps penetrate some cool, rocky grotto, in which the second of these classic streams takes its rise. This stream empties into the Hudson at Tarrytown, and flows through the dreamy, delectable region of Sleepy Hollow. It was no sleepy hollow to Ichabod Crane, when, on a Saturday night, long ago, he rode furiously along the lonely road, pursued by the headless horseman. But this haunted stream has also, among the country people, a very common-place name: it is called Mill river. To say nothing of designating such a tiny tributary of the Hudson a river, mill rivers are almost as common as mills. The name, indeed, is pleasanter than Saw-mill river, which grates a little harshly on the nerves; but, fortunately, we have left us the Indian name of the stream, and no combination of syllables, hardly, could have a more brooky fall upon the ear—the Pocantico.

"Now let us return to the Whip-poor-will hill, and travel thence in a northeasterly direction toward Bedford and Poundridge, and so on to the Connecticut line. Observe that we are keeping upon the high grounds, and that on our right the streams flow southeasterly toward the Sound, and on our left they take an opposite course toward the Croton. We have some hard climbing over and along these hills, but the wildness of the scenery more than repays us, and we have the satisfaction of treading the highest land south of the Croton.

"But before returning to the Whip-poor-will, let us follow one of these rivulets leading northwestward,—say the Beaver Dam,—down to the Croton. A little below the mouth of the Beaver Dam there flows in, on the opposite bank, a considerable stream. It is the Muscoot. Let us swim over and ascend this stream. A tortuous course it leads us under the shadow of hills that look frowningly upon the adventurers. At last we reach one of its sources, the famed Lake Mahopac, and though this beautiful water lies just beyond the bounds of the county, yet, as we have seen, all its connections are with Westchester, and to Westchester, therefore, it may be said to belong; for do not the fair Manhattanese, who haunt the indented borders of this lake all the long summer, drink its limpid waters from leaden pipes all the winter?

"Climbing the hills westward of Lake Mahopac, we look down the course of streams running in the same general direction as the Bronx, Neperan, and Pocantico; we know, therefore, that the hills north of the Croton, have the same trend as those south of it; the Croton cuts across them, stealing around through the hollows.

"Standing here, near Lake Mahopac, we are under the very shadow of the noble Highlands. And these hills that run southward through Westchester—what are they but spurs of the Highlands? Let us image this mountain land,—so full of powerful repose,—as a great couchant lion that with careless majesty extends a paw down to the ocean's edge; the hills of Westchester are the sinews of this paw. And what, again, are the Highlands but a part of the great Alleghany mountain system? And what, once more, are the Alleghanies but a part of the great continental system, which includes the Rocky Mountains of the west, and subordinates the Mississippi and the Mackenzie to mere valley streams. Having thus tacked these mountain systems upon our Westchester hills, let us return to the Whip-poor-will and sit down upon some soft rock; after our rapid journeys we shall need a little rest.

"But soft rocks are not easily found in Westchester; indeed they are for the most part of the hardest and roughest kind, and no wonder, for through what countless ages have they stood the wear and tear of the world's changes. Cross over into New Jersey, and the soft red sandstone crumbles beneath your feet; but your Westchester rocks have the true grit. And look at them! see how they sparkle in the sun! age has not dimmed their luster.

"These rock-hewn hills over which you gaze have, then, a history—a history which antedates by myriads of years the earliest epoch of human history, and it becomes you to know the outlines at least of this history, so far as it is yet understood.

"If you should take the steam-cars here at Sing Sing, and go northward, after you had passed the Highlands you would observe a great change in the appearance of the rock through which the road cuts its way; you would perceive that above the Highlands the rocks are arranged in layers, which, however much contorted, are always distinct, and nearly parallel, and you would infer—if you are disposed, as a rational being should be, to submit the facts which your eyes furnish you to the cross-examination of thought—that the materials of which these rocks are composed were slowly deposited from water in a soft condition, and only after a long period of time and under great pressure attained their present hard consistency. You would also observe that the rocks above the Highlands have a dull, opaque look, while those that compose those noble mountains and these picturesque hills sparkle with brilliant crystalline faces of various tints,—some like frozen rose-water; some a tender pearly hue; some a soft white, streaked with green; some a creamy flesh-color, like that of Venetian Madonnas. These rocks, also it is true, show more or less distinct traces of an original deposition in layers or strata, yet they evidently were formed under different conditions than those which attended the composition of stratified rocks, or, at least, have had a different subsequent history. But you will understand this matter better when you come to the studies of your senior year.

"It will serve you for the present if you learn, that, of these two kinds of rock, the crystalline which you see here around you, and which underlies the leafy mold of these hills, is far older than that other stratified kind, and owes its origin to a period in the world's history when fire and water yet contended for the supremacy; while the latter variety shows only the more peaceful sovereignty of water, though fire had not, at the time of its formation, nor has it yet, wholly yielded the sway to its opponent.

"But why are not these old crystalline rocks, of which these hills are formed, covered up and hidden from view by the later stratified rocks? Because Fire, shut up within his subterranean dungeon, swelling with wrath, strove with great power to break the inclosing walls. And he did indeed raise, first the Canadian heights, and then, little by little, the long rolls of the Alleghanies, including these very hills; nay, in some places he broke his way through, as along yonder High Torn range and the steep Palisades which you see vanishing southward; but, sputtering and foaming, he was driven back by his old enemy. Thus it was that these rocks, broken and rolled up into hills as you see them, were rescued from the sovereignty of Water before the later depositions had time to accumulate upon them.

"It was not till many ages had passed that Fire, lashing himself into fury, like a caged beast, again strove to burst his dungeon walls. This time he raised the great Rocky Mountains from the surface of the water. And, before his energy was spent, that great valley between the Alleghanies and the Rocky Mountains, which under the quiet waters had accumulated strata upon strata of sand and clay, was, after many vicissitudes of elevation and depression, rescued at last from the domain of ocean.

"Thus, if Fire did not gain the mastery, he succeeded in establishing the dry land as a neutral ground; the power of his old enemy was effectually crippled. And thus, in their blind contest, did these two foes unwittingly prepare the conditions for the rise of that Promethean power, which, by its wiles, should filch the sovereignty from both. This power is Man.

"As you see, I have gone pretty far back to seek the

beginning of Westchester history and legend, some sketches of which I propose to give you; but I have as an excuse the excellent example of that old chronicler Diedrich Knickerbocker, who, in his famous history of New York, philosophically begins with the creation of the world. The events of the present are determined by a long chain of antecedent causes, which must therefore be investigated. Do you think if the Alleghanies had not sent forth this expedition of hills down to the sea, and had not opened a path for the waters of the Hudson, that Westchester County would hold the important place it now does in the world's destinies? No, indeed," said the Principal, with great gravity. "See," he added, with assumed grandiloquence, "this line of hills forms a great pen, of which the city is the sharp nib; and by this pen, held in the mighty grasp of this great Union of States, the destinies of empires shall perhaps be written.

"But my task," he continued—"that of telling you something of the history and legends of this bit of land—is not one of such magnificent pretensions; nevertheless, I shall have to defer undertaking it till to-morrow afternoon."

CHAPTER XXXIV.

TRADITIONS AND LEGENDS OF THE NEUTRAL GROUND.

The following afternoon we thronged again to the library in larger numbers than before, and eagerly gathered about the Principal, who, having spread the map out on the table, began as follows:—

"Yesterday, my young friends, having adjusted our wings, we took flight over the Chappaqua hills, across the Dark Valley, where rises the Bronx, and alighted on the Whip-poor-will hill; thence we surveyed with a bird's eye the hills and streams of this picturesque country from the Highlands to the sea. Put on now the sandals of Mercury, or your seven-leagued boots, or whatever else you have of more modern invention, for we have rapid journeys to make this afternoon.

"And first, again to Whip-poor-will hill. The region which we now overlook is not so new in the annals of man that his joys and sorrows and superstitions have not had time to attach themselves here and there, like ivy, to its rocky hill-sides, and to give to many localities something of an old-world interest. The echoes of historical and legendary footsteps are heard in the hollows and ravines. More than two centuries have passed, since Hendrick Hudson sailed up the waters that bear his name, and cast anchor off the mouth of the Croton, and within that time how has human story woven here its mist-like veil of romance!

An entire race of men, whose cheeks reflected the fading hues of an autumn sun, have vanished from these woods and the borders of these streams. Armies have dragged their weary way northward, leaving blood-stained foot-prints. Marauding bands have stolen along under the shadow of these hills and desolated solitary homes. Battles have been fought, and lonely encounters between man and man have darkened the glens, and the young violets at the base of the rock have fed on blood, and superstition hovers about haunted nooks, and legends have grown over old graves.

"There is indeed more of sadness than of joy in the interest that attaches to this region, notwithstanding that the inimitable Irving has invested the life of the Dutch settlers with such an atmosphere of quaint humor.

"It was in 1614—was it not '35'?—that the first boatload of Dutchmen touched the rocky shore of Manhattan Island. It was a serious business that they had before them, and their humor must have been of a grim sort. If not a graceful and beautiful people, they were certainly stout-hearted; they were the children of a race that had made themselves masters of the ocean, and were pushing their enterprises into every sea,—a race too, that claim our gratitude as the earliest defenders of civil and religious freedom. We can not afford always to laugh at them. Nevertheless these early settlers of Manhattan and the river counties were a quaint people and had quaint, comfortable ways with them, many of which their buxom sons and daughters retain even down to the present day, albeit I fear our American-Dutch, in losing something of the rotund, well-poised proportions of their ancestors, have become more close-fisted, and have acquired a certain forward stoop, which is often suggestive of a grasping disposition.

"But they have their apology, if any be needed; for hardly had the Dutch in America succeeded in establishing themselves as a thriving community, capable of development into a well-organized and cultivated state, when they found themselves hemmed in, isolated, and finally reduced to a subordinate condition by a more powerful race, alien in language and habits. The animus of independent growth was gone, and it is not therefore wonderful—if it be the fact—that their descendants have degenerated.

"New Amsterdam fell into the hands of the English, August, 1664, and the poor humiliated Dutchmen must thereafter hear their city of many gables called New York; and though the colony, after a lapse of nearly ten years, again fell into the possession of the Dutch Republic, their hold of it was so brief that the Dutch ascendency may be considered to have ended with the first surrender. But I am not going to relate the colonial history,—that you can read for yourselves.

"Let us set out on our travels. It seems in our talk about the early Dutch settlers, we have been led from our favorite resting-place—the Whip-poor-will hill—away down to the island of Manhattan. Let us make haste to escape from that doomed region; its green woods shall be cut down and its wood-nymphs frighted away, its mossy rocks shall be torn up, its hills leveled, and great dead walls of brick built thereon, and countless throngs shall pass and repass where once a beautiful solitude reigned; let us haste away, for we love not the city. We cross Spuyten Duyvil creek at King's bridge. But stop, let us pause midway on this bridge. 'Spuyten Duyvil!' What a fine, vicious name! It was here, according to the veracious Diedrich Knickerbocker, that the stout Dutch burgher, Anthony Van Corlear, the trumpeter, met his luckless fate. It was a dark and stormy night, according to the chronicler, when the good Anthony arrived at the famous creek,—sagely denominated Harlem river—which separates the island of Manhattan from the mainland. For a short time he vapored, like an impatient ghost, upon the brink, then swore most valorously that he would swim across 'en spyt den duyvil,' and plunged into the stream. But scarcely had he buffeted half-way over when, according to an old Dutch burgher who witnessed the fact, the duyvil in the shape of a huge mossbunker was seen to seize the sturdy Anthony by the leg and drag him beneath the wave,—but not till he had instinctively put his trumpet to his mouth and had given a vehement blast, that rung far and wide through the country round and brought the alarmed neighbors to the spot. It is said that the restless ghost of the unfortunate Anthony still haunts the spot, and that his trumpet is often heard on a stormy night, mingling with the howlings of the blast.

"It was off the mouth of Spuyten Duyvil creek that the first blood of the red man in this part of the new world was shed by the hand of the white, for it was here that a number of the Mahicanni, who had their hunting-ground in Sleepy Hollow, and of the fierce Manhattans, who have given their name to the island on which New York is now built, angered by the perfidy of Hendrick Hudson's crew in making some of their race prisoners, assembled to intercept the *Halve Maen* on her return. The Dutch ship being compelled by the unfavorable wind and tide to come to anchor, the painted savages sallied forth in their canoes, and shot their arrows at the bulky sides of the monster—as it may have seemed to them. But the monster belched forth fire and smoke, and many of them, struck as if by an invisible hand, leaped maddened into the waves; the rest returned in affright to the shore, and betook themselves to the woods.

"It was at the mouth of this creek that the early Dutch settlers first proposed to found their city, tempted probably by the natural strength of the situation and its adaptability to fortification.

"Under the Dutch government and the earlier years of the English, a simple ferry was sufficient to meet all the wants of travel. It was not till 1692 that his excellency the governor of the province, out of great favor to the city of New York, proposed the building of a bridge at the '*Spiken Devil Ferry*.'

"In revolutionary history, King's bridge was a point of great interest. It was across this bridge that Washington led his army on his retreat from Long Island. You will remember that he had established his lines along the Harlem river—as the channel is called which separates Manhattan island from the mainland, and of which Spuyten Duyvil creek is a part. He was, however, soon forced to abandon this line, not indeed by direct attack, but by the measures which the enemy, under Lord Howe, were planning in order to outflank him. The British, taking transports at New York, landed on the extremity of Throg's Neck, but finding their progress cut off by the destruction of the bridge connecting that point with the mainland, they crossed over, October

18th, to Pelham Point, and marched the same night to the high ground near New Rochelle. Their object was to obtain command of the routes leading to the east, and thus isolate Washington's army and cut off his supplies, which were principally obtained from that quarter, and thereby force him to a general battle. But the wary commander-in-chief anticipated this movement; he had already sent on a detachment to erect fortifications at White Plains, and as soon as the design of the enemy was fully developed, left his head-quarters at Fort Washington, crossed King's bridge, and moved toward White Plains, with the Bronx on his right, which was defended at every assailable point.

"Soon after the check which the British received at White Plains, they returned to Dobb's Ferry, and thence by way of King's bridge to New York. Thereafter, during the remainder of the war, King's bridge constituted an outpost of the British lines. The lines of the Continental army were maintained along the road from Tarrytown to White Plains till February, 1780, when they were re-established along the Croton as far as Pine's bridge, and thence to Bedford. All the intermediate country constituted 'the neutral ground.'

"The poor people of this region were unfortunately situated. Included within the lines of neither army, they fell a prey to marauding bands, which were restrained from robbery and outrage by no military authority. These were known under the names of 'Cowboys' and 'Skinners.' The former found shelter and protection within the British lines. The British post at King's bridge was their great rendezvous. Thence nightly they issued forth on their work of rapine and outrage, and thither they brought their booty, principally consisting, I suppose, of cattle, which they sold to their British allies. The Skinners pretended to espouse the American side, but their only object was plunder, and they cared not whence it came; they were, in fact, in league with the Cowboys, and through the latter their spoils generally reached the British lines. These lawless wretches, of either name, hesitated at no outrage when outrage served their purpose, and many is the deed of horror which they perpetrated, the memory of which still clings in tradition to the solitary wayside homesteads and the sequestered hollows of this region.

"But, in addition to the attacks of these cowardly enemies, the unfortunate inhabitants of this district were liable to be harassed by foraging parties from the British lines, which at one fell swoop would perhaps deprive them of all the results of their summer's labor. The troops selected for this purpose consisted generally of refugees, who, as is generally the case with traitors, constituted the most merciless of foes. The principal corps of these refugees was stationed on the right of the British lines, under the protection of the works on the Harlem river, and was commanded by Colonel Delancey, a renegade American, but brilliant cavalry officer, whose exploits we shall hear of frequently as we traverse the neutral ground.

"After a year or two of such warfare, the condition of the people was truly deplorable. Their homes were scenes of desolation,—walls, floors, and windows shattered by violence or eaten by decay,—furniture plundered or broken to pieces, cattle gone, fences plundered for fuel or thrown down, fields grown over with weeds and wild grass. The high roads, which had once been enlivened by frequent travel, were deserted, and the grass grew of full height for the scythe over the old carriage tracks.

"But let us cross the bridge and continue our journey northward. The high ground on our left, as we set foot on the mainland, was known as Berrian's Neck, or Tippet's hill. Here are yet to be seen the remains of fortifications thrown up by the Americans, from which in the year 1777, while the lines of our army still extended from White Plains to the river, and the British were in winter-quarters in New York, our troops, under General Heath, occasionally cannonaded the rifle-pits of the Hessians, encamped on the opposite side. The old Tippet mansion was located on the eastern side of this neck of land, and was still standing not many years ago; half hidden behind gaunt poplars, its antiquated and lone look was well fitted to suggest the popular superstition that it was haunted by the ghosts of the old Tories. In the time of the Revolution much of this region must have presented the original unreclaimed wildness of nature, for we hear of deer being shot in the woods along the river side as late as 1782.

"Proceeding northward toward Yonkers, we pass on our left the Van Cortlandt hill, upon which lay the wide estate of a branch of the Van Cortlandt family that figures so largely in the colonial and revolutionary history of New York, and which we shall hear more of as we go northward. The plain, substantial manor-house, which was built in 1748, still remains.

"North of this lies Vault hill; it was here in the summer of 1781, when the British pickets had been driven within the lines on New York island, that

Washington stationed his troops and lit his camp-fires for the purpose of deceiving the enemy, while he secretly withdrew his forces across New Jersey to join the French in Virginia.

"The valley from Vault hill to King's bridge, through which a small stream flows, called Tippet's brook, was the scene of many a fierce encounter. It was down this valley that the daring cavalier, Colonel Armand, having ridden rapidly under cover of the night from his quarters on the Croton, charged at full speed and fell upon and destroyed a company of the 'Green Yagers,' encamped near King's bridge. The British bugle sounds to horse, but before the pursuit is well begun, the dashing trooper is far on his way to the Croton.

"Here, too, occurred a more sanguinary affair. In the vicinity of the 'Indian Bridge,' which spans Tippet's brook where the stream crosses the road, a party of Stockbridge Indians were decoyed into an ambuscade. Driven among the rocks west of the stream they were surrounded and cut to pieces, only four of them succeeding in escaping to the American lines. Nehman, their chief, when he saw the British cavalry in his rear, called out to his band to fly, 'he himself was old and would die here;' and he died bravely, wounding with his own hand the leader of the enemy. An opening in the Van Cortlandt woods, where the dead were buried, was, within a few years, still known as the Indian field; and it is reported by the neighboring rustics that the old sachem still haunts the spot.

"On the right of this valley, as we pass on between it and the Bronx, lies Valentine hill. Ascending this, we shall overlook the country east of the Bronx to the

Sound, beholding far in the distance the blue line of Long Island. Southward we shall look down the graceful slope of the Tippet valley as far as New York; and westward, through the breaks in the hills that skirt the river,—the Cortlandt, Vault, and Bear hills,—we shall catch glimpses of the dark and wrinkled Palisades. We are again on historic ground, for it was on Valentine hill that Washington, when cautiously withdrawing his troops from the Harlem line to White Plains, held for a short time his head-quarters. From this height he could watch with ease the movements of the enemy on the opposite side of the Bronx, and could direct the attacks which were made upon the flanking parties of the enemy, or take measures to anticipate any advance across the Bronx, if that should be the intention of the enemy.

"As the general stood one day, leaning upon the pommel of his saddle, talking with Thomas Valentine, the owner of the estate on the hill, he perceived at a distance of three or four miles over the river, the heads of the British columns, apparently directing their march toward the hill. Soon, however, it became evident that the enemy were taking the road toward White Plains, and Washington, who had anticipated this movement and had already thrown up works in that quarter, pushed on his left wing to that place, while Valentine hill now constituted his right; when the design of the enemy was still further developed, he called in all his detachments along the line of the Bronx, and prepared to defend his position at White Plains. These movements from King's bridge filled the interval of time between the 11th and 27th of October, '76. The battle was fought on the 28th of that month.

"Valentine hill was frequently occupied in the course of the war by divisions of the one or the other army. In the absence of the regular troops, it was much visited by marauding bands of Cowboys and Skinners, and suffered much from their depredations. On one occasion a party of the former forced an entrance, in the dead of night, into the Valentine house, and rousing the proprietor, Thomas Valentine, they demanded his money. Disregarding his protestations of a moneyless condition, and turning a deaf ear to the cries and entreaties of the women of his household, they dragged the old man forth to the foot of a cherry-tree, which may be seen still standing in the corner of the old garden, and driving back his frantic wife and daughter, placed the cord around his neck and were about to fling the loose end over a branch of the tree, when the stout-hearted patriot suddenly shook himself free from the clutches of his base enemies, and, throwing the cord from his neck with an air more of indignation than of fear, exclaimed: 'Don't be such fools as to hang a man when he hasn't any money.' His coolness and evident sincerity convinced the robbers that they would better wait until another time; perhaps when they made their rounds again in that quarter, old Valentine's money-bags might be replenished; nothing was to be made out of a dead man. But they were not always so reasonable, and frequently, in the anger of disappointment, carried their experiments to a fatal end.

"Among the number of the heroic women of the Revolution, Susan Valentine, the daughter of the old man whose adventure I have just related, deserves an honorable mention. On one occasion, in the absence of the master of the house, when a gang of these maranders burst open the door, this young lady seized a large oven shovel,—a formidable weapon in those days of great brick ovens, capable of containing a large brood of generous loaves with room to spare,—and, brandishing this weapon aloft, threatened to split the head of the first man that dared to cross the threshold. The vile intruders shrunk away thoroughly intimidated. On another occasion she was not so fortunate. A friend of hers, a Mr. Snider, who was about to set out on a distant journey, intrusted £30 in gold to her keeping— a considerable sum in those days—which it would be hazardous to carry about his person. The brave young woman accepted the charge, and for greater security, concealed it in her gown. But on the very evening of her friend's departure, a party of Skinners broke suddenly into the house, and before she had time to devise means of defense, burst into her bedroom and demanded her money. She denied that she had any, and called upon her brother for help; the latter rushed in, and though unarmed, vigorously set upon the ruffians. While the struggle was going on, the undaunted girl slid unobserved from the foot of the bed, and was about escaping through a side door, when she was perceived and seized. In her violent struggles to get free, the money was loosened from her clothes and fell with a loud ring to the floor, or, as she herself described it, "was fairly shook out of her." The delighted Skinners were well content to make off with their prize without further molestation of the occupants of the house.

"From Valentine hill we look down upon a beautiful lowland adjoining the Bronx river, which was known during the Revolution as Mile Square. The spot was a favorite camping-ground with the troopers of both armies. There they would tie their horses to the apple-trees in the orchard adjoining the Ryche mansion, while, to guard against surprise, vedettes were stretched along the neighboring hills, on the summits of which the remains of earth-works are still visible, and which often, doubtless, gave back the echoes of the bugle as it sounded 'to horse,' when perhaps some troop of the enemy was descried turning the brow of a distant hill.

"On the road leading from Mile Square to Yonkers the remains of an old inn were still visible not many years ago, which was kept by a Frenchman, named Gainos. When Washington retired to White Plains, Monsieur Gainos, who was enthusiastic in his attachment to the American cause, and had made no concealment of his detestation of 'les Anglais' took refuge within the American lines, leaving his hotel in charge of a trusty tenant. Occasionally, however, under the cover of night, he would steal down the valley of the Bronx, and hiding himself among the rocks near his house, would make known his presence to his tenant by certain signals, imitative of natural sounds: for, accustomed to the wild life of nature, he had learned to mimic to perfection such notes as those of the owl or the whip-poor-will, or those other feathered or furry creatures that haunt the lonely places, and thrill the night with their penetrating voices. On hearing the response agreed upon, announcing to him that the inn was free from dangerous guests, he would hasten with eagerness to enjoy its homely comforts. One night, however, he had not long ensconced himself comfortably by his fireside, when a loud knocking was heard at the door, followed by a demand for instant admittance. Peering through a loop-hole in the wall, Gainos discerned by the dim light, a party of four or five rough-looking fellows, whom he easily recognized, by their accouterments, as Cowboys. No response was made to the threatening demands that were meantime repeated, but muskets were brought from their place of concealment, and old Gainos produced a heavy sword, which had seen much service in French wars. Meanwhile, the assailants had taken measures to burst open the heavy oaken door. When, at last, the door fell in, Gainos, his tenant, and the stout stable-boy, fired simultaneously upon the marauders, and before the latter had recovered from their surprise, the valiant Frenchman rushed through the smoke, and with one blow of his sword struck off the head of the leader of the band; he then, with the prudence of a good general, who always sees to it that his base is protected, retired within the house. The guns had discharged much noise, without discharging the Cowboys; but these midnight heroes, seeing their luckless comrade shorn of his head, felt no desire to offer themselves for similar tonsorship. Dragging the headless body with them in their retreat, as far as the adjoining well, and seeing that life was utterly extinct, they threw it in head foremost, for so the tradition tells.

"When, a few years ago, I passed the old hostel, it was evidently falling rapidly to decay. Situated on a lonely spot, surrounded by gnarled cedars, it presented a gloomy, desolate look. The curb-stones of the well were overgrown with moss, and there were no foot-prints of living man within a wide circle of the ground encompassing it, which in truth was overgrown with coarse grass and rank weeds; but it is said that on dark nights the old marauder may be seen seated on the stone of the well. Be this as it may, the country people never permit themselves to be overtaken by the night in the neighborhood of the ruined inn; or if they are compelled to pass it, do so with averted heads, and at their topmost speed. And let us also hasten to leave the precinct, for though it is not yet night, it is a lonely spot, and these dark rocks seem to be invested with a certain strange mystery.

"Let us take the road over the hill to Yonkers. The name of this ancient village is a quaint one, and had a quaint origin. Early in the history of the Dutch settlement of the New Netherlands, this site fell into the hands of Adrian Van der Donck, who afterward became famous as the author of a learned work, entitled 'Beschryvinge van Nieuw Nederland'—description of New Netherland. The domain of Heer Van der Donck extended from Spuyten Duyvil creek to the mouth of the Neperan—where the first village was established—and as far inland as the Bronx. Here he founded a colony—known as Colen Donck—over which he was invested by the home government with all the rights and authority of the Dutch patroons. The good patronus soon had the satisfaction of seeing a goodly population settled on the hill-sides of the domain, over whom he exercised a patriarchal sway, and he looked forward with honest Dutch pride to the time when the Jonge Heer—young lord—who was already showing the signs of manhood on his plump chin, should succeed him in the obedience and affection of his people. But, alas! the Jonge Heer was a wild, rollicking fellow, and disturbed the whole country round by his mad pranks, leading a band of riotous companions as far north as the 'Slanpy Haven kill,' and southward to the 'Haarlem' river;

this he would often cross, and cause the good burghers of New Amsterdam to shake their heads at his unseemly revels, though much was pardoned the Jonge Heer, and their buxom daughters were not forbidden to smile upon him. He, in short, became the town and country talk. The Jonge Heer was in the mouth of every one; it was always, 'What is the ast prank of the Jonge Heer?' Thus it was that the village, of which his father's house was the center, became identified in the thoughts of the people with the Jonge Heer, for he was its life and its spirit; and thus did it get its name, for Jonge Heer being corrupted, is Yonkers. The 'J' in Dutch has the sound of our 'Y,' and, indeed the title itself was often written and pronounced Jonkheer, so that the change is more one of spelling than of sound.

"Van der Donck obtained this land by grants from the Indians, a numerous tribe of whom—belonging, in common with all the tribes on the east bank of the Hudson, to the powerful Mohegan race—were settled about Yonkers, to which place they gave the name of Neperah, or Neperan, transferring to their village the name they had given to the stream that here empties into the Hudson. The word Neperah, in the Indian language, means, it is said, 'rapid water.'

"In a quiet nook of the Hudson, not far above the mouth of the Neperan, there lies, a little out from the shore, a huge bowlder, which the Indians called Maceakassin, which name we are told means 'copper stone.' This great dark-hued rock, so mysteriously separated from its original resting-place,—thrown by the power of some mighty being, and from some unmeasured distance, into this shadowy recess,—was to the Indian mind a charmed memorial of Deity, and with wild rites and discordant song they worshiped it. Among other relics of that forest-born race, whose thoughts and life reflected the gloom, the mystery, and the fierceness of the wild nature around them, not the least interesting are the 'tawasenthas'—places of many dead—several of which are found within a few miles of Yonkers. In one of these was recently exhumed the skeleton of a woman, discovered in a sitting posture, with her child in her arms. How touching is the picture which this incident at once awakens! How one is startled with this image of divine motherly love in the midst of a grim setting of savage woods!

"The great estate of Van der Donck was sold under the English to Vreedryk (peace-rich) Felypsen, or, as the name was Anglicized, Frederick Philipse, and constituted, along with all the rest of the land on the east bank of the Hudson, extending northward as far as the Croton and inland as far as the Bronx, the great lordship and manor of Philipsborough, holden of the king of England by feudal tenure. And we shall perceive as we go on, that much the greater part of Westchester County was thus, under the English colonial rule, divided up among a few families, which, fortified by the law of entail, constituted a powerful landed aristocracy, and were invested with important privileges, such as the authority to hold baronial courts, exclusive right to game, etc.

"The influence of such an aristocracy will explain the strength of the Tory element in Westchester County on the outbreak of the Revolutionary war. All of these families, however, did not side with the English government; a few resisted the strong temptation, growing out of their position as grantees under the crown, to sustain the power which accorded them the privileges they enjoyed. Not only did these patriots stake their possessions, but they must have foreseen that even in the event of success they could not hope to retain, under the republican form of government which was foreshadowed, the aristocratic privileges that were then theirs.

"But let us resume our journey. Keeping on the old post-road, we pass the manor-house of the lords of Philipsborough, with its broad stone front, through which a long line of windows peer, and with numerous door-ways in the quaint Dutch style. Here, on great rent days, the lords of the manor, aided by a retinue of fifty servants, feasted their tenants. Here was born that famous beauty, Mary Philips, who was the animating spirit in the lordly festivities of those gay colonial days, and who was said to have captivated by her charms the heart of a young Virginia colonel,— one George Washington.

"Going northward from the village, we climb Wild Boar hill—now the site of many a quiet home nestled among trees and vines, but once, as its name shows, the savage haunt of the wild boar. So troublesome was this animal in colonial times, that the provincial government was compelled to pass against it a decree of outlawry, and set a price on its head.

"This hill, and indeed the whole country north of Yonkers for many miles between the Hudson and the Neperan, was covered in Revolutionary times with dense forests. These wilds, with their numerous rocky hiding-places scattered along the shore, afforded shelter to the American water-guard, whose duty it was to watch, and as far as possible obstruct, the movements of the enemy upon the river. In the day-time they patrolled the river-side, but when night had set in they issued forth with muffled oars from one and another rocky recess, and glided like shadows under the shadows of the hills, or pushed boldly out into the mid-stream on some adventurous enterprise against the enemy's shipping.

"One August night of '76, the woods that border this part of the Hudson were strangely illuminated. The brave water-guard had sallied out in their gun-boats from the mouth of the Neperan, having in tow a couple of old hulks which they had filled with combustibles. The night is beset with thick clouds, and the boats steal out silently and are lost in the darkness, while from a rocky prominence of Wild Boar hill several general officers of the American army anxiously wait the result. Off this hill the two British frigates, the *Rose* and the *Phœnix*, lie at anchor, and against these the enterprise is directed. The sentinels on board the ships break the midnight silence by their cry, 'All is well;' the echoes have scarcely died away along the shore, when suddenly the fire-ships burst into a blaze, and are seen floating up with the tide toward the British ships. The waters flash from their surface the reflected fires; the rocks and woods by the river-side leap from the darkness; the rigging of the ships is drawn in lines of light against the dark Palisades; the clouds begin to unroll in great volumes overhead. In a few minutes the fire-ships are in contact with the frigates, but the British tars are already at their post, and after a struggle of ten minutes, during which cannon are discharged into the fire-ships, to sink them, the frigates succeed in getting loose from their terrible foes before any harm is done. In the mean time the American gun-boats, pursued by the grape and canister of the enemy, have regained their covert in the Neperan. Their enterprise has proved unsuccessful. But what would you not give to be transported back to those times, and see with your own eyes that glorious night-scene, privileged to stand among the Continental officers who are grouped on some one of the rocky projections of Wild Boar hill?

"But the woods that darkened the sides of this hill, and the ridges of rock into which its surface was broken, afforded shelter and concealment to other than the water-guard,—to Washington himself, who frequently traversed the Neutral Ground in disguise. On one occasion, finding himself suddenly in the presence of the patrol of the enemy, he was compelled to flee from capture up the steep front of a rocky ledge that cropt out on the hill-side. And not many years ago a tree was still standing,— one of the few extant representatives of the original forest,—in the hollow trunk of which the great chief, wearied by a long journey, slept for two or three hours, while his trusty guide, Martin Post, stood guard over him.

"Crossing over Wild Boar hill we descend into the valley of the Neperan. At the foot of the hill, near where a bridge spans the stream, stood the old parsonage, or, as it was called during the Revolution, the Babcock House. It was occupied at that time by the fascinating widow of the Rev. Luke Babcock, and by Miss Sarah Williams, sister of Mrs. Frederick Philipse. At various times during the war, troops of one or the other army were stationed here, partly because the position was favorable for encampment, but also because the society of the ladies was much sought after by the officers in command.

"Miss Williams doubtless favored the royalists, but the charming widow's heart beat with patriotic fervor, and though many an epauletted red-coat contended for her hand, it was reserved for the gallant Colonel Gist, of the Continental army to win the honor of the favored suitor. But the devotion of the colonel nearly cost him his life, for on one occasion, having taken advantage of an opportunity to encamp his force in the valley of the Neperan at the base of Wild Boar hill, he was tempted to cross the stream and spend a few hours of the evening in the society of the ladies. But the enemy had gained information of his movements, and had chosen the time for an attempt to cut off both him and his command; and their eagerness in the enterprise was not a little stimulated by the fact, that some of the officers were greatly piqued at the advances of Colonel Gist in the affections of the fair occupant of the parsonage.

"The enemy, consisting of a considerable force of cavalry and light infantry, set out from King's bridge in two columns, the one moving around Valentine hill to a point east of Gist's encampment, the other stealing along the Cortlandt ridge to a point on the west, while a detachment was sent forward to secure the road leading northward through the valley of the Neperan. The object was to cut off every avenue of escape; but either through some mismanagement or through the alertness of Captain Odell, who had been left in command of the camp, the small American force were able to make their escape, on the first alarm, by an unfrequented pass through the woods west of the Neperan. At the same moment the enamored colonel receiving timely warning, flung himself upon the charger which stood at the door of the parsonage, and dashing across the bridge, closely pursued by the enemy's horse, rejoined his companions in arms on the hill-side.

"Meantime the undaunted widow had stationed herself at an upper window of the house, where she could overlook to advantage the movements of both parties; by waving her handkerchief she encouraged the Americans in their flight and signaled the position and advances of their foes; nor, when the British officers, after the bugle had sounded the recall, presented themselves as her guests, could she refrain from manifesting her exultation at their ill success, nor they from concealing under a show of bravado their feeling of chagrin.

"Farther up the valley of the Neperan we come upon the old homestead of the Odells. Here to a good old age lived a veteran of the Revolution, Jacob Odell, who was fond in his old age of gathering a group of boys about him and recounting the exploits of his younger days and the sad story of the Neutral Ground. A gleam of quiet satisfaction would light up the wrinkles of the old man's face, whenever his mind reverted to that bright spring day of '76,' when, in his twenty-first year, with three cousins of his own name, and like him just come to man's estate, he stood under the famous white-wood tree near Tarrytown, and enlisted in the Continental army, vowing in his heart fidelity to his country's cause.

"In the absence of this youthful patriot the maranding Cowboys frequently visited the old homestead; on one occasion they dragged his aged father from his bed and hung him, till life was almost extinct, to a tree on the road-side, in hope to extort from him a confession of concealed money. Not succeeding in their object, either because the old man had no money to surrender, or was too stout-hearted to yield, they were about to repeat their cruel experiment, when his frantic spouse broke from the cellar in which they had confined her with the rest of the household, and seizing what weapon she could reach, suddenly assaulted the ruffians with such vigor that they released their hold of the old man and gave up their attempted extortion.

"Crossing the range of hills east of the Neperan we descend into the valley of the Armenperal or Sprain Rook. Beyond this, bordering on the Bronx, lie the heights of Tuckerhoe. This singular name is of Indian origin, and was applied to a kind of bread made from certain roots that grew in abundance along the streams that drain this region.

"On the western slope of these heights took place one of those minor incidents of the war, which were of so frequent occurrence in Westchester County. A company of Delancey's refugees, under command of Captain Barnes, had issued from their quarters under the protection of the forts on the Harlem, and had gone up the Bronx on a plundering expedition. Major Leavenworth, of the Massachusetts line, learning through his scouts of the enemy's movements, determined to cut off their retreat. Accordingly he posted his force in ambuscade near the base of the hill. At the same time he sent a few men to the brow of the hill with instructions to display themselves conspicuously on the approach of the enemy, and in such a manner as to present the appearance of a considerable force prepared to meet attack. The stratagem was successful. The enemy abandoned the hill and took the lower route, and thus fell an easy prey to an inferior force; on the first volley, poured into them from behind the rocks, they laid down their arms.

"This hill was the scene of another neat little stratagem. A marauding party of the enemy, one dark, cloudy night of autumn, had taken up their quarters in the old school-house. Benjamin Hunt, and six or eight other Westchester patriots, determined to attempt their capture. Hunt took upon himself the office of captain, and assigned to his compatriots the rank of lieutenants and sergeants. Their force of privates was an imaginary one; but with this they, nevertheless, boldly surrounded the school-house, issuing the necessary orders in loud tones of command. When their fictitious arrangements were complete, Captain Hunt burst open the door and bade the enemy surrender at once, or his men, enraged by their depredations, would show no quarter. The panic-stricken marauders yielded their arms and marched out, thirty in number, as prisoners of war.

"These incidents are only instances of many similar ones which are still extant in the traditions of the Neutral Ground.

"But descending from the heights of Tuckerhoe to the creek of the same name that flows along at their base, let us recross the hills that intervene between this stream and the Armenperal and—climbing the more formidable range, which lies beyond, and which in the time of Van der Donck was covered with an almost impassable forest, the undisputed haunt of bears, wolves, wild-cats, and rattlesnakes—descend into the valley of the Neperan. Following the windings of this stream northward for a few miles, let us swing ourselves across it on this old willow that has half lost its foothold in the loose earth and droops low over the opposite bank; then we shall strike boldly across the hills in the direction of Dobb's Ferry.

"Ah, we have missed our reckoning a little and have come out a mile below Dobb's Ferry, near Edgar's Lane —a section of the Albany post-road. Let us pause on the hill-top a moment, to take breath after our tough scramble over the hills, before we descend to the beaten road. Hark! Do we not hear the tramp of horse. See, there they emerge from behind that bend in the road. It is Colonel Sheldon with his troop of Continental dragoons. The gallant colonel rides at their head with his trusty guide, Isaac Odell, by his side, with whom he is in consultation. They halt; the colonel surveys the grounds, and the guide points to a bridle-path leading to the river. They turn off into this path and disappear behind some rocks among which the path winds and in the clefts of which cedars have taken root. Again all is silent.

"But let us not leave our covert on the hill; there is something ominous in these preparations; like the wild deer we may snuff danger in the air. Hark, again there is the low heavy tramp of horse; it comes from below, from the direction of Yonkers, where Emmerick's troop of British cavalry is encamped. Now they ascend the hills and appear in sight. By their accouterments and their stolid looks they are Hessians. They spur their horses and are passing us on the gallop. A shrill whistle from behind the cedars! The officer who leads the Hessians is startled, and reins in his steed. But hardly has he turned his head when a discharge of fire-arms is heard and little puffs of smoke jet forth here and there from the cedars. The Hessians are thrown into confusion, and many a poor fellow topples from his saddle, and many a riderless horse, snorting with fear, gallops with flying rein up and down the road. And to add to their confusion, Sheldon's cavalry, having turned the base of the rocks, are seen charging impetuously upon them from above and below. How their swords flash in the sunlight and clash and clang together! How they lean forward to give the far-reaching stroke! How they bend backward on rearing horse to avoid the blow! The surprised and discomfited Hessians, their retreat cut off, seek to make their escape by the bridle-path leading to the river; but here a second volley is poured into them by the dismounted dragoons among the rocks, and the path is strewn with horse and man, dead or dying. And of all that company of hard riders, only one stout trooper breaks through the line of his foes, and speeds down the road to carry the story of his comrades' fate to the camp at Yonkers. Emmerick starts his whole force in pursuit; but Sheldon with his prisoners is far on his way to the American quarters at North Castle. Let us descend. Have no fear; these are but apparitions that we have seen, and all this happened long ago: Edgar's Lane is now a race-course.

"Following the post-road we soon reach the ancient village of Dobb's Ferry—situated at the mouth of a stream which is called in the Indian tongue, Wysquaqua, which pleasant sounding name the English-speaking settlers corrupted into Wyckus creek, which again they jocosely lengthened into William Portuguese creek. The name of the stream was doubtless affiliated with the name of the Mohegan village which was situated on its bank—Weckquaskeck, which word, being interpreted, means 'the place of the bark kettle.' The site of the aboriginal village can still, it is said, be traced by the numerous 'shell beds,' that are found here, varying from two to three feet in depth. The place seems to have been a stronghold of the Weckquaskeck Indians, for they had here no less than three intrenched forts, one of which was still held in 1663 and was garrisoned with eighty warriors. The hunting-grounds of the Weckquaskecks extended over the whole region between the Bronx and the Hudson, and from Spuyten Duyvil creek to the neighborhood of Sing Sing. They were consequently brought into frequent contact with the Dutch, and wars ensued, in which the latter were generally the aggressors.

"It was not till 1641 that these hostilities broke out, but the incident that evoked them was of much earlier occurrence. The story will illustrate the Indian's tenacious memory of wrong. In 1626, years after the Dutch had laid the foundations of New Amsterdam, when one of the Weckquaskecks, accompanied by his nephew—a mere lad—was on his way to the Dutch fort to sell some beaver skins, he was met by three Dutchmen, rough fellows, who, doubtless, had been compelled to seek refuge in the New World to avoid the punishment of their crimes, or else were waifs from some one of the buccaneering craft that then infested the seas. On the Indian's approach their greed was immediately excited by the rich load of beaver skins which he bore on his shoulders; and when he refused to surrender his hard-earned wealth, they assaulted and slew him. The Indian boy had meantime fled to the border of the neighboring wood, and when he saw his uncle fall, fearing that the murderers would pursue him, he buried himself in the depths of the forest and by secret paths sped homeward. But that terrible picture could not be erased from the boy's brain, and his uncle's spirit seemed ever to haunt him, and to whisper in his ear, that the wandering shade would never rest in the happy hunting-grounds till his death had been avenged, for the wild religion of the Indians made revenge a duty. The boy brooded over the matter in secret and bided his time. When at last he had grown to manhood, he could no longer restrain the spirit that possessed him. Three lives must be sacrificed to the shade of his uncle. Claes Cornelisz Smits, the 'road-maker,' is selected as the first victim. The poor road-maker is taken unawares and slain with one blow of the tomahawk. Another and another victim follow. The Dutch are in arms and demand the surrender of the murderer; but the old sachem of the Weckquaskecks, reminds them of the murder of the young man's uncle fifteen years ago, and will not surrender the culprit.

"War follows. An expedition is fitted out by Director Kieft, and while the snow is yet on the ground a secret advance is made up the Bronx and the Armenperal into the heart of the Indian country, but the wary savages are on the alert and retreat to their fastnesses, and the attacking party returns unsuccessful. The Dutch now resort to a mean stratagem; they concoct a treacherous treaty of peace, and in the following winter, when the Weckquaskecks are attacked from the north by the formidable warriors of the Huron race and, being driven southward, beg assistance from the Dutch, Kieft seizes the opportunity to advance upon them in the dead of the night, and, surrounding their huts, begins an indiscriminate massacre of men, women, and children, which does not end till daybreak: more than a hundred of them are slaughtered.

"But the cruel white men will rue the event of that night. The red men of the Hudson form a league with the kindred tribes of Long Island, of the Connecticut valley, and of the New Jersey shore, eleven tribes in all, and from the Connecticut to the Raritan the tomahawk and the scalping-knife are seized. The Dutch, whose farms extended in Long Island, Westchester, and New Jersey to a distance of twenty and thirty miles from Fort Amsterdam, are driven in on all sides; their houses and farms burned, their crops destroyed, their cattle butchered. 'Mine eyes saw the flames of their towns, the frights and hurries of men, women, and children, and the present removal of all that could to Holland.' Such are the words of Roger Williams.

"The Dutch are forced to sue for peace. Yet during two or three succeeding winters, irregular hostilities were carried on. At last, however, in the summer of 1645, the chiefs of the Weckquaskecks, the Sint Sinks, and the Kitchawans,—who inhabited the hills of the Croton,—together with the high sachem of the whole Mohegan race, on the one side, and the director-general of the Dutch and his council, on the other, seated themselves in a circle before the fort at New Amsterdam, and, silent and grave, smoked, 'in the presence of the sun and the ocean,' the great calumet of peace.

"Peace being restored, let us return to the village of Weckquaskeck, for so it continued to be called for some time after the settlement of the place by the Dutch. It was not till the Dutch farms had become numerous on the other side of the Hudson, and the passage of the river at this point became a thing of daily occurrence, that in the year 1690, or thereabouts, one 'Jan Dobs, en zyn huys vrou' settled here and established a ferry. Dobs, or Dobbs with the two b's, since the added 'b' is more becoming,—one 'b' was probably hardly adequate to the Dutch portliness of the original Dobbs,—seems to have been an important personage in the 'place of the bark kettle,' for ere long he gives his own name to the village. And I guess the name will stick; it has good sticking qualities. But if, as may chance at some future day, the bran-new people of the town turn up their noses at the stout honest old name, then, if you will, let the place be called 'Snobbs.'

"In Revolutionary history, Dobb's Ferry holds a prominent place, though it does not appear to have been the scene of any of those local contests which were of such frequent occurrence in Westchester. It was here, however, after the retirement of the English from White Plains, that the right of the American lines rested till the depletion of Washington's force compelled him to withdraw his outposts as far back as Croton. Here the Americans had erected redoubts, from which, when subsequently in the course of the war the place was taken permanent possession of, they were able to seriously annoy the enemy's shipping. It was here, finally, on the suspension of hostilities, that the American and British generals-in-chief, attended by their respective suites, met to arrange the preliminaries of peace.

"Leaving this ancient village and following the river northward, we shall, after a walk of a few miles, pass the old Van Tassel place, better known as Wolfert's Roost. But the quaint history of this quaint old homestead—how its founder was a comfortable old Dutch burgher who called it his 'rust,' or 'place of ease'—how during the Revolution, under Wolfert's doughty descendant, Jacob Van Tassel, it became the secret rendezvous of the water-guard, and all the bold lads of the country round, who made themselves a terror to Cowboys and skirmishers,—all this has been told in an inimitable way, and I need not repeat it. And how this Rust, or 'Roost,' to which the English ear and speech humorously transformed it, has since become a shrine of genius, is also well known to you. Let us not, however, disturb by our presence the serenity of this quiet retreat, pausing only to train a laurel wreath about the gateway, while meantime we peer through the trees at the quaint Dutch gables, surmounted by weathercocks and trailed over by the affectionate ivy.

"East of Wolfert's Roost, in the valley of the Neperan, lies the little hamlet of Greenburgh, and thither let us now turn our steps. In this region lived another branch of that patriotic, stout-hearted race of Dutchmen—the Van Tassels. The two brothers, Peter and Cornelius, co-operated with the famous Jacob Van Tassel, of Wolfert's Roost, in many a bold enterprise. Their temerity, however, at last brought down upon them the vengeance of the British refugees, a detachment of whom, belonging to Delancey's corps, sallying forth one November night of '77 from their quarters on the Harlem, and riding rapidly up the valley of the Neperan, succeeded, before the alarm could be given, in cutting off all the avenues of escape from the house of Van Tassel, and, waking up the household in the dead of the night, robbed the women and children of the clothing necessary for their protection from the cold, and dragged the two brothers off to New York as prisoners of war.

"But their ally, Jacob Van Tassel, and his associates of the water-guard, did not allow the outrage to go unrevenged. A party of them took advantage of the first favorable night, when the sky was darkened with clouds, and, setting out from Tarrytown in their stout gun-boat, coasted noiselessly down the Hudson, passed the enemy's forts at the mouth of Spuyten Duyvil, eluded the enemy's guard-boats, glided unchallenged by the enemy's ships-of-war, and, hiding their boat in a secluded bend of the shore, made their way to the house of General Oliver Delancey, uncle of the cavalry officer of the same name, burnt it to the ground, and succeeded in regaining their boat and in returning in safety to Tarrytown.

"In fact, according to good authority, in no part of the Neutral Ground could a more redoubtable set of fighters be got together than in the country about Greenburgh. They knew the peculiar crack of each other's muskets, and awaited no other call. To give an instance of their alacrity and prowess: one morning when, at break of day, a large party of Cowboys were returning through the valley of the Neperan, laden with the spoils of a midnight foray, John Dean, a brave young farmer, posting himself advantageously behind the rocks by the wayside, picked off one and another of the marauders, and, while retreating before them, held them in check till the report of his gun had summoned to his aid a considerable number of his neighbors, who poured so hot a fire into the ranks of the Cowboys that they were compelled to abandon their plunder and beat a hasty retreat. Doubtless among the gallant youth who enlivened the valley of the Ne-

peran with their musketry that brisk morning, Isaac Van Wart, John Paulding, and David Williams—names familiar to you as household words—and (if not at the time abroad on some expedition) those famous rangers and guides, John and Isaac Odell, were not the last on the field.

"Continuing our course eastward, we leave the valley of the Neperan, and, climbing Chatterton Heights, tread historic ground, for here and not at White Plains was fought, October 28, '76, the battle which takes its name from the latter place. Chatterton hill lies, as you see, on the west side of the Bronx, while White Plains is situated on the high ground rising from the opposite bank of this stream.

"Washington's right occupied Chatterton hill, while his main body was drawn up on the heights of White Plains. Fortifications of a temporary character had been thrown up at both places. The object of the commander-in-chief was simply to hold the enemy in check till works of a more formidable nature could be completed a mile or two further northward, among the hills of North Castle, for it was Washington's policy, as the general himself expressed it, 'to intrench and fight with the spade and mattock.' Yet his troops were in good spirits and eager to meet the enemy, for since their defeat on Long Island they had been inspirited by their invariable success in the several local encounters that had taken place during the march of the enemy from Throg's Neck.

"On the morning of the 28th, Washington, attended by several general officers, rode out to reconnoiter the high grounds on the left of his position. While on the way thither, a light horseman came up on the full gallop, and addressed the commander-in-chief with the startling words—'The British are in the camp, sir.' The general turned with calmness to his officers and said: 'Gentlemen, we have now other business than reconnoitering,' and putting spurs to his horse, galloped to head-quarters. Arrived there, he was informed by his adjutant-general that the guards had been all beaten in, and that the whole American army were drawn up in order of battle. 'Gentlemen,' said the commander-in-chief to the attendant officers, 'you will repair at once to your respective posts and do the best you can.'

"Chatterton hill was held by a few regiments of regulars and militia, under General McDougal, and against this position the British directed their attack. Under cover of their artillery, they threw a bridge over the Bronx and began the crossing. In this operation they were much annoyed and impeded by the fire of a couple of pieces of artillery, posted upon a table-rock half way down the hill, and commanded by the famous Alexander Hamilton. Their first step, after the passage of the river was effected, was to make a charge upon Hamilton's artillery, but such was the strength of his position, that, as he described it in after years on visiting the spot, 'for three successive discharges the advancing column of British troops was swept from hill-top to river.' The enemy's force on this part of the field, finding the American position impregnable, turned to the left and joined the second column of attack, which, under General Rahl, had crossed the Bronx about a quarter of a mile below. The united body then moved forward with the view of turning McDougal's right flank. The latter retired slowly up the hill, contesting the ground at every point. On the summit a decided stand was made, and the British infantry and cavalry were twice driven back; but finally, the militia on the right giving way before a cavalry charge, Washington dispatched to McDougal's aid a few regiments from the main army, under cover of whose fire he succeeded in withdrawing his force over the Bronx to the heights of White Plains.

"The enemy spent the three succeeding days in an effort to draw Washington from his position and provoke a general engagement, but without success. On the night of the 31st, the American commander, leaving his camp-fires burning, withdrew to his new position on the hills of North Castle. The British, giving up all further offensive operations for the year, retired to Dobb's Ferry, and thence behind their defenses along the Harlem river.

"The house which Washington occupied as his headquarters at White Plains, is still pointed out: it lies a little north of the village, amid a deep solitude of woods and hills; but it was the scene of a busy life during those eventful days, when the general's horse stood caparisoned at the door, and the steeds of his staff pawed the ground, hitched fast to the scattered trees, or held by the hand, ready to be mounted at a moment's notice. It is a quaint old house, with small windows and wooden shutters and low roof—one of those Dutch structures, which seem to hug the ground with a kind of humble, homely affection. The old fashioned sideboards upon which the hero's table service was deposited, are still preserved in their accustomed places.

"White Plains is endeared to our memory by still other, earlier associations. It was here, in August of '74, that the Whigs of Westchester met to appoint deputies to the Continental Congress; and here, again, in the spring of '75, other meetings were held for a similar purpose. But their proceedings did not pass without protest. We read of the lord of Philipsborough attending at the head of a large body of his tenantry, and, with others from other sections, protesting that 'we meet here to declare our honest abhorrence of all unlawful congresses or committees.' Poor man! With all his tenantry, he finds himself in a minority, and can only hold up his hands in pious horror. Alas, the days of the house of Philipsborough are numbered! When the storm comes on, the unfortunate lord knows not on which side to turn for shelter. He can not, like the Van Cortlandts, obeying a clear sense of duty and a native patriotism, sacrifice his aristocratic pride and his hopes of a powerful family, to the claims of his country, and boldly espouse her cause; nor can he, tender-hearted man that he is, imitate that bold dragoon, Delancey of Mamaroneck, and take up arms against his former friends and neighbors. He will retire to his castle Philipse at the mouth of the Pocanteco, and there let the storm, if it will, blow past him. But in times such as these, no man can remain neutral; he must show his hand as friend or foe. So, after a few years of vacillation, the good man escapes from the turmoil to a refuge beyond the sea, and his lands become confiscate to the state."

At this moment Mr. Ellery's discourse was interrupted by the ringing of a bell, which called us to evening prayers. But before we broke up, we exacted a promise from him that we should be allowed to put on our seven-league boots again, the next afternoon, and under his leadership continue our travels over the Neutral Ground.

CHAPTER XXXV.

TRADITIONS AND LEGENDS OF THE NEUTRAL GROUND.

(*Continued.*)

THE following afternoon, on the dismission of the school, not finding Mr. Ellery in the library, we issued out upon the parade-ground, descried him under a distant apple-tree, charged upon him in a body, captured him, and brought him in.

The good-natured Principal submitting to his destiny, produced his map, and, putting his forefinger on White Plains, thus led the way in our journey from that point.

"Taking the Tarrytown road leading northward and westward, once more passing the Bronx and ascending the hills, we pause at a crossing of the road, where, in Revolutionary times, was situated the hamlet of the 'Four Corners.' This spot, as all of you who have read Cooper's 'Spy' will remember, was the site of 'Betsey Flanagan's Hotel.' Betsey and her hotel were inseparable. The hotel, in fact, consisted simply of a cart which the hostess was accustomed to drive about to the American posts, stored with liquors and a beggarly array of sutler's goods. As the 'Four Corners' was, for many years of the war, the frequent camping-ground of the Continentals, Betsey's hotel was much seen there.

"Till the year 1780, the lines of the American army, extending from White Plains to the Hudson, had been maintained with some success; but in the winter of this year, in consequence of the weakness of our army, a force of only two hundred and fifty men could be detailed to protect the region intervening between these lines and the Croton. This force was placed under the command of Lieutenant-Colonel Thompson, a man of approved bravery, but one, whose courage, as was afterward shown, was not sufficiently tempered by discretion. The lieutenant-colonel had been instructed to keep constantly on the move, in order to make up by increased activity for the inadequacy of his command, and thus render surprise by a superior force a matter of the greatest difficulty. He had, however, in the dead of the winter of 1780, taken post for some days with a portion of his troops, at 'The Four Corners,' or, as the place was subsequently known, 'Young's burnt house,' for the house and out-buildings, which formed the quarters of the Americans, were the property of Samuel Young—a patriotic farmer, who, having been captured by the refugees, had become the recipient of British courtesies in the old prison-ship of New York. The remainder of the colonel's troops had been sent out as flanking parties to the right and left. While thus stationed, intelligence was brought of the approach of a hostile force. The colonel was advised to withdraw and concentrate his troops upon the stronger ground in his rear, but he was confident that the enemy were only a body of horse whom he could easily disperse, and refused to quit his ground. The enemy's horse soon appeared, making their way slowly through the deep snow; they were soon, however, followed by a considerable body of infantry. The action was a brief one. Our troops finding themselves greatly outnumbered and unable to return with effect the enemy's fire, soon broke and were pursued by his cavalry. The flanking parties, reaching the ground at this moment, could do nothing more than cover the irregular retreat by a fire at long shot. The enemy having collected a considerable number of prisoners, among whom were Lieutenant-Colonel Thompson and several other officers, set fire to Young's house and outbuildings and returned to their quarters.

"After this disaster, it was judged inadvisable to attempt to defend so wide a region, and accordingly the American posts were withdrawn to the line of the Croton.

"But this region was the scene of an affair of a little more sprightly character, which did not have so unfortunate a termination.

"In the summer of 1779, Captain Hopkins, in command of a company of light dragoons, obeying the orders of his superiors, set out from North Castle to watch the movements of Colonel Emmerick, who was known to be advancing by way of White Plains. Emmerick, hearing of Hopkins' movements, determined to cut him off, and accordingly dispatched Major Bearman with a body of light cavalry to gain his rear, and sent a courier to the yagers at Tarrytown with orders to guard that avenue of escape; he himself advanced directly from White Plains. Hopkins, however, was on the alert. Riding rapidly southward from the 'Upper Corners,' to the Tarrytown road, he concealed a portion of his command in the woods by the roadside, and rode with the remainder to meet Emmerick.

On perceiving the latter advancing at the head of a body of cavalry, Hopkins feigned a retreat, and drew the enemy on, till at a given signal, the flanking fire of the body of men whom he had placed in ambush was poured in upon them. He himself, at the same moment, charged with such effect, at the head of his troopers, that all, except Emmerick himself and a few of the better-mounted dragoons, were killed or taken prisoners. Hopkins pursued Emmerick so closely for the distance of half a mile that many sword strokes were exchanged between them; the British officer gained a stone wall, over which he leapt his horse and behind which he had a body of infantry concealed, which as soon as their own commander was out of the line of their fire, simultaneously discharged their pieces at Hopkins and his guide, Isaac Odell, who had meantime overtaken him. Strangely enough, Hopkins was untouched, and Odell received but a slight wound. Both instantly turned their horses, and soon rejoined their party. Hopkins now determined to retreat with his prisoners by the Neperan valley road to the 'Upper Corners'. He had gone, however, only a short distance when he discerned in the distance the cavalry force which had been sent out under Major Bearman to intercept his retreat. Hopkins turned quickly about with the intention of making his escape by the Tarrytown road. But here again he found Emmerick drawn up to dispute his progress. With the enemy in front of him and the enemy behind him, and grounds impassable to cavalry on the right and left of him, there only remained the alternative to surrender or cut his way through. He at once chose the latter, and, still keeping his prisoners under guard in the center of his force, he charged upon Emmerick's infantry and horse, and succeeded in breaking through their ranks with only the loss of a few prisoners. He now sped rapidly toward Tarrytown, closely pursued by the enemy's troopers. When, however, he had reached the junction of the Sleepy Hollow and Tarrytown roads, he found them both guarded by well-posted and strong bodies of the enemy's yagers. But the gallant captain did not intend to be caught; he cleared the roadside fence, dashed down the declivity, crossed the Pocanteco, and led his dragoons, with the prisoners safe in their possession, out upon the post-road a little above the old Dutch church, the whole body of the enemy's horse following in close pursuit. Hopkins led his command at their topmost speed till they had reached a point in the road near where the aqueduct now crosses. Judging then that the best horses of his pursuers were far in advance of the main body, he left his prisoners to continue their present route under a sufficient guard, and turning his horse's head became himself the pursuer. Continuing the chase as far as the brook which crosses the road in the Beeckman wood, he captured two or three of the enemy in the very face of the main force which was rapidly approaching, and wheeling around made good his retreat.

"This certainly was a spirited affair, and the memory of the flights and counterflights of the captain's little band, snapping up prisoners on the way, now dashing down through the ranks of the astonished enemy, or now unexpectedly outflanking him and slipping out of his jaws at the very moment they are about to close on him, then after all turning suddenly around and, so to speak, striking out two of his teeth to carry off as trophies,—the memory of all this gives a kind of sparkle to the region which we are traversing.

"Let us now follow in the course of the gallant captain toward Tarrytown; and yet I am greatly tempted to lead you up the Neperan,—which here crosses our road,—and through the somber glen of the Raven Rock, where the ominous croaking of that bird of ill was wont to be heard, as it skirted in its flight the black and beetling brow of the cliff, around which so many superstitions—themselves birds of night—still float; it is said that the apparition of a lady in white is often seen in the dark glen, and that, of a long winter's night, her shrill shrieks are often heard, invariably presaging a coming storm. Perhaps, long ago, chased from her home by the merciless marauders of the Neutral Ground, she perished, crazed with fright, somewhere in this wild glen, and the driven snow became her shroud. Let us, however, avoid this forbidden ground, and go on our way to Tarrytown.

"Tarrytown is another instance of the humorous and sometimes grotesque turn which English speech has, often quite innocently, given to the old Dutch names. The original word—half Dutch, half English, an evidence that the town was founded at a time when the Dutch language was getting supplanted by the English —was Tarwe-town. Tarwe means 'wheat,' and Tarrytown is, therefore, if this derivation be correct, the same as 'Wheat-town.' Doubtless these hills in early days produced abundant crops of this cereal, and in the fall of the year, before the river closed, the honest country people—tenants of the lord Philipse—drove many a wainful of the golden grain to the mill which the noble lord had built near the mouth of the Pocanteco.

"Yet that judicious chronicler, Diedrich Knickerbocker, gives a different and very plausible origin to the name of the town. He says, and he professes to have good authority for his statement, that the Dutch farmers were wont to tarry over long, smoking the peaceful pipe and quaffing the generous beer, before the broad hospitable front of the inn, so conveniently placed near the road-side, thereby bringing upon themselves the reproaches of their hard-working *vrouwen*, who meantime had much scrubbing and churning to do at home, and who, not content with upbraiding their good men, vented their sturdy indignation upon the place itself, stigmatizing it as Tarrytown. Whether this is the better derivation of the name, or whether the chronicler was not, in his sly way, merely nudging the fat sides of the old Dutchmen, I leave you to decide.

"Yet there seems to be good ground for the veracious chronicler's story, for we find that in later times, these vigilant, shrewd Dutch women, discovering, perhaps, that their remonstrances were unavailing, executed a clever flank movement of their own; they succeeded in ousting the portly old tavern-keeper, and in setting up as mistress of the house, one of their own number, who, when her guests tarried over long, with mop and broom soon, doubtless, made a clean swash and sweep of the premises.

"The name of this redoubtable hostess was Elizabeth Van Tassel. Her dispensation lasted down through the Revolutionary times, and her house was frequently the scene of stirring events. On one occasion a party of British refugees took possession of it despite the bold opposition of the good woman, and proceeded at once to make a jolly night of it. They helped themselves to her liquors, piled fagots on the fire, drew the heavy oaken table to the center of the room and, throwing aside their arms and cumbrous accouterments, produced the well-thumbed pack of cards, and were soon deep in the game, breaking the silence only with muttered oaths, or, when, after drinking deeply, they smacked their lips and set the great tankards of ale upon the table with heavy thumps. The enraged hostess looked in at times from an inner door, shook her fist at the marauders and unnoticed, silently withdrew again, with an expression of face that meant mischief. On her last appearance the look of wrath was replaced by a gleam of satisfied vengeance, and she nodded her head and compressed her lips with an air that said,—'I have you, my lads.' In fact she had succeeded in warning the patriots of the neighborhood of the presence of the refugees in her house and had instigated an attempt to capture them. At that time Major Hunt, a Continental officer engaged in some secret service, was spending the night near by, attended by only one of his men, a well-known patriot of Westchester, known as John Archer. Only a few weeks before, Major Hunt's brother, having been met in a lonely glen in the valley of the Neperan by two British refugees, was assaulted and slain. The major, thereupon, on hearing of the presence of the party of refugees at Mrs. Van Tassel's, was eager to undertake their surprise, particularly as it was suspected that the slayers of his brother were among them.

"Hunt, Archer, and a few patriots of the neighborhood noiselessly approached the house about midnight, while the troopers were still deep in the game, and deep in Mrs. Van Tassel's good ale. Hunt first peered through the crevice of the half-closed window-shutters, to observe the disposition of the enemy, then instructing his party how to act, and providing himself with a formidable club from the neighboring wood-pile, he rushed at the head of his men into the room, and raising his weapon, exclaimed 'Clubs are trumps in this game.' The struggle was a short one, for the patriots had immediately possessed themselves of the arms of the refugees, which had been carelessly flung aside. Archer, who was much devoted to the major, was about to inflict summary punishment upon two of the refugees, whom he recognized as the murderers of the major's brother, but the humane officer interposed and saved their lives. The whole party were led off prisoners to the American camp, to Mrs. Van Tassel's great exultation.

"But the enemy also know how to plan a surprise, for when a small Continental guard is stationed at this inn, Colonel Emmerick, at the head of his light horse, dashes down upon them so suddenly that several are killed and the rest made prisoners. On this occasion, Polly Buckhart, a buxom lass of the neighborhood, having just before the surprisal, merrily placed a trooper's hat on her head, is shot in the act of making her escape across the fields, being probably mistaken for one of the troopers.

"Following the post-road northward from Tarrytown, we advance but a short distance when we come upon a little brook, that with much brawling crosses our way. It is evidently a very self-important little stream, garrulous in its own glorification, and with good reason, for this spot has been made forever memorable in the history of our country, as the one where Major André was captured with the evidences of Arnold's perfidy on his person. Near at hand stood the famous white-wood tree, beneath whose ample shade the Indians doubtless held war councils long before the *Halve Maen* appeared in the waters of the Hudson; and under which, in the early days of the Revolution, the drum of the recruiting sergeant was beaten, the reverberations of which among the hills called forth many a sturdy farmer's boy to do battle for his country. But André's capture, and his subsequent melancholy death, threw an atmosphere of gloom about this region, and strange tales were told of apparitions seen hovering between the brook and the tree, in the dusk of September evenings.

"Do you mark that group of oaks and chestnuts, matted thick with wild grapevines, within which the brook loses itself and becomes silent, even as a life is lost in the mystery of death? It was in this covert that the patriots were hid when the doomed André rode up from Sleepy Hollow early in the morning of the 23d of September.

"But I shall not repeat the familiar story of André's capture. Do not, however, be misled by the current pictures of the event into the fancy that the young men who were fortunate enough to do their country such important service, were so comfortably arrayed after the fashion of well-to-do yeomen. They were a ragged and shoeless set; and no doubt, in planning their wayside ambuscade, had—and quite pardonably—as much in thought the bettering of their own condition, at the expense of the enemy, as of doing their country any important service. I am not sure that it was not Major André's boots to which that gallant officer owed his misfortune, for, as he approached the hiding-place of the patriots, one of them said in a low voice to Paulding, 'There comes a well-dressed man with boots on; better stop him if you don't know him.' Boots in those days, in the estimation of the poor farmers of Westchester, were plainly a great mark of distinction.

"Descending the hill, we find ourselves upon the borders of the beautiful Pocantico, which, flowing gently down through the haunted region of Sleepy Hollow, here empties into the Hudson. Below us, near the river, we discern the walls of Castle Philipse; but do not look for ivy-crowned towers, frowning over the brink of some rocky height, for the castle is a very plain brick building, comfortably placed, with a Dutch partiality for the flats, close to the smooth waters of the Pocantico. Nevertheless, it is a strongly built structure, with massive walls, in the lower part of which may still be seen the embrasures through which, in the early colonial days, cannon were pointed to guard the approaches against hostile Indians. Within these ample walls the lords of Philipsborough maintained for nearly a century, a state that was deemed in those simple days one of great magnificence. Here, on great rent days, they received their tenants and generously feasted them in the great halls; here they held their baronial courts and decided the disputes that, sooth to say, sometimes disturbed the serenity of even those quiet, comfortable country people.

Hard by the manor-house stood the old mill, to which the farmers brought their grain to be ground, and whence the opulent lords of the manor shipped the accumulated miller's toll in the stout bottom of the famous *Roebuck*. The hulk of this honest Dutch-built boat lay, for many years after the Revolution, near the ruined mill, and supplied the last of the millers with an incredible amount of wrought nails and old iron.

"After the forfeiture of the manor to the State, the 'castle' became the home of Mrs. Cornelia Beekman, daughter of Lieutenant-Governor Pierre Van Cortlandt, a lady of noble spirit, who, in the course of the war, by her letters and personal influence, did much to keep bright the flame of patriotism among her countrymen. Here in this pleasant retreat she lived to a good old age, proud of the success of the republic—a genuine example of the strong, high-minded lady of the old school, an instance of a class of women not infrequent in those trying days, to the earnest spirit and indomitable will of whom the Continental cause owed much of its strength.

"Standing on the bridge that spans the Pocantico, we behold before us on the swell of the hill that rises from the farther side of the stream, that 'old Dutch church,' which is so frequently mentioned in the early annals of the county. Erected by 'Frederick Philipse and Catharine Van Cortlandt, his wife,' in 1669, it is now the oldest church that still remains in the State. The brick of which its walls are partially built, had to be imported expressly from Holland; for it seems the settlers had not yet acquired the facilities for brickmaking. Its hipped roof and open belfry, surmounted by the indefatigable weathercock, its narrow windows and weather-stained walls, and close-shaven eaves—all have a quaint, venerable look, as if the old church, while conscious of the dignity of its years, peered out from its past upon the pageantry of the present, with a twinkle of merriment lurking somewhere in the corners and crevices of the walls and the angles of the small windows. Verily, the passing world is as queer to the old church as the old church is to the world.

"Following the indolent windings of the Pocantico, we penetrate the shadowy recesses of Sleepy Hollow with, it must be confessed, somewhat of secret trepidation, for we are treading haunted ground. Happily it is yet broad daylight, and we have not to fear an encounter with the headless horseman, who nightly rides up and down the vale 'like a rushing wind.' Yet even in the broad noon, a certain, mysterious spell rests upon this region; let us therefore resist the temptation which steals upon us to pause and rest in some one of these shady nooks, through which the stream drones its quiet tune, lest we be overcome by an enchanted sleep, and glide from the memory of men.

"Yet, by the way, it was not here, as the unlearned sometimes think, that the good Rip Van Winkle took that long nap of his; that was in the Sleepy Hollow of the Kaatskills—a more fearful spot. In this beautiful valley one's slumber would be visited by troops of soft dreams; but in that sunless abyss, scooped out in the side of the great mountain, where no bird trills a random note, and the wind but lightly stirs the thickly-hanging leaves, even dreams droop their wings, touched by the heavy spell of sleep.

"Let us push boldly on, inwardly petitioning the genii of the Pocantico to be favorable to us, for we have undertaken a hazardous enterprise. A certain mystery enshrouds the whole course of this stream, and I have yet to hear of the adventurer who has followed its strange windings to their remote beginning; whosoever essays it, some unseen influence diverts him and leads him astray mid unfamiliar wilds. It is ours, however, to make the attempt." * * * * * *

At this point in the Principal's discourse a long pause ensued, during which he seemed to be lost in abstraction; while we boys stood silent and motionless around him, as if the sleep of enchantment were stealing upon us.

At last the Principal raised his head with a startled air, and rubbed his eyes as if just awaked. It was all done to the life. Gradually recovering himself, he exclaimed,—

"Well, we have succeeded! We have wended our way through the haunted region. But," he continued, with hushed voice, "let us not whisper to mortal ear the strange sights we have seen amid the mazy folds of the hills, lest we offend the spirits of the stream that have guided us along its mysterious course. We have touched our lips to the twofold source of this magic current, yet we dare not speak of the mystic virtues of its waters as they bubble fresh from the earth.

"Skirting now the wild and gloomy Chappaqua hills, we discover the nestling-places of still other rock-hid fountains, and, following their startled waters, descend with them to the Kitchawan, or—as the moderns name it—the Croton, finding ourselves at a spot famous in Revolutionary story—Pine's bridge.

"As this bridge was an important channel of communication between the upper and lower country, and, as the river was fordable a short distance below the bridge, a strong guard was always maintained in this quarter. In the year 1781, the command of this post was intrusted to Colonel Green, an officer who had already greatly distingushed himself as the generous conqueror of Count Donop, and who was much respected by the commander-in-chief, and beloved by his fellow-officers, and was the favorite of his men. His career, however, was cruelly cut short.

"As the colonel never dreamed of the enemy's venturing to approach this distant post by daylight, it was his custom to observe the greatest vigilance at night, but to withdraw the guards at sunrise. This custom, however, having been betrayed by a deserter—in revenge for a well-deserved punishment—to Colonel Delancey of the British refugees, the latter determined to attempt a surprise.

"This officer had been much chagrined at the success of several recent attacks on his own quarters, near the present High Bridge, on the Harlem. To give one or two instances: In the spring of the preceding year, Captain Cushing, with a detachment of Massachusetts troops, guided by Michael Dyckman, who had succeeded in learning the countersign of the enemy's guard, surprised Delancey's troop in their quarters and captured over forty of them. Delancey himself, the seizure of whom was the particular object of the enterprise, owed his escape to his having absented himself for the night from his head-quarters. Again, in January, 1781, Colonel Hull forced a passage to the Harlem, cut away the bridge in the rear of Delancey's post, captured over fifty men, burned their huts and forage, and brought off a great number of horses and cattle without suffering much injury. The enemy, starting in pursuit, fell in with a covering party and were driven back with the additional loss of thirty-five men.

"Smarting under the humiliation of these and like surprises, Delancey determined to have his revenge, and in this he was only too successful. Setting out in person, with a company of about one hundred and fifty dragoons, he succeeded in secretly making his way through the lines extending from White Plains to the river, and in reaching the vicinity of Pine's bridge about daybreak. Colonel Green's quarters were at a house lying a short distance below the bridge, and opposite the ford. Delancey awaited in concealment the customary withdrawal of the guards at sunrise, then, dividing his men into two bodies, he ordered the greater part to cross as rapidly as possible and attack the colonel's quarters; he himself remained behind with the rest to guard the ford and cover the retreat.

"The first intimation Colonel Green received of the enemy's approach was the tramp of his horse; but it was already too late to attempt an escape; the house was surrounded, and in a moment more the door was burst open. The colonel defended himself bravely, and with his sword struck several of his assailants to the floor, but finally, weak with the loss of blood, he was overpowered and slain. In another room, Major Flagg, the colonel's second in command, was in like manner cruelly murdered. The colonel's body was found near the river, so mutilated as to be scarcely recognizable. Altogether, this was one of the saddest affairs in the history of the Neutral Ground, and illustrates the truth that traitors are always the most merciless and brutal of foes.

The house in which this unhappy encounter occurred is still standing, and its present occupant points out the spot where the bed of Colonel Green stood, and the window from which Major Flagg discharged his pistols at the assailants; the old-fashioned window and wainscoting are pierced with numerous bullet-holes.

"In the spring of the following year a body of American regulars under Major Woodbridge, and of volunteers under Captain Hunnewell, completely surprised Delancey and cut to pieces his entire force; they did not, however,—as they hoped to do, in retaliation for the slaughter of Colonel Green and Major Flagg,—effect the capture or death of the commander of the post.

"At Pine's bridge we intercept again the route of Major André. Having been unable to regain the deck of the Vulture, André crossed by the 'King's' ferry, then plying between Haverstraw and Verplanck's Point, and by the aid of the pass with which Arnold had supplied him, traversed the works at Verplanck's, crossed the Collabergh hills to Crompond and took thence the road to this point. From Pine's bridge he followed the Chappaqua hills a few miles in the direction of White Plains, and then turned off upon a road leading to the river, and came out on the Albany post-road near the village of Sparta,—a classic site with which you are well-acquainted, lying but a short distance below Sing Sing. André's original design was to make his escape by way of White Plains, but hearing from a chance word, that the Cowboys and refugees were out on the river road, he turned his horse's head thither, and thus rode into the ambuscade at Tarrytown, as if it had been purposely set to entrap him.

"Having now reached the banks of the Croton, we have attained the northern limit of what was known as the Neutral Ground. North of the Croton the country assumes a more and more mountainous character; the traveler is, as it were, borne up upon great land-swells from which he sees not far distant the threatening waves of the Highlands, the approaches to which the American forces kept guarded, and among the fastnesses of which the American army often lay during the long dark days of the Revolution.

"It were, however, too bold an undertaking to seek to penetrate these mountain wilds at this late hour of the day. Let us be content to follow the Croton through the deep and dark clefts of the hills, till we once again reach the more open region of the Hudson; nor shall we pause long at the Croton dam, which lies in our course, for this is a work of modern structure, which most of you have already visited.

"We have crossed the river at Pine's bridge and have taken the road which leads along the north bank, and we are therefore following the southern border of what once constituted the great Cortlandt manor—an estate which extended northward as far as the Highlands, and from the Hudson eastward to the Connecticut line, including an area of 80,000 acres. This princely domain was acquired, through purchase from the Indians, by Stephanus Van Cortlandt, a merchant of New Amsterdam, who was subsequently confirmed in its possession by royal charter, and at the same time invested with feudal privileges and obligations.

"A walk of a few miles brings us in view of the mouth of the river, and on the right of the road we presently discern, shadowed and half-hid by magnificent forest trees, the old manor-house of the Van Cortlandts. It is a plain hospitable-looking house of moderate size. The founder, unlike the lords of Philipsborough, was evidently a man of simple, democratic tastes, and cared not to establish a claim to lordly grandeur. Like Castle Philipse, the house was built with massive stone walls, in the embrasures of which cannon were mounted as a protection against hostile Indians. It is now, however, surrounded with broad generous piazzas of wood, which conceal the antiquity of the walls and give it an expression of simple, unostentatious hospitality and of peaceful days.

"Here may be seen, pictured on canvas, the noble head of Pierre Van Cortlandt, third lord of the manor, and first lieutenant-governor of the State of New York,— a man distinguished for firm patriotism and wise counsels during the trying times of the Revolution. The head is not unlike Benjamin Franklin's as well in massiveness as in fullness and detail of expression.

"Here too is seen the portrait of his son, General Philip Van Cortlandt, who in the outset of the war, when visited at the manor-house by Governor Tryon and tempted by him with the offer of a major's commission in the royal army, as an inducement to ally himself with the enemies of his country, at once declined, and soon afterward proferred his services to the Continental Congress, by which he was tendered a lieutenant-colonel's commission.

"On the opposite wall may be traced, on a canvas darkened by time, the grim and tawny features of a redoubtable adversary of Colonel Van Cortlandt,—the celebrated Indian warrior and chief, Joseph Brant. In the winter of '78 Colonel Van Cortlandt was ordered to protect the frontiers from the depredations of the Indians, who, accepting the bribes of the English, were waging their merciless warfare along the valley of the Mohawk, firing the isolated farm-houses and the villages, and driving the terror-stricken and defenseless inhabitants before them. In one of the encounters that ensued on the arrival of Colonel Van Cortlandt, Brant ordered a rifleman to fire at the colonel who was leaning against a tree on an opposite hill, awaiting the closing up of his men; fortunately the ball buried itself in the tree a few inches above his head. The Indians being driven from their ground and dispersed, the colonel engaged in personal pursuit of the hostile chief, but the latter succeeded in making his escape in the thicket that bordered an adjoining swamp. But here, on these old walls, they are again brought face to face.

"Let us now leave this time-honored mansion—one of the few remaining memorials of an heroic past—and follow the path leading to Croton, or Teller's Point. On the narrower strip of land by which this point is united with the mainland, running between a marsh on the north and salt meadows on the south, once rose the fort of the Kitchawans, behind which they were accustomed to retire, when hard pressed by hostile tribes. The great number of arrow-heads and other Indian missiles, that are found here, show that this spot has been frequently the scene of savage conflicts; many a time, doubtless, has the frightful war-whoop startled the silence of the woods, and awakened unearthly echoes among the recesses of the hills that here overlook the Hudson.

"Between the fort and the mainland, on the brow of a wild glen, was situated the Kitchawan buryingground. It is said that the old Indian warriors have been observed, in all their paint and feathers, lurking behind the trees and rocks of the glen below or stalking about the site of the old fort; and so frequently have these apparitions been seen by the good people of the neighborhood that they speak familiarly of them as 'the walking sachems of Teller's Point.'

"It was off this point of land that the British frigate Vulture rode at anchor, while André, having landed under cover of darkness on the opposite shore, spent the long night of September 21st, 1780, concealed among the bushes, and engaged in conference with the traitorous Arnold. The next morning a boat's crew from the Vulture having attempted to land on the Point, they are fired upon and driven off; later in the day, as the farmers of the neighborhood are fearful of a descent upon the coast, Colonel Livingston at Verplanck's sends down an artillery-piece, the fire of which compels the Vulture to unfurl its sails and drop down the stream below High Torn. Meantime André is still on shore, concealed in the house of one Smith,—a *quasi* accomplice of Arnold's,—from the windows of which he beholds with considerable misgiving the withdrawal of the Vulture, under whose wings, when night had again set in, he had thought to take shelter.

"But for this little circumstance the conspiracy might have proceeded to an unhappy termination, for André was compelled by the Vulture's change of position, to cross the river at King's Ferry and seek to regain the British lines by a hazardous journey through the Neutral Ground. 'Old White,' the field-piece which did our country this important service, is still preserved in Sing Sing, and on Fourth of July's is brought out, and patted on the back and invited to make a speech, which he does with a voice a little hoarse and rusty, it is true, but still lusty and valorous.

"Croton Point was the scene of another and very spirited little affair, in which the celebrated spy, Enoch Crosby, figures. A sloop of war being at anchor off the Point, Crosby, concealing five or six men among the bushes and rocks, proceeds to the open shore and displays himself conspicuously in the uniform of La Fayette's corps. A boat manned by eleven men, under the command of a lieutenant, immediately puts off from the sloop; and as it touches the shore, the marines leap out and pursue the retreating strategist. When Crosby has drawn them far enough on to suit his purpose, he suddenly turns about and exclaims, 'Come on, boys! now we have them!' At this signal his comrades raise a great shout and make such a stir in the bushes that the British, thinking themselves surrounded by a superior force, surrender at discretion and are marched off by the triumphant Crosby to the old Dutch prison-church at Fishkill.

"Returning from the Point we pass by the old ferry-house,—where a Continental guard was stationed,—and cross the river over the long bridge, which looks in the distance like the bony framework of some huge antediluvian serpent. Our road now leads through a thickly wooded hollow between the hills that here descend with steep banks to the Croton and the Hudson.

"We pass by the old Orser place, where a body of Americans suffered themselves to be surprised by a superior force of British cavalry. The American dragoons, under the command of Captain Williams, were returning from a successful foraging expedition in the neighborhood of Morrisania, and, having now nearly reached their quarters on the Croton, they deemed themselves secure from farther pursuit, and halted at the old house to appease their morning appetite,—to which their ride of forty miles or more had given an edge as sharp doubtless as that of their own broadswords—and in their haste neglected to post the usual guards. In the midst of their culinary preparations they suddenly find themselves almost surrounded by the British cavalry. Some of the Americans are cut down within and about the house; others rush down the bank to the river and escape on the ice to Croton Point. Captain Williams being closely pursued down the hillside by a single trooper, suddenly stops short, and before his enemy can check his horse deals him a blow which ousts him from his seat; the captain vaults into the empty saddle and makes his escape to the banks of the Croton.

"And let us also make haste to escape from this gloomy hollow, for the weird twilight hour is upon us, and it is said that the place is haunted. The story is that the luckless trooper whom Captain Williams unseated comes nightly forth from the tangle that now doubtless covers his bones, and, as fast as a horseless dragoon can, chases down this lonely road to the brink of the Croton, when, seeing the redoubtable captain ascend the opposite bank on the very steed of which he himself was dispossessed, he turns away, pale with ghostly wrath, and drags his misty legs wearily and slowly up the hollow, vanishing in the dank tarn at the very moment that the morning breaks and the cock crows."

CHAPTER XXXVI.

TOM, NED, AND "SEVENTEEN."

Notwithstanding our eagerness to begin the exploration of the region to which the narrative of Mr. Ellery, by linking with it so many historical and legendary associations, had given a new interest, the unsettled state of the roads compelled us to wait yet awhile. Besides, the Easter holidays were rapidly approaching, and most of us had our thoughts upon the "Star" and "Double Star" honors, which were to illustrate their advent; we were accordingly pushing our studies with a zeal that increased as the day of decision drew near.

Military exercises also, remitted in part during the winter, were now occupying a portion of our time; still we were permitted and found opportunity to wander about in small parties within limited distances. Altogether, notwithstanding the necessity of close study, it was a gay time with us. The season itself with its sunshine and shower, its genial airs, its full streams, its expanding buds pregnant with the promise of summer, opened all hearts. Add to this the nearness of the holidays, always welcome to boys, and the hope which many of us entertained of gladdening the hearts of our friends at home, by the decorations which should testify to our industry and success; and it will be seen that there was plentiful cause for good spirits.

When at last we had entered upon the closing week, the Major, finding our good humor contagious, yielded to the solicitations of those who, for one fault and another, had been denied the liberty of leaving the school grounds, and permitted them to enjoy the same freedom that was accorded their comrades. "17's" old associates in evil were quick to avail themselves of this privilege, and were admitted, or rather tolerated, as companions in the many unpremeditated rambles that were undertaken by one party and another. But "17" himself still held aloof; he seemed to be too proud to accept his liberty as a boon; or else, disdaining to associate on equal terms with the more common and coarse natures, he yet found it impossible to break down the wall which his own consciousness erected between him and the good. He thus stood alone, an object of curiosity to some, of fear to others, and of secret sympathy to very few.

Yet even in the heart of "17" the stirrings of the spring were experienced, and he felt an impulse to shake off the fetters that bound him. One Wednesday afternoon, finding himself left quite alone on the parade-ground, all his school-mates having wandered off in one direction and another, he yielded at last to the temptation to take advantage of his liberty; for he was not without a certain passion for nature, whose silent life seemed to favor his brooding disposition. He would not, however, he thought, go where his school-fellows would be likely to cross his path; he would, as always, keep to himself; he wished neither to disturb them nor to be disturbed by them. He knew that if he passed through the village he would almost surely meet some of them; therefore, on issuing from the court-yard, he turned to the right, and in a few minutes found himself in the open country below the village, and quite alone.

Whither now should he turn his steps? He could go southward without fear of falling in with his school-companions, but then the road was muddy and unattractive; he would turn, he thought, toward the river; there following the railroad, or picking his way among the rocks along the water's edge, he would find drier footing, and the thought of the waves breaking upon the shore vaguely suggested to him an analogy to his own life, which had hitherto dashed itself in vain spite and rage against the good, and had recoiled at last in conscious impotence; the noise of the tossing and breaking waves would, he felt, be a sympathetic undertone to his own thoughts. Striking off from the road, he crossed an open field and entered a belt of woods. His path led him to a little water-course; following which, letting himself down from rock to rock, over which the stream descended in petty cascades, he soon found himself by the river's side. He crossed the track and sat down to rest himself on a large rock, the base of which was washed by the tide, now nearly at its height.

Here, for some time he remained, almost without moving a limb, while his mind drifted about without guidance, sometimes amid brooding recollections of the past,—his childish life, his mother dead and gone, his severe guardian, his defeat and disgrace at school,—sometimes dwelling upon the moral distance at which Tom and Ned and all the better sort seemed to stand from him. With all this was mingled an indolent observation of the scene before him,—of the restless and flashing waves, roughened here and there by gusts of wind,—the snowy sails of the schooners and small sail-boats dipping before the wind,—the hills on the opposite side, softened by the distance and the haze that settled about them,—the light, airy clouds and the serene blue under which they floated.

At last "17," wearied with the monotony of his thoughts, rose, and leaping from the rock, strolled up the river-side. Seeing none of his school-fellows in sight, he proceeded as far as the village wharfs, and watched the arrival of a steamer and the discharge of its passengers and freight.

When the boat had pushed off from the wharf, and had now turned Croton Point, "17," animated by the busy spectacle which he had witnessed, began to wish for some more active amusement. The thought occurred to him to hire a sail-boat, and go out on the water. This the boys were forbidden to do, except on special permission, but "17" was not troubled by conscientious scruples; all he cared about was to get back to the school in time, and thus avoid the disagreeableness of all questions. He found no difficulty in procuring the boat, and was soon skimming the smoother waters that lie off the mouth of Croton river, and under the protection of the Point.

"Seventeen" had had but little experience in sailing; but his natural aptitude sufficed for the proper guidance of the boat while the winds were blowing as fair as they then were. His little bark, as it bore off toward the extremity of the Point, gayly tossed the spray from its sides and sped along upon the waters with a certain dancing motion, as if conscious of freedom. "17's" spirits began to rise, and for the first time for many a day, that oppressive load that weighed upon him, lifted like a cloud, and permitted him to look out into the free heavens. He caught himself patting the sides of his little boat with an affectionate spontaneity new to him. Oh, that he might be always thus! he inwardly sighed; that he might loosen the bonds of his nature, and flow forth in generous feeling, and be like such boys as Ned and Tom! His little boat seemed at that instant to give an unusually sprightly bound, and tossed up the spray from its prow with increasing animation. "17" could not help smiling at the vivacity of his companion.

By this time he stood off the extremity of the cape. Finding that he had yet a good deal of the afternoon before him, and the wind favorable, he was loath to shorten this the first pleasure he had enjoyed for a long time; he determined, therefore, to round the point and sail a little way up the river. When "17" was fairly out on the open stream, he found the waters much rougher than he expected; but his little boat seemed to be inspired with fresh zest, and leaped upon each advancing wave with saucy effrontery, and "17" was pleased with its lively spirit, and took care to keep it close to the wind. Tacking and retacking, and enjoying a happiness of mood quite new to him, he stood gayly up Haverstraw bay.

Tom and Ned, since their reconciliation, were even more fond than before of strolling off by themselves, whenever the opportunity favored; they seemed never to get enough of each other's society. Sometimes I was their only other companion; but it often happened that I was separated from them by accident or the companionship of others; for, though naturally so retiring, I had been gradually drawn into a less constrained mood, and had added largely to my circle of friends.

On the present afternoon Ned and Tom had strayed away from their companions, and were amusing themselves in a quiet way. The stroll of the two friends had led them to the bank of the river, about a mile and a half below the village, where a wharf had been built for the shipment of the marble which was quarried in that neighborhood. A little distance below this wharf the railroad had cut its way through a high hill of precipitous sides. In this cut Ned and Tom loitered for some time, wondering at the grotesque contortions of the rocky layers which were exposed to view, and at their singular burnt look. Their imaginations animated the rock with a kind of "life in death," and they fancied that, remote ages ago, it had writhed in dumb agony over the internal fires that then burned, till at last in the midst of its contortions it grew rigid and cold.

They became so interested in their examinations of the rock, and in their speculations, that they did not note that the heavens had darkened over with clouds; and they were greatly surprised when a few scattering drops betokened the approach of a storm. They hastily clambered up the side of the hill and placed themselves under the shelter of a shelving rock. They had not been long ensconced in their eyrie when the storm burst forth. The rain poured down in torrents, but they found themselves pretty well protected, and at the same time so placed as to command a view of the river, from Croton Point over the full length of the Tappan Zee, and, congratulating themselves on their own security, they watched the effect of the storm on the water and adjacent hills with a lively interest.

Youths of their age often feel a wild exultation in the sublime and semi-chaotic action of nature's forces; an exultation which we of a maturer age can no longer appreciate. It is at these moments, when nature seems to be breaking loose from her chains, that their own strong sense of freedom, their creative will, finds expression and sympathetic scope. When, then, Ned and Tom listened to the crashing noise of the rain driven in gusts along the waters, and beheld the wild swaying of the trees, and saw the lightnings glitter over the opposite hills, and heard the leaping thunder, deafening for the moment the roar of the storm, they seemed to feel themselves in their element, and often shouted aloud, as if ambitious to become partakers in the grand outbreak.

In one of the lulls of the storm when the rain, pouring down with diminished force, permitted the surface of the river to be more clearly scanned, Ned called his friend's attention to a sail-boat that had just appeared off Croton Point, and which was floating down the river seemingly unguided, its sail flung loose in the wind.

"It has probably escaped from its fastenings," said Tom. "Surely there can not be any one in it!"

"Yes, there is," said Ned, "I am sure I see some one in it. And there! he has taken in the sail. He will be safe now, if he is strong and has oars. But see, he is floating along at the mercy of the waves. He certainly has not oars, or can not use them if he has!"

The boys, wrought up to a high degree of excitement, watched the boat in silence.

At length Tom broke the spell of fear which rested upon them.

"Ned, something must be done. Whoever he is,

man or boy, he will be drowned if assistance does not reach him."

"What can we do? He will be carried away beyond our reach, before we could get to the village. But let us run." Ned started up as he spoke.

"Wait," said Tom. "Don't you remember seeing a boat at the wharf down there? I am sure I saw one. Let us go at once."

The boys found the descent of the rocks much more difficult than the ascent and not free from danger, especially as they had been rendered slippery by the rain. Impelled, however, by their fears for the safety of a fellow-being, they did not hesitate long in choosing their footholds, and in a few moments were on the wharf. The boat—for there was one—floated between the wharf and a stake, to both of which it was fastened. Fortunately the oars had been left in it. The boys swung themselves, hand over hand, upon the rope which held the boat to the wharf, quickly detached it, and pulled with determined energy for the mid-stream. Such was their excitement that they had not spoken a word since leaving their shelter.

"Steady! Steady!" said Tom, "we must not waste our strength! no bad strokes! Both together now."

Animated by a common understanding of what the circumstances demanded of them, they rowed down rather than up the river, as only thus, could they be sure of reaching the mid-stream in time to intercept the boat.

They pulled on in silence, amid the driving rain, only now and then looking around to watch the course of the boat, which, floating helplessly with the tide, was bearing a soul—perhaps to eternity. The frail bark was evidently either in a leaky condition or was filling with the waters that dashed over its sides, for they could see that its occupant was busily, almost frantically, engaged in efforts to bail it.

The boys pulled on with renewed vigor as they neared the middle of the current and as their hopes of success increased.

"Good Heaven!" exclaimed Ned. "It is one of our boys, I see the blue coat. And the boat is settling fast. Pull, Tom, pull, for life's sake!"

Tom merely turned his head to verify the observation of his companion and rowed on with set teeth.

It was, indeed, no other than their school-mate "17," whom we left an hour ago sailing under a joyous spring sky, and surrendering himself to its liberating influence with an openness of heart quite new to him. He had been surprised by the storm in the midst of Haverstraw bay, had tacked about and had hoped to turn the Point, before it came on in its full fury. As he was unprovided with oars his only hope of success in this effort was to leave his sail standing and keep as close as possible to the wind. For a short time he bore on bravely thus, the wind remaining steady; but unhappily a sudden gust from a new direction pounced upon him with such violence, that he only saved his boat from being capsized, by quickly loosening the sail and allowing it to swing round with the wind. The storm now descended in all its fury, and he was completely at the mercy of the winds and waves.

As he passed the Point, he succeeded in lowering the sail, which, swinging about at will, had greatly increased his danger; he also loosened the mast from its hold. All that now remained possible, was, so far as the boat would obey the helm, to keep it from being turned broadside to the waves, and, floating down with the tide, trust to the chance of rescue. All this time the necessity of action had been so imperative, that "17," though greatly alarmed, had not seized the full peril of his situation. But now, as he sat there at the stern, holding the ropes of the rudder in his hand, and looked out into the rain, which with its thick veil almost hid the shores from sight, and as he looked forth upon the waves leaping up wildly and with foaming crests all around him, and, turning his gaze upward, saw no ray of light in the heavens, saw the heavens themselves seemingly settling down upon him, and felt his boat swayed to and fro almost at the scorn of the waters, his heart sank within him, and a voice in his soul seemed to cry out, so that he almost heard it with his ears,

"Lost! Lost!"

"Lost? This then is the end! Here, all alone, alone," he gasped; and his hands were relaxing their hold of the rudder ropes and the boat was swinging its full broadside to the waves.

But a new terror arouses him from the stupor that was stealing upon him. The boat is filling with water! It had already shipped a great deal, but now it is filling fast! It must have sprung a leak! A fresh peril, in the midst of despair, is often as effective in exciting to action, as gleams of hope from an unexpected quarter. "17" grasped the rope of the helm firmly in one hand and with the other doffed his military cap and began bailing out the water.

Instinct led him to concentrate his whole mind upon this simple action, that he might thus keep out the thought of death and eternity, that seemed to hover like an engulfing night over him. Thus occupied, it was not till Ned and Tom had nearly reached the middle of the current, that, lifting his head to watch the direction of the waves, "17" caught sight of the boat coming to his rescue. So sudden was the hope that entered his heart, so violent was the emotional change he underwent, that, in a vain effort to shout, his tongue clung to the roof of his mouth, his hand relaxed its hold upon the ropes of the rudder, and for the moment he became as powerless under hope as when he yielded to an access of despair. Making a great effort, he recovered himself and returned to his work.

But the water has gained! it is gaining still, the boat is settling! Ah if it should yet be too late! "17" cast an appealing look toward his rescuers. That instant as if by a common instinct, and as if the moment was one when soul could speak to soul without the aid of speech, both Ned and Tom, turned their heads and recognized their old enemy, and he them. Who can say what flashed through the soul of "17" in that dark moment of time? Did not some ray of heavenly light pierce the cloud that enveloped him, revealing the divinity of self-sacrifice, of love?

"Pull! Tom, pull! Quick for life's sake."

"Steady, Ned, steady! You are losing strokes."

"Ah! God! it is sinking! it is sinking! We shall not save him!"

The boats were not two oars' length apart, when "17's" swayed a little on one side and sank. It was impossible for Ned and Tom to turn their boat, which had its broadside to the current, in time to reach a hand or an oar to the struggling, despairing boy. Alas! at the very moment of rescue he is lost!

No! Tom has jumped from his boat! Two manful strokes and he is by the side of "17;" he grasps him by the arm; he supports him! Alas! how the waves buffet them! They sink! they sink!

No! no, thank God, Ned has got the boat to their side;—he grasps them both;—he leans back to steady the boat:—they are saved!

CHAPTER XXXVII.

TRIUMPH AND BEWILDERMENT.

By this time the storm had greatly abated, and the boys had scarcely headed their boat toward the shore, when the sun broke through the clouds and beamed right across their path. The wind had fallen, but the waves swept tumultuously across the prow, and they had to pull with vigor to stem the downward current.

"Seventeen," exhausted as much by the emotions that had crowded up in his soul, as by his bodily exertions, and thoroughly chilled by the cold waters from which he was rescued, lay in a half-fainting condition, propped up against the stern of the boat, and poorly protected by the wet coats of his companions. Tom, exerting himself manfully at the oar, soon drove off the chill which his bath had given him.

The two friends did not exchange a word except where their necessities compelled them to do so, and then they spoke briefly and with lowered voices; the hearts of both were too full for speech. They directed the boat straight toward the village wharf. As they approached they saw a large crowd of men and boys standing there, and apparently awaiting their arrival. In fact "17's" peril had been observed at the village, though not soon enough to anticipate Ned and Tom in rescuing him, or even in time to afford any assistance. The news, however, had been communicated from one to another, and very many, among them some of the boys of the school, watched with breathless and speechless anxiety the brave and steady efforts of the two rowers, and when at last they saw them reach the sinking boat, and rescue the poor youth from the waters, they could no longer contain their joy, and by their shouts called many others around them. In fine, before the rescuers had reached the wharf, the news of their achievement had spread throughout the village.

They had no sooner struck the wharf than helping hands were reached to them, and they were lifted from the boat, and actually borne in the arms of the men to a carriage which had been brought for the purpose from the adjacent railway-station; dry coats were wrapped around them, and they were driven at once to the school, being escorted up the hill, through the main street of the village, and to the very door of the school-building, by a vociferous crowd of men and boys, that gathered force by the way, and which, on depositing them in the care of the principals, testified its appreciation of the heroism of my two friends, and the general gratification at their safe return, by three unanimous cheers, that made the various buildings surrounding the court-yard clamorous with echoes, and the very window-panes rattle.

The next morning Tom and Ned rose refreshed, and felt none the worse for their exertions of the day previous. Naturally, they were centers of great interest,— an interest which their comrades had no opportunity of personally manifesting on the preceding evening, because the principals, solicitous to guard against any ill effects from their exhaustive efforts, had insisted that they should be left undisturbed to gain that rest which they so greatly needed. Now, however, the enthusiasm and curiosity of their school-mates could not be repressed, and such was the talk and excitement that the performance of school duties was often seriously interfered with. The names of Ned and Tom were in the mouth of every one. They were compelled to repeat over and over again all the details of their achievement, and their youthful hearers were always disappointed when the end was reached, and secretly wished the story begun again; thus they instinctively strove to make the heroic deed their own.

In the evening there was a little extemporized social gathering in the parlors, and Ned and Tom were invited in, and were introduced by Mrs. Blaisdell as "the two heroes," and were of course the recipients of renewed attentions. Indeed, if they had not been so seriously impressed by the experiences of that hour of peril; if, at that dread time, when death, the dark shadow of life, floated near them, life itself had not stood forth with a sublime significance never before realized, their heads would have been turned by the flatteries which they received. Happily the halo of that experience still encompassed them, and their hearts responding to the genuine sympathy, which gave warmth to the applause, did not take an empty delight in its mere echoes.

"Seventeen" was seemingly too much exhausted to rise that morning and attend to his school duties. Yet the physician, when called, discovered no symptoms of fever; additional rest was all, he said, that was needed. In truth, "17" was still under the spell of that awful moment, when, in the midst of the waves, life, like a lightning flash, shot with blinding and searing force across the clouds and darkness of his moral death. Ever since the fearful moment when, just as the measureless wave of eternity seemed about to surge over him forever, his eye met the eyes of the school-mates whom he had wronged, the terror of a new revelation rested upon him; he lay on his couch unable to move, and in a kind of stupor. He spoke but mechanically to those who approached him and hardly seemed to recognize them. Only once—when the names of Ned and Tom were uttered, and their wish to visit him was mentioned—did he rouse from his seeming apathy; the thought of seeing them seemed to call forth actual terror; he cried out, "No, no!" and, with a gesture of aversion, turned hastily to the wall.

CHAPTER XXXVIII.

THE FLIGHT.

The last few days of school preceding the Easter holidays were devoted to a private examination and review, in the several class-rooms, of the work accomplished since the Christmas vacation. Its object was to sum up in the minds of the pupils all that they had gone over, and, at the same time, to enable the instructors to decide, in connection with the weekly records, upon their comparative proficiency. This examination was now completed, and the last day of school was come.

In the mean time, "17" had been growing stronger, and there was, apparently, no longer any sufficient reason for his absenting himself from the routine of the school. There was still, however, in his manner, a certain abruptness, and in his eye an occasional look of fear, which showed that he had not yet recovered his strength of nerve. The Principal, therefore, did not urge his presence in the school; he had, in all probability, decided to keep "17" in the seclusion of the sick-room till the boys had left for their homes.

But "17" took the determination of his case into his own hands. On the morning of the last day of school, the matron, on paying her customary visit to the sick-room, found "17's" bed empty. He was gone. She immediately reported the fact, and an inquiry was at once made. "17" had not been seen by any of the boys that morning; he was not to be found about the premises. An examination of the dormitory, in which his wardrobe was kept, showed that he had visited it in the secresy of the night, and provided himself with a portion of his clothes. Soon afterward, a note was brought the Principal, which had been found lying open on the table of the sick-room. It was addressed to Ned Eldridge and Tom Manning, and read thus:—

"My School-mates: Forgive me, forget me. Farewell. C—— H—— N——."

These were the initials of "17;" I shall forbear to give his name in full.

The Major hoped that "17" had taken the earliest train for home, but, observant of the disturbed state of his mind, he knew not what wild project might have entered his brain. Information obtained at the railroad station, to the effect that no boy of his description had been seen, increased the Major's fears. Later in the day a telegram received from "17's" guardian, in response to one sent by the Major, still further disquieted him—"17" had not appeared at his home. The anxious Principal devoted himself to discovering the whereabouts of the runaway. He was only partially successful on the first day of his search, and it was several days before he was able to find full traces of him.

"Seventeen," it would seem, had effected his escape from the school long before daylight, as, when he was first seen, which was quite early in the morning, he had already gone a considerable distance. Instead of turning his steps toward the river, where he might have taken an early boat or train, he struck the road that led most directly into the back country. After daybreak, his great object seemed to be to avoid observation, and his course consequently led him to the most unfrequented regions. Indeed, for some time his irregular wanderings seemed like the flight of one who is driven about from one region to another in vain effort to escape from himself—to escape from some pursuing demon of his own mind, from some ever-present thought. At last, however, he seemed to have taken a more direct course, which was tracked to a small station on the Harlem railroad.

The station-master remembers selling the boy a ticket for New York; he wondered, at the time, at the boy's strange appearance. The Major is half a day behind time; nevertheless, he follows "17" to New York, hoping against hope to find some trace of him. Here he meets "17's" guardian; but for many days no trace of the runaway is discovered. Finally, however, in response to an advertisement under the head of "Lost," information is received that a boy of the description advertised had appeared at the office of a company engaged in the China trade, and had taken service in one of their ships, which had subsequently sailed from port.

Thus ended the search, and thus ended the school-days of "17." Thereafter, life was his school. His singular experience had given him an early maturity, whether for good or for evil. When this vivid consciousness of the divine life—of Life—has seized upon a trembling soul, who can say that it ever releases its grasp? The poor victim may wander hither and thither, and plunge into all sorts of sin, in vain efforts at escape, but must he not, at last, succumb? Who, then, is the more powerful, man or God?

CHAPTER XXXIX.

STARS THAT SHOOT MADLY FROM THEIR SPHERE.

Notwithstanding the interest we felt, not unmingled with anxiety, in the fate of "17," for whom of late considerable sympathy had been awakened, our joy at the near prospect of the holidays could not be restrained. The thought of "17's" sad destiny could not outweigh the thought of home and its loved ones, and while the Major was anxiously engaged in his first inquiries concerning the whereabouts of our lost comrade, we were busy with our preparations for departure. Besides, we were to learn that morning who were to be recipients of the honors for which we had been striving, and in many a heart expectancy was on the stretch.

We were assembled in the school-room that morning an hour later than usual. By this time all our preparations had been completed, and when we appeared, it was in our most showy regimentals, our brightest buttons. We were not, as usual, detailed to our several class-rooms, nor were the reins of discipline held very tight. For half an hour or more there was a hum of voices rising and falling all over the room, while our teachers, grouped about the desk, were engaged in earnest conversation. In the mean time the Major's family, and some invited guests, entered the room and took the seats provided for them.

We were called to order by Mr. Ellery, who, with a few pleasant remarks about stars, wandering and fixed, and those that would soon shoot madly from their spheres, proceeded to read the names of those boys who were entitled to the starry honors. Each boy, as his name was called, came forward and received a beautifully-worked silver-lace star, which Mrs. Blaisdell pinned to his breast. The honored youths on receiving their decorations took places in line upon the floor, and a gallant appearance they made. Those who were entitled to the "double star" were then called forward, and were decorated by the same gentle hand. When among these, the names of Ned and Tom were pronounced, a torrent of applause burst forth from all parts of the room, and the ladies, having learned by whispers, rapidly passed from one to another, who the favored youths were, saluted them with smiles and the waving of handkerchiefs. The happy fellows were suffused with blushes. The "double stars" were arranged in front of the others.

Mr. Ellery then made a little congratulatory speech, ending with an allusion to the noble exploit of Ned and Tom, whereupon a new shower of plaudits broke forth, in the midst of which the signal for dismissal was given. The officers formed their various divisions along the aisles and marched them out in due order, each youth bowing to the ladies.

Not many hours had passed before most of the boys had departed in various directions of travel, a few only, whose homes were at a great distance, remaining to spend the short holiday week in rambling over the hills of Mount Pleasant.

CHAPTER XL.

THE ENCAMPMENT.

There was so little during the two remaining months to disturb the happy flow of our days, that few passing incidents cling to my memory. Nothing certainly occurred to interrupt or modify our agreeable relations; indeed as to Ned and Tom, their sad experience during the winter had given them such an insight of themselves and of each other, and had lifted their friendship to so serene a height that it seemed impossible that a shadow should ever afterward cross it. Their particular associates caught somewhat of their elevation, and emulated them in the art of being happy. The genial influence spread throughout the school, and an atmosphere of peace and good will was everywhere diffused. Even those unruly spirits, who had followed the lead of "17," seemed to border upon a sense of what is beautiful in decorous manners, and tempered their own accordingly.

Nevertheless, as we neared the close of the term, a little cloud of anxiety rose that threatened to cover our sky; it was an anxiety in respect to the examination in our studies to which we were to be subjected,—an examination to be conducted, not in the comparative privacy of the class-room, as was the last, but in the presence of the assembled corps of teachers, before school trustees and invited guests—gray-beards of wisdom.

This advancing cloud might have saddened our days, if the anticipation of a novel pleasure had not, so to speak, illumined its edges.

The examination usually filled up all the last week of school, but this period was also characterized by a great change in our mode of life; it was "camp week" with us. It was no child's play in which we were to engage, but a regular military camping out, by night and day, conducted with all the precision of military discipline.

The prospect of this novel life, was of course very agreeable to us and made us to a certain extent unmindful of the terrors of the contemporaneous examination; and as the day approached which was to be the last of the old school routine, our enthusiasm knew no bounds.

We had a merry afternoon of it, pitching our tents. Of course all the young soldiers took part in this work. Our camp covered a considerable portion of the parade-ground contiguous to the school-building; it was governed in due conformity to military usage; guards were posted night and day, rounds were made, counter-signs demanded, arrests pronounced, confinements in the guard-house enforced; in short, every thing was done in strict military fashion.

To us boys, this kind of life, with its mock seriousness, was rare sport. The play of youth is the comic side of the serious pursuits of men. Our camp life was a joke, a satire, and we enjoyed it greatly; we entered into all its details with admirable spirit, and that the play might be complete in all its parts, we would run the guard and commit other military sins, which brought us to the guard-house. For the discomforts of the guard-

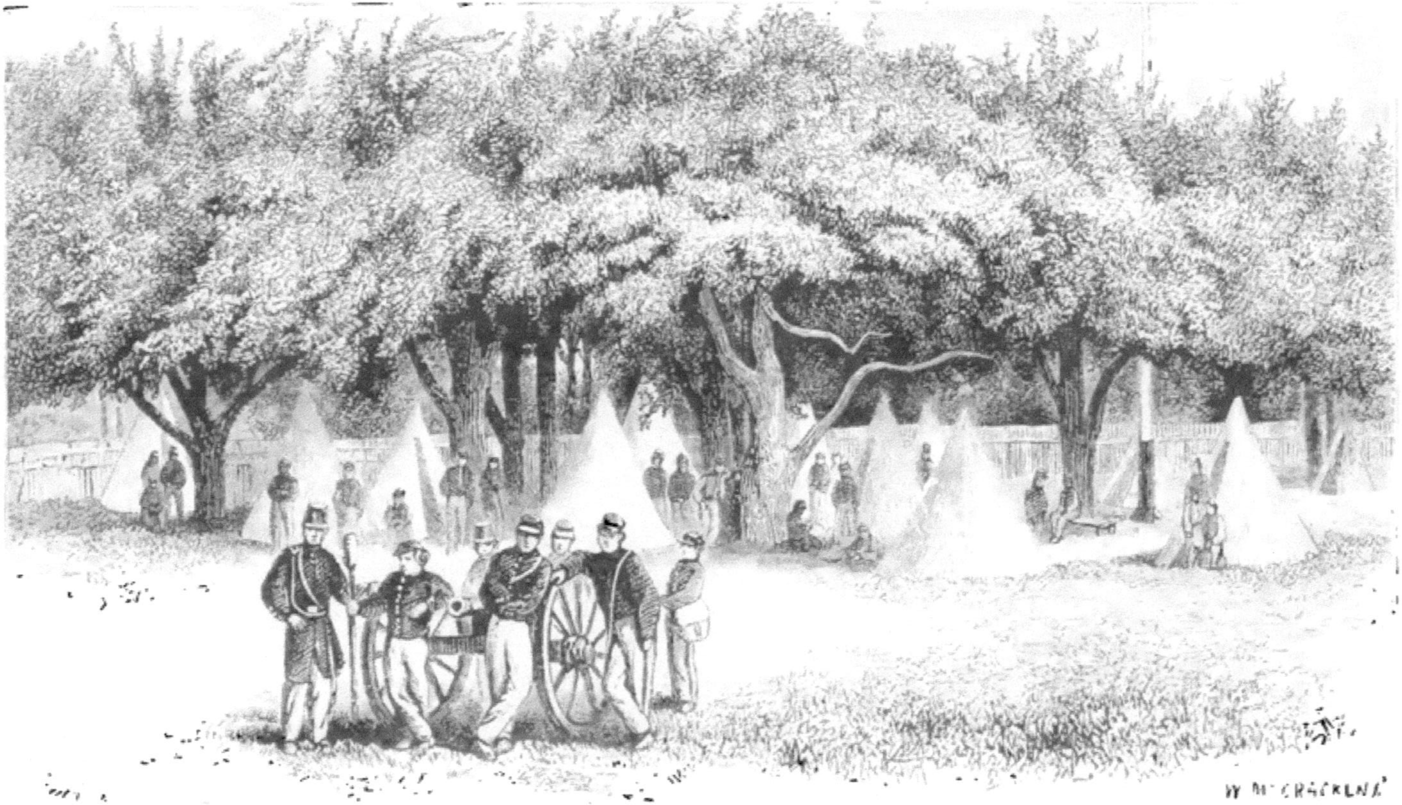

house—and they were real—we had a genuine zest, and even the best-behaved boys made trial of them. The nights were glorious; to lie on the hard ground, with only a blanket for bed and coverlet and a knapsack for pillow, to be half awakened from time to time by the cries of the guard, such as "twelve o'clock and all's well," to hear the officer of the guard making his rounds, or to be one's self a sentinel and tramp to and fro under the stars—all this was "grand." But since that peaceful time many a bearded man has found such life a very serious thing, and only the inspiration of a great cause has relieved its monotony, thrown a veil over its hardship, and given it a grandeur not its own.

We were not allowed, however, a great deal of idle time. Between guard mounting, guard duty, morning and evening drill, and artillery practice, our day was pretty well occupied.

In the mean time within doors the examination was progressing, class after class being called in from the camp at specified hours, in accordance with the printed programme. There was no play in this at all—it was a grave affair. To stand up before a platform covered with dark-browed men, clad, as it seemed to us, in the blackest of black broadcloths,—with here and there a bright lady's face, to observe your confusion,—and have dark questions poked at you, is not less than terrifying; and even such brave soldiers as we were, may be excused if we nervously fingered the seams of our pantaloons and felt our knee-joints a little weak.

But custom blunts the edge of such trials, and I, for my part, found that the second ordeal of this kind had lost much of the terror of the first, and the further course of the examination gave me no alarm. I even had sufficient presence of mind to observe, toward the last, that many of these sedate men before me were occupying themselves with their own thoughts, and I fancied they sometimes nodded, but perhaps this was a sign of their approval. In short, in examinations as in a battle, it is the first volley that terrifies.

I shall not attempt to narrate the incidents of that week of camp-life. All the intervals of time between examinations and camp duties were filled up with fun and jollity. Stories, songs, practical jokes, *jeux d'esprit* of every boyish sort, gave to the passing hours a tripping measure, and even now they make the memories of that time, as seen from the gray present, bright and winsome, albeit upon other ears than mine the recounting of them would probably fall stale and flat. The trivial incidents of one's boyhood are regarded by the bearded man from a stand-point which he alone occupies, and they have for him a half comic, half pathetic interest, which he alone can feel. He looks along the silver thread of a consciousness, which binds together moods so strange and contrasting; and no other eye than his can follow this line of light. It is not the outside, but the inside view of the incidents of the early past that has so singular an interest; it is not the mere events that give to memory so sad a pleasure, but the impressions and sensations which attended them.

Perhaps the word which will best express the mature man's view of his own childhood is "queer." It is all so queer. It is so queer that one should ever have been a child in arms, so queer that he should have toddled about in swaddling clothes, so queer that he should have been a chunky school-boy, with round, fat flanks and shining morning face. But equally queer to him are the moods and impressions whose ghostly apparitions inhabit that past,—his outlook upon the world, and the world's inlook upon him through those wide-open boy's eyes of his. And peering back through his consciousness he seems to see the ghosts of those moods —of his old self, grimacing and beckoning to him; and they are so queer. And in those images of one's self, there is so exquisite a combination of the comic and pathetic, that in our smiles there lurk always—tears.

The last day of school was marked by ceremonies which, to our boyish eyes, possessed great grandeur. The examination was now closed, and all the anxieties which it brought with it vanished like a mist. After the customary morning drill, the remainder of the morning was devoted to making preparations for departure. The camp was forsaken for the dormitories, and during an hour or more the agitation of feet and hands on the third floor was something alarming, and the babble confounding. The cause of excitement was not simply the prospect of home, but the anticipation of the exercises of the afternoon and evening.

For the afternoon, the order was a grand dress-parade and review. Already parents, brothers, sisters, and cousins were arriving in great numbers; the parlors of the school were filled with guests, and many more were finding entertainment at the hotels and elsewhere in the village.

I shall not attempt to convey to the reader an adequate impression of the grandeur of this parade, and of the military evolutions that preceded it. Think of a regiment of soldiers with heads held as high as the legs of boyhood will permit, and with hearts beating a great deal higher; not, indeed, "bearded like the pard," nor with visages grim and scarred, fit to "chop off strange oaths," but—well, fierce enough for the occasion, when not a serried foe was before us, but a gay host of friends and relations.

We were reviewed by an officer of high rank in the United States army, who, after we had gone with great success through all the evolutions, and had deafened the air with our volleys of musketry and artillery, and were at last drawn up on parade, addressed us in a neat little speech, which greatly flattered our vanity and inflamed our martial ardor. The gallant array then broke, and the gay company dispersed to consummate their preparations for the evening—for the grand ball.

The ball was of course "a splendid affair;" but the witcheries of that occasion are too subtle for my pen; in truth, at the time I was so much bewildered by the suffusion of feminine loveliness, that only a general impression remains. I doubt, however, whether we boys showed to so good advantage as on the tented field; our military discipline did not serve us in the presence of so many radiant eyes, and we were speedily resolved into the condition of an "awkward squad."

By midnight the festal halls were deserted. A few hours' sleep, and then came the parting. There were no tears shed, for youth is too much enlivened by change, too full of hope, to be saddened by leave-taking. Besides, for myself, I had exacted from my two particular friends, Ned and Tom, the promise of a visit of a week or two at my father's country place, and we parted gayly, with many anticipations of the pleasure in store for us.

Alas, for the too confident hopes of youth! events took quite a different course. I learned, on reaching home, that my father had been appointed to an office under our government, the duties of which required him to live in Germany. It was necessary that he should depart immediately, but as he would undoubtedly remain abroad several years, he determined to take his family with him; we accordingly had to busy ourselves at once with our preparations. I wrote to my friends of the sudden change that had occurred in my present destiny, promised to write to them from Germany, and to seek them out immediately on my return, and I begged them not to forget their school-mate. A few weeks thereafter, standing on the deck of the steamer, I watched with straining eyes the shores of my fatherland as they vanished in the blue distance.

CHAPTER XLI.

TATTOO.

We remained in North Germany a little more than two years, during which time I attended one of the excellent German schools, or gymnasia, as they are called. It is not my purpose, however, to dwell on this epoch in my life, or seek to contribute to a knowledge of the German educational system. A great deal has been written recently on this interesting subject, though not perhaps enough to convince Americans of the folly of self-glorification in matters of education. The school systems of our country are not "the best in the world," nor are we "the best-educated people on earth." Intelligence here may be more widely diffused, but that is owing to the popular nature of our governmental institutions, not to our ill-digested methods of education.

On leaving Germany, my father engaged rooms for us in Paris, where we remained nearly half a year. We reached home about the first of July. I had during my absence kept up a correspondence with Ned and Tom, and knew consequently that they were still at Mount Pleasant, where they were now completing the last year of their course. Accordingly as soon as we were fairly settled in our old home, I made haste to visit them, eager also to refresh myself with the sight of the grand region in which I had spent one of the happiest years of my life, and which was hallowed in my memory by the association with it of a rare and beautiful friendship, and by the sacredness of the first fresh feelings of youth.

Of course, on reaching the school, I first paid my respects to the principals and to Mrs. Blaisdell. Mr. Ellery divining my eagerness to hasten to my old comrades and friends, soon led the way to the department of the seniors, whither he said he had occasion to go, and pointed out the room which Ned and Tom held in common. The door of their apartment stood open, and so intent were they upon their books, as they sat before their tables, that they did not pay any heed to my entrance.

"Ned! Tom!" said I, imitating as nearly as I could the old familiar tones. They started simultaneously as if, as they afterward said, they had been awakened from a dream and found that after all they were still juniors. They turned at once full toward me, and then their greetings were as warm as I could desire.

I found them, of course, much changed in appearance,—taller, manlier; but a few words of conversation, the deepened echoes of the old tones, and that mystical speech which the eye utters, soon bridged over the intervening years, and they were the same old comrades.

Both of my friends stood high in rank. Tom was now senior captain, and also the acting adjutant; Ned was captain of the first company. Nor was their advancement in their studies less marked. In French and German I was naturally a good deal more proficient than they, though they conversed with considerable ease in the former language: in other branches, however, I had no reason to congratulate myself on any superiority.

Their book-shelves showed that they were developing a taste for the best English reading. Among other works I discovered a volume of Wordsworth, over which Ned was very enthusiastic; the simple piety of this poet, and that sentiment of identification with nature which is diffused throughout his verse, supplied Ned's heart with the kind of food most congenial to it.

Tom was of a more analytic turn, and already showed in his literary selections a taste for positive science. He had determined, he said, to study geological surveying, as this pursuit would, he had heard, afford a grand field for observation, and serve as an introduction to the wider domains of science.

My interview with my two friends was necessarily brief; their school duties, now that these were drawing to a close, were especially exacting and left them but little spare time.

On departing, however, I promised at their urgent solicitation, to spend with them the approaching camp-week, the last week of their life at school.

I made good my word; and that I might not seem a bird of strange feather among my old school-mates and might the better revive old times, I procured a uniform and enrolled myself in Ned's company. A little practice soon refreshed all my former familiarity with military exercises, so that I was able to go through my part without disgracing my commander.

My week of camp life was a delightful one; to me doubly delightful, for in it I enjoyed not only the passing, but the past time. But I must not dwell upon the closing scenes of these reminiscences, of which, the reader is doubtless well weary; let him, however, remember his own boyish days and pardon my prolixity.

Camp week ended with the usual grand parade and ball. On all occasions throughout these ceremonies I was delighted to observe the marked respect and honor with which Ned and Tom were received, on the part of both their associates and their teachers. In the ballroom they shone conspicuous stars, and were pointed out to strangers as the two youths who a few years ago bravely risked their own lives to save that of a schoolmate; and the incidents of the affair were buzzed about from one to another, though Ned and Tom seemed unconscious of the observation of which they were the centers.

But alas, poor "17"! what of him? As I stood in the midst of the gay throng, the thought of him rushing out into the night to escape the pursuing eyes of his comrades and of his own conscience, and the thought of him as still, perhaps, driven about over the world, a prey to conflicting passions, was saddening.

And now, patient reader, farewell! The ball is ended—the lights are out—the tattoo is beaten.

The Merchant of Venice

A Memento of the Old Winter Garden.

The Text as arranged for the Grand Revival by EDWIN BOOTH, at the late Winter Garden Theatre,

AND WITH

ILLUSTRATIONS OF THE SCENES.

Royal 8vo, cloth, full gilt, $2.

BOOTH MEMORIALS.

Passages, Incidents, and Anecdotes in the Life of

JUNIUS BRUTUS BOOTH,

(THE ELDER.)

BY HIS DAUGHTER.

ILLUSTRATED WITH A STEEL ENGRAVING

OF

BOOTH AS RICHARD III.

12mo, 184 pp., paper, 50c.

Upon the receipt of the price, any of the above books will be mailed to any part of the United States.

HENRY L. HINTON, Publisher,

680 Broadway, New York.

www.ingramcontent.com/pod-product-compliance
Lightning Source LLC
Chambersburg PA
CBHW030006240426
43672CB00007B/845